THE WHIPPET

C. H. DOUGLAS-TODD
F.Z.S.

Revised by Kay Douglas-Todd

POPULAR DOGS
London

Popular Dogs Publishing Co Limited
3 Fitzroy Square, London W1

An imprint of the Hutchinson Publishing Group

London Melbourne Sydney Auckland
Wellington Johannesburg and agencies
throughout the world

First published (as *The Popular Whippet*) 1961
Second edition, revised (as *The Whippet*) 1973
Third edition, revised 1976

Printed in Great Britain by litho by The Anchor Press Ltd
and bound by Wm Brendon & Son Ltd
both of Tiptree, Essex

ISBN 0 09 127360 9

Contents

Illustrations

IN THE TEXT

Foreword to the first edition

BY LORD NORTHESK

Chairman of Cruft's

This book will certainly find its place on the bookshelves of all those who breed or own Whippets. Written by such an expert in the breed as C. H. Douglas-Todd, it is a 'must' for breeders and owners throughout the world.

Mr Douglas-Todd writes in such a charming way of this most attractive breed, and also of other aspects of breeding and of the Dog Fancy in general, that I feel sure *The Popular Whippet* will command a very wide number of readers.

The author is to be congratulated on the great care which he has so obviously taken to check all his facts and to present a thoroughly reliable volume for all dog lovers.

Author's Introduction

All my life I have loved Whippets. For much of my life they have been my companions, so much so that they are, indeed, part of my life. To me they have long since ceased to be just 'dogs' but have become 'little people'; it is not surprising, therefore, that for a very long time I have wanted to write a book about them.

This book, then, has been written for three reasons: firstly, because of my deep affection for my own dogs; secondly, to fulfil a promise I first made in 1934, both to myself and others who also love Whippets; and thirdly, because, out of my long experience with the breed, I feel I may be able to help others who own Whippets and want to maintain the high standard of the breed.

What I feel about Whippets, and any promises I have made, will be of only incidental interest to those of you who have bought this book and, indeed, had I written it for those reasons alone it might be of little value to any reader. At the same time my book about the Whippet would be colourless and completely valueless unless my own deep affection for the breed had not impelled me to write it.

What I have set out to do is to write a friendly, simple and sincere book that will be helpful to all dog lovers, but especially in the hope that it will stimulate a wider interest in the Whippet. If the book succeeds in this object I shall be well contented.

Writing a book, however, calls for a lot of patience, not only on the part of the author, but also on the part of others. My grateful thanks go out to all who have so generously helped me, to my many friends at home and abroad who have supplied me with information, especially those who have sent me photographs

—alas, not all of them could be accommodated in a book of this size—and to those whose enthusiastic encouragement enabled me to overcome the many difficulties I encountered.

Special thanks are due to Mr Peter Weir who, although a very busy man, spared many, many hours checking up my work and putting me right when I tended to deviate from my set purpose; also, to my veterinary surgeon who, out of his crowded day, still found time to look at various points in this book that are more in his field than in mine. I would also especially thank the Secretary of the Kennel Club, Mr E. Holland Buckley, for his very kind help in checking many details.

1960 C.H.D.-T.

Reviser's Notes

It was with considerable humility that I undertook the task of revising this volume. Mr C. H. Douglas-Todd's great knowledge and sincere love of the breed are undeniable, and his request that I should undertake the revision of his book was indeed a great compliment.

Although several minor changes have been made in the original text, revision of the author's wording in certain chapters (particularly those concerned with the Breed Clubs and noted Whippet kennels) could detract from historical accuracy. Therefore much of the revision has been undertaken in my additional Chapter 13 and in the appendices. Some of the photographs have been replaced by six new blocks.

I should like to acknowledge the assistance received from the Secretary of the Kennel Club, Lieutenant-Commander J. S. Williams, and members of his staff, who kindly made available facilities for research. My grateful thanks, also, for help received from many dedicated Whippet breeders. I am sure that all will forgive the omission of their names: to make individual acknowledgements would require a further chapter.

1972 K.S.

Sadly, 'The Maestro', as many called him, has passed away. His request that, once again, I should revise for its third edition this well-loved book on the breed gave me particular pleasure. After his return to these shores I formed a closer connection with the author. I took his name and shared in his everyday life, all of which brought me even closer to these little dogs which we both loved. Charles might have undertaken the revision himself.

However, it was his wish that, having started the work, I should continue and I take pride in the confidence placed in me.

In this third edition I have tried to bridge the gap between 1972 and the present time simply by adding a few observations and by bringing up to date the breed records and certain other information, and I should like to thank those people who have assisted in any way.

1976 K.D.-T.

I

The Origin of the Whippet

THE Whippet of today is one of the most popular of British dogs. In the Kennel Club Registers it has averaged fifth place in the Hound Group over the last seven years. This rise in popularity took place despite the fact that Whippet racing declined with the advent of Greyhound racing. For fully a decade after the end of World War II Whippets were raced only in isolated places, whereas at one time Whippet racing was a sport which had thousands of devotees all over the country. It was particularly popular in industrial areas where it ranked second only to horse racing.

Whippets are such charming little members of the canine race that it was only natural their sterling qualities would survive even when the new sport of Greyhound racing took the country by storm in the 1920's.

There is, to my mind, no more elegant dog than a Whippet, no dog with a more lovable disposition, none which gives its unstinted affection for man more fully. No dog is easier to house and keep, being a very easy dog to feed and keep clean. In consequence, the Whippet is the ideal house-dog. In addition, as a gay and lively little sportsman he most certainly has no equal.

The Whippet, therefore, is a dog to suit every taste and, although somewhat sensitive to cold winds, the breed is as hardy and as free from catching cold and/or disease as any of the more robust-looking breeds.

There is no doubt that as a separate breed Whippets have existed for very many years—long, long before dog shows were thought of! F. C. Hignett, writing on the breed, in *The New*

Book of the Dog, in 1907, stated that he thought it certain that the Greyhound has a share in the genealogical history of the Whippet because, not only is the Whippet a Greyhound in miniature, but the purpose for which he was bred was very similar. The only difference between them, Hignett claimed, was that rabbits were coursed by Whippets and hares by Greyhounds.

B. S. Fitter in his book *The Show and Working Whippet*, 1947, goes deeper into the origin of the breed. He writes that the miners of Northumberland and Durham produced the Whippet for racing purposes.

It will be noted from the foregoing that in forty years two writers on the breed put forward two different viewpoints, for Fitter in his book goes on to say that Whippets are descended from 'out-crosses' from the following breeds: Bedlington Terrier, Manchester Terrier, the Old English White Terrier and the Italian Greyhound. Fitter further claims that the Terrier blood gives the Whippet his gameness and tenacity, the Greyhound blood his speed, stamina and beautiful conformation.

Other eminent writers on canine matters have put forward similar views. For instance, Freeman Lloyd, in 1894, in his *The Whippet and Race Dog*, says that 'A Whippet is nothing else but a Greyhound reduced in size by the cross of the Terrier and the Italian Greyhound'. He also says that it was 'straight racing' coming into fashion that inspired men to produce the Whippet.

Like many others who have submitted similar views of the breed's origin, no real proof of any kind is given to substantiate these claims which, so often repeated, seem to have become accepted generally. In fact, some dictionaries give as their definitions of a Whippet: 'a cross between the Greyhound and the Terrier!' I have never found any proved authority for stating how Whippets were evolved, furthermore, I do *not* agree with the theories I have quoted.

I will admit, however, that I am not certain how the breed originated or even when Whippets, as we know them today, became standardized and bred true to type. I incline, however, to the view that they have been kept as sporting dogs, and pet dogs, for very many years—perhaps for centuries. In support of this I would submit that there is no doubt that dogs of the Greyhound type have been kept for sport for thousands of years. Actually, in Proverbs xxx, 31, King Solomon refers to a Greyhound as being one of the four things which 'go well and are comely in going'.

The Greeks depicted Greyhound-type dogs on pottery and statues. The smaller type of these dogs were very like Whippets in size and shape and, indeed, many of them seem to have the typical Whippet rose ear.

There is no doubt that the Graeco-Roman 'Group of Dogs' (now in the British Museum) found at Monte Cagnolo, near Lanuvum, is a beautiful work of art depicting two dogs, more like Whippets, to my way of thinking, than any other breed, and, what is of more significance, they are shown in typically characteristic Whippet poses. These dogs are certainly *not* Greyhounds, neither are they Italian Greyhounds as we know them, but, as I think, Whippets which come halfway between those two lovely breeds.

From a fairly close observation of works of art over the ages I am of the opinion that the *first* dogs were mostly of the Greyhound type. Later came the Mastiff type—the guard dogs and the war-dogs type. It seems only natural to me that different localities should require different types of hound or dog. These requirements may have been brought about by differing climates, the type of work for which the dog was required—mostly in connection with the chase, of course, which means hunting over varying types of terrain and so on. Whether the dog lived with nomadic tribes, semi-wild hillmen or more civilized types of folk residing in towns or country houses and so on, would also have its bearing upon the evolution of the dog most suitable to requirements.

If deer should be the main quarry, then the size of hound required to chase and bring them to bay would be a main consideration. It would ultimately depend on the size and weight of the animal to be hunted, its speed and so on. Likewise, if the quarry was of a smaller type, such as the gazelle, hare or rabbit, a smaller type of hound would be suitable and, indeed, necessary.

It is, I suggest, this variation in the size of the hunted animal which made necessary the breeding of differing sizes of hounds of the same type.

So we have, for large deer, a strong, fast dog such as the Deerhound, for the gazelle-type of quarry the Saluki, and for the smaller ground game, the smaller Greyhound or Whippet, and so on all through the various breeds of hounds.

Now it is only natural, I think, that the smaller type of hound should be given privileges which the larger dog did not enjoy. The women and children would naturally make friends of these smaller types of dogs and soon they would be given the run of their dwelling places. One can picture them coming in after the chase on a cold day and cuddling in for warmth, for, as I said at the beginning of this chapter, Whippets are not only ideal house-dogs but also, because of their affectionate natures and sporting instincts, they endear themselves to all.

Again, in a period when food was certainly not so readily obtainable as it is today, a dog that was a favourite for its character and was also able to help in the hunt for food would become very popular in any establishment.

This may be an appropriate place to mention that, in Salisbury Museum, there is the skeleton of a dog known as the 'Windmill Hill Dog'. These are the oldest remains of a dog found in this country I am given to understand, and it is of interest to note that the skeleton is very similar in every way to that of a modern Whippet.

Those particularly interested in this subject will find much to interest them in a study of 'Joachim with the Shepherds' by Giotto 1350; 'The light of the World' by Memline 1450; the Greek terra-cotta vases, fifth century, in the British Museum; and the 'Vision of St. Hubert' by Dürer, fifteenth century. There are of course very many other works of art depicting Whippets, among them some very old and beautiful tapestries which show very clearly the Whippet in various phases.

There is also another point to consider which, I think, should have some bearing on this question of origin—namely type. There is no doubt that Whippets have changed very little, if at all, for almost a century in either make, shape or type. There are still some veteran breeders with us today who can remember Whippets for over seventy years. They tell us quite emphatically that the breed, then as now, came true to type in breeding, which points to the fact that Whippets, as a well-established breed, had been evolved for some considerable time prior even to *that* period.

I myself have been interested in the breed since I was a lad of twelve years of age, and I can see no real difference in the type of Whippets of today and those of my boyhood, except perhaps in front movement.

Again, *if* the Whippet of today is the result of recent and various 'crosses', as is suggested by so many writers, surely we should occasionally hear of some breeders getting peculiar specimens in litters now and again? Something akin to a 'throw-back'—a puppy with a long coarse coat for instance or one obviously of incorrect type, perhaps hound-eared and so on. During all my experience in the breed I have never bred one of these 'throw-backs' nor have I ever heard of anyone who has, and this is another reason why I do not subscribe to the generally accepted 'cross' theory.

To sum up this very interesting subject, which I am certain can be one of surmise only, it seems that a Whippet is a small dog of Greyhound type of great antiquity. That, from what the ancient artists show us, a dog similar to a Whippet has been a favourite model for their various types of artistic creations: sculpture over the centuries, pottery and so on. That he is closely akin to the Greyhound and the Italian Greyhound, and that there is no evidence to prove him otherwise.

Incidentally, at Windsor Castle, the Royal Collection contains a delightful portrait of Ann of Denmark, Consort of James I, surrounded by dogs which are definitely *not* Greyhounds nor Italian Greyhounds, but Whippets.

There is, however, every reason to believe that, with the advent of Whippet racing, crosses with Terriers were frequently operated. This doubtless came about because it was thought that the introduction of new blood would give more courage to the dog in running its race to the end. But I doubt if this became a recognized general rule, as the dogs would have been seriously impaired in the matter of their speed, the first essential, of course, of the race dog. It was certainly not carried far enough to alter the type to any great extent, whatever introductions may have been made in isolated instances.

Therefore, the true Whippet, having been bred to a definite type and established for so many generations, soon came back to its original appearance. Certain is it today that no traces of supposed 'crossings' remain; all of which, I think, goes to prove my theory, and try as one may, it is almost impossible to breed *out* the true Whippet type. Actually, if one looks back to the Bedlingtons of the early 1900's it will be found that *they* are not unlike Whippets in appearance, whereas today that breed has many points that we most certainly do not look for, or want, in a Whippet. A photograph, in the possession of the late Lewis Renwick, of one of these old-time Bedlingtons—Mr Harold Warnes' Cranley Blue Boy, I think it was—showed, so Renwick claimed, body characteristics remarkably like those of a Whippet, and he often used to say that he wondered if the Whippet was not used to make up the Bedlington way back in the eighteenth century, instead of vice versa. An interesting point indeed.

The dictionary definitions of Whippet are also of some interest. It has had various meanings at different times, but in its general sense it means something that is quick and fast. For instance, 'As quick as a Whippet', 'Whippet-like in movement', 'With the agility of a Whippet'; and modern sports cars are sometimes termed 'Whippet' to denote their speed, quickness and handiness in many ways.

The Lurcher. This is a recognized type of dog generally accepted as being, for the most part, a cross between a Greyhound and a Whippet, and used for little else than poaching. Now your true Lurcher, that is one that comes from a long line of Lurchers and, maybe, owned and bred by a 'Lurcher lover', of whom I am definitely one, probably comes as near to qualifying as a 'true bred' as many of the accepted Kennel Club breeds shown in the ring today. Frankly, I am only too glad that we have at least two types of dogs that are recognized for what they are but not accepted by the Kennel Club as recognized breeds and, therefore, not eligible for exhibition. What this really means is that they are not of sufficient interest to the modern dog breeder to warrant his, so-called, 'improving'. These two types are the Border Collie and the Lurcher. The former is often the product of an unbroken line which goes back over sixty years and is fully recorded, as, for example, the Border Collie bitch, Shane—owned by my daughter Jennifer—and a wonderful working dog she is too.

The Lurcher is a definite type. He is much favoured by gypsies—and gets a bad name accordingly—and their like. He is essentially a worker, bred and used for that purpose, and is in no sense a pet. In fact, and I have known many, the Lurcher is a dog who does not like a lot of petting and fussing. He likes, and acknowledges, a word of praise or encouragement, but goes no further than that; almost an undemonstrative type of dog one might say. He is a quiet dog in every sense, yet very alert at all times and, let me hasten to add, the devotion and singleness of purpose of a Lurcher towards its owner is indeed something to marvel at. Bred long in the leg to course a hare; long in the neck to pick her up; harsh of coat to withstand any weather and any conditions; eagle-eyed to see the slightest signal; keen of ear to pick up and instantly obey that thin, almost supersonic whistle which emanates from a grim-faced master's tight lips, the Lurcher has a clean and functional beauty all his own. Many a Lurcher owner will proudly claim that his dog is 'Bulldog bred', yet the long muzzle, slim raking shoulders and general racy build, quite apart from his size, might cause many a disbelieving shake of the head. Yet, as it is claimed, the Bulldog played an important part in his make-up. The foundation of the Lurcher, in fact, may well have been a Bull bitch many generations back; many Greyhounds may have played their part in his lineage in building up his speed; and undoubtedly a Scottish Deerhound passed on his harsh, weather-resisting coat. But deep down it was the Bulldog that gave the Lurcher his basic character, which is so highly prized. Stories, strange and true, are told of Lurchers and their ways and deeds, and one will hear them if one is fortunate enough to count among ones friends those who spend their lives in caravans wandering from place to place, always accompanied by their Lurchers. These silent, watchful, grey-coated hounds who lie under the caravans, whose orange-coloured eyes watch strangers thoughtfully through narrow slits, the gypsies will tell you, if they will talk with you at all, are, among other things, the finest baby-watchers, the quietest and the most reliable in the whole world. So do not accept the statement that the Lurcher is a mere Greyhound/Whippet cross. He is not; he is a hound, bred to an ideal, and for a purpose which he nobly fulfils. As such I admire and respect him.

Reviser's note: Mr Douglas-Todd's theory that the Bedlington originated from the Whippet is further supported by a modern pictorial chart which clearly shows the evolution of the many and varied breeds of dogs. In this the Bedlington Terrier is depicted as stemming from a union between the Whippet and the Dandie Dinmont Terrier—an explanation which, as a devotee of both these breeds, I find particularly interesting.—K.S.

2

The Whippet of Today

ALTHOUGH there is nothing certain about the origin of the Whippet, we do know exactly what the dog has looked like for the greater part of a century. Just as in other breeds of stock, fashions in dogs change from time to time, and these changes in popularity often bring about changes in conformation. To illustrate what I mean, consider the Foxhound. A Foxhound, wherever he is found, cannot be mistaken for any other breed; but there are different types. A hound with a hill-pack is quite different in build from one found in a pack in what we call 'the Shires'. The reason for this is obvious. To hunt a fox over the Fell country of Cumberland requires a different animal from the one that goes at racing pace over the grasslands of the Midlands.

In Whippets, the only things which seem to change in popularity are size and, to a lesser degree, colour. The variation in height has been with us for many years and has probably been the most hotly discussed of all Whippet topics.

For over fifty years the approved height agreed by the Whippet Clubs has been eighteen and a half inches for dogs and seventeen and a half inches for bitches. These are the *ideal* heights recognized and accepted by the Kennel Club in their official standard. A slight variation either way is left to the discretion of the judges.

The question of height is of the utmost importance, for a Whippet must not be confused with a small Greyhound or a large Italian Greyhound. If it is too big, the Whippet becomes coarse, and if under the standard height requirements too much of a toy, which it is not.

This all important matter has been fully discussed many times by breeders at club meetings and friendly gatherings, but always the result has been the same, namely, a definite urge *not* to alter the recognized heights.

My good friend the late Lewis Renwick, when he was breed representative on the Kennel Club Liaison Council, was instructed by the ruling body to get each of the Whippet clubs to send a representative to a meeting to endeavour to draw up a breed standard. This, when agreed on, was to be submitted to the Kennel Club for its consideration so that a standard for each breed of dog could be approved by the Council and the whole recognized as official breed standards. The meeting of the club representatives duly took place, and when the question of height was raised, unanimously and without discussion, it was immediately agreed that the height for each sex should remain for the future as it had been for the past fifty years or more. I think it is very important to appreciate this point fully for, from time to time, newcomers to the breed raise the height question. Older and more experienced breeders and exhibitors, however, are convinced that it would be a great mistake to make any changes. My own observations are that in height, the top-class dogs of today more nearly conform to the Standard requirements than they have done at any time during the last thirty years. The following is the approved Breed Standard, published by courtesy of the Kennel Club, and I suggest that it is read in conjunction with the Points of an Exhibition Whippet illustration (facing page 20):

General Appearance. Should convey an impression of beautifully balanced muscular power and strength, combined with great elegance and grace of outline. Symmetry of outline, muscular development and powerful gait are the main considerations; the dog, being built for speed and work, all forms of exaggeration should be avoided. The dog should possess great freedom of action, the forelegs should be thrown forward and low over the ground like a thoroughbred horse, not in a hackney-like action. Hind legs should come well under the body giving great propelling power, general movement not to look stilted, high stepping or in a short mincing manner.

Head and Skull. Long and lean, flat on top tapering to the muzzle, rather wide between the eyes, the jaws powerful and clean cut, nose black, in blues a bluish colour is permitted and in livers a nose of the same colour and in whites or particolours a butterfly nose is permissible.

Eyes. Bright, expression very alert.

Ears. Rose-shaped, small and fine in texture.

Mouth. Level. The teeth in the top jaw fitting closely over the teeth in the lower jaw.

Neck. Long and muscular, elegantly arched.

Forequarters. Shoulders oblique and muscular with the blades carried up to the spine, closely set together at the top. Forelegs straight and upright, front not too wide, pasterns strong with slight spring, elbows well set under the body.

Body. Chest very deep and plenty of heart room, brisket deep and well defined; back broad, firm, somewhat long and showing definite arch over the loin but not humped, loin giving the impression of strength and power, ribs well sprung; well muscled on back.

Hindquarters. Strong and broad across the thighs, stifles well bent, hocks well let down, second thighs strong, the dog then being able to stand over a lot of ground and show great driving power.

Feet. Very neat, well split up between the toes, knuckles highly arched, pads thick and strong.

Tail. No feathering. Long, tapering, when in action carried in a delicate curve upwards but not over the back.

Coat. Fine, short, as close as possible in texture.

Colour. Any colour or mixture of colours.

Size. The ideal height for dogs is 18½ inches and for bitches 17½ inches. Judges should use discretion and not unduly penalize an otherwise good specimen.

Front and Shoulders. Weak, sloping or too straight pasterns, pigeon toes, tied elbows, loaded or bossy shoulders wide on top and straight shoulder-blades, flat sides. An exaggerated narrow front not to be encouraged.

Head and Skull. Apple-skull, short foreface or downface.

Ears. Pricked or tulip.

Mouth. Overshot or undershot.

Neck. Throatiness at join of neck and jaw, and at base of neck.

Body and Hindquarters. A short-coupled or cramped stance, an exaggerated arch, a camel or humped back (with arch starting behind shoulder-blades), a too-short or over-long loin. Straight stifles, poor muscular development of thighs and second thighs.

Feet. Splayed, flat or open.

Tail. Gay, ringed or twisted, short or docked.

Coat. Wire or broken coated, a coarse or woolly coat, coarse thick skin.

It will be readily recognized, I feel sure, that it is not easy to put into a few words a clear definition of what a dog should look like and how it should move. It has been done very satisfactorily in regard to the Whippet, however, but a more detailed explanation will be helpful in discovering why a Whippet should conform to that Standard. In this connection the diagram opposite will be useful for identifying various parts of a Whippet's anatomy.

Note first its general conformation. Bear in mind that a Whippet is *not* a ladies' pet, although its special characteristics make it the perfect house-dog. Remember, too, that the Whippet is a *Sporting dog* and has been from its very beginning. This is most important, and I feel that I cannot stress the point too often or too strongly in order that many of the points raised will be more readily understood.

The Whippet has been evolved for great speed over short distances, great stamina, a good eye and a quick brain combined with intelligence of a very high order; a dog which can catch a rabbit on its own ground, one capable of hunting for hours on end if necessary, and one not unduly out of its element if it should put up a hare.

I am not much in favour of coursing hares with Whippets, but they are used in this connection, and some are very efficient at it. For my part, however, I have had many experiences which make me regard the hare as too big a quarry for a Whippet to tackle in the general way. I have seen too many hares coursed and caught by Whippets who were unable to despatch their kill

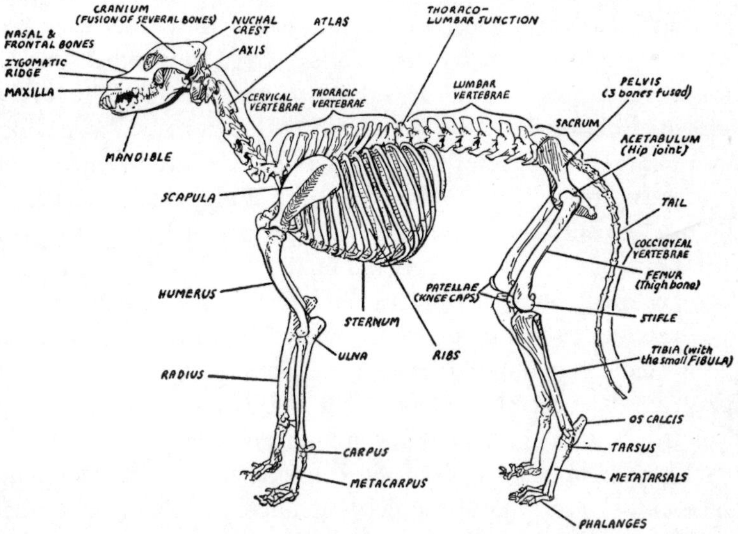

Bone structure

quickly and cleanly. I loathe and detest causing pain to any living thing. I hate the killing of any animal unnecessarily, and for that reason alone I would veto coursing hares with Whippets. I have seen Whippets coursing a hare and actually running beside it in play—not that I suggest the hare regarded it as fun! They made, on a particular occasion I have in mind, no attempt to kill the hare, but made repeated efforts to get 'puss' to go again when, eventually, bewildered and scared almost to death, the hare stopped. If any tender-hearted reader wonders what eventually happened to this hare, may I say that I rescued her, picked her up and let her go in a nearby spinney—getting beautifully scratched for my pains! We often saw what we liked to believe was 'our hare' on subsequent occasions when we visited that particular field, but she never gave the dogs another chance to pit their paces against hers, for which I was very grateful.

It must not be overlooked that the hare is capable of making an extraordinary sudden 'turn', a characteristic of the animal when hard pressed, and that in doing so it can easily break the neck of a Whippet if at the moment of 'turn' the dog should snatch at it while at top speed. I am convinced that is the reason Whippets are injured when engaged in coursing hares, notwithstanding the reports that they 'ran into some wire' or 'a post' when out of sight. It is significant, at least I think so, that when a Whippet is picked up injured, the incident is invariably described as having taken place out of sight of its owner. No, I am of the opinion that it is asking too much of a Standard-size Whippet to expect it to become a really proficient, and safe, courser of hares. Still, as I say, some of our best breeders and exhibitors find it a great sport and get much enjoyment from following it, and no doubt they will roundly condemn me for my views. Be that as it may, I still hold them. I should add, as regards sporting Whippets, since it may not be generally known, that Whippets work well with ferrets, and that as a breed they are not gun-shy.

Keeping in mind that it is in connection with the foregoing sporting aspects that the official Standard of Points has been drawn up, let us now examine the various points mentioned.

First, the *head*. I will say at once that I *do* like a refined slim head and often refer to this point in such terms in the critiques I write after judging these dogs. At the same time the head must be wide enough for brain development and reasonably wide between the ears, not so refined that it resembles a Collie. A good head is a 'balanced head', flat at the top of the skull, with a very slight 'stop', and the foreface well filled up below the eye. A good guide is to estimate the distance from the occipital bone to the corner of the eye, for that distance should be the same as a line drawn from the eye—the inside corner in both instances—to the tip of the nose.

The *eyes*. Bright and alert. This implies the need for

exceptionally good sight. This is essential, for a rabbit on its own ground is clever and quick and is very difficult at times to run down. A poor-sighted Whippet would be of little use in rabbiting. I knew of a famous Whippet, one belonging to the late Stanley Wilkin, which used to run after hares with the 'Tiptree pack' when he was *stone blind*! This dog used to run with his shoulder pressed as near as he could get it to one of the others and, as Stanley used to say, 'The old blind man goes with them, and unless he falls into a ditch he is there at the kill!' I have actually seen 'the old blind man' going with 'em, and although I must admit that the sadness of it distressed me, he seemed to enjoy the game and was as keen as any of them. That dog was Tiptree Monk whose name appears in so many Whippet pedigrees.

The *jaws and teeth*. The jaws must be strong, and the teeth likewise, and level; that is, the teeth in the top jaw must just close over the bottom ones so that the dog can grip and hold its quarry when caught. In a Whippet, an overshot or an undershot mouth is a dreadful fault and one possessing such a blemish should never be bred from. Happily, the 'wrong-mouthed 'un' is a very rare bird indeed in Whippets and so need not cause undue worry.

The *neck*. It is absolutely essential that the neck should be strong and muscular and slightly arched. It should have great power and be very flexible, to enable the dog to 'stretch', catch and kill his rabbit. It must never be forgotten that Brer Rabbit does *not* run straight but jinks from side to side when he is at speed, and it may well be that a Whippet has to make a 'side catch' when making his kill. This calls for a neck, flexible, strong and lengthy, such as the Standard lays down.

The *shoulders*. Here we come to one of the most important and, I think, one of the most misunderstood points in the breed. The shoulder angle should be sloping. The blades should lie back and not be upright. Why? Because unless this is so the dog cannot use his full strength in propelling himself over the ground, neither can he move smoothly when he is walking, or moving up and down the show-ring. A straight or upright shoulder on a dog will never do other than cause him to be restricted in movement; whereas a shoulder-blade that is laid back, as the Standard calls for, allows the front legs to swing forward in that lovely flowing movement which is such a delight to behold. Watch your 'hackney-like' moving Whippet and then examine his shoulders. I give here (facing page 28) a snapshot of a Whippet which conveys perfectly the correct forward movement of the breed. The dog in question is Wingedfoot Hildebrand (never shown because of his size), a brother of Ch. Wingedfoot Claire de Lune and a son

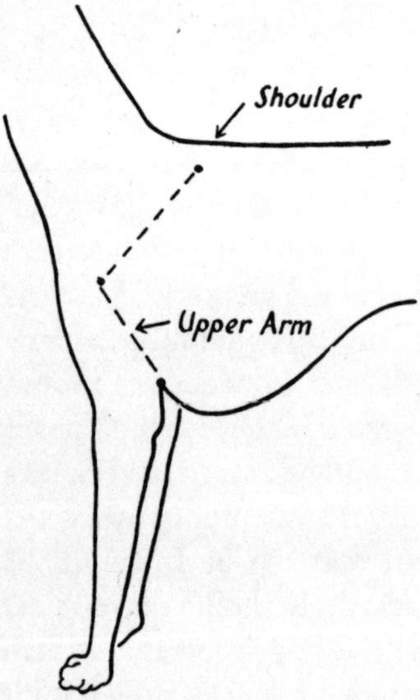

A correct shoulder. Well-laid blades, sloping well back and a good fore-upper arm

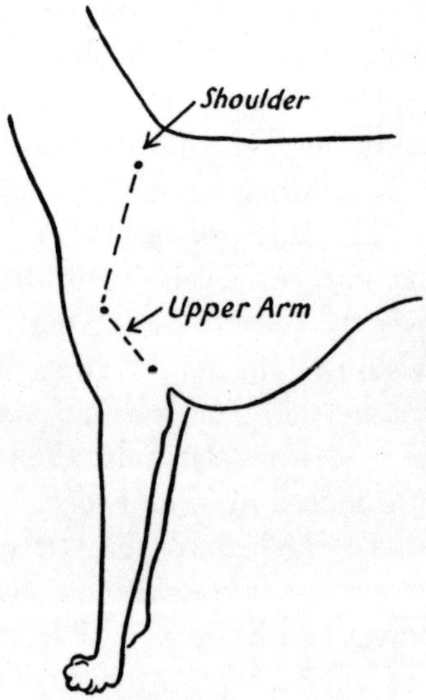

A badly laid shoulder. Blades short and too upright

of Ch. Wingedfoot Hildegarde whose movement was always accepted, by all judges under whom she was shown, as being as near perfection as possible. Study this photograph carefully and you will sense that grand, flowing front movement. Note the low-carried 'daisy clipping' forward thrust of the paws (no 'hackney-like movement' here) and the length of the dog's stride. This dog is an exceptionally fast animal as the photograph clearly shows.

This then is the perfect forward action desirable in the breed and the illustration might well be studied by those judges who have so little conception, from what they say and write at times, of how the breed should move.

An upright shoulder in a Whippet is like a man with hunched shoulders. Just try hunching your shoulders and then, with your shoulders up round your ears as it were, try to walk forward smartly and see how you feel. Now 'walk high', i.e. with your head 'scraping the clouds', in the same manner, and note the difference. So it is with a dog having upright, as against 'well-laid' shoulders. Get your shoulders in your strain right and your movement problem, if you have one, will be more than half cured. There is *no other way*.

The requirements go on to indicate that shoulders should be well muscled. Here again we have a confusion of thought on the part of some who set out to judge the breed. They do not seem to be able to differentiate between well-muscled shoulders and 'loaded' shoulders. Every Whippet should possess well-muscled shoulders, otherwise it cannot possibly do its work. Remembering that the strong, tremendously powerful hindquarters (discussed later) develop terrific forward thrust, unless the dog has shoulders which are powerful enough to resist that thrust and 'hold the ground' while his body passes over it (forming a fulcrum as it were), each hindquarter drive will pitch the dog on its nose. Think this over and you will see how obvious it is. For that reason, a dog must be as strong in front as it is behind and Nature invariably makes this adjustment.

To illustrate what an important part the front legs play in movement at speed study the wonderful action picture of Greyhounds (facing page 28). Greyhounds were used in this illustration because their size enables the picture to be studied in more detail —the Whippet's movement is, of course, the same. Dog No. 7 is in full flight, all feet are off the ground, and he is at the maximum of his speed. Dog No. 4, in the next position, is just coming to earth, as will be seen by the near forefoot touching the ground; the moment for the strength of the shoulders and the front legs is beginning. Dog No. 2 has just collected himself, taken hold of his ground with both forefeet, and is holding his ground while his hindquarters have begun their powerful forward thrust. *This* is the moment when the strength of the shoulders and the forefeet are taxed to their limit, the illustration demonstrating it to perfection. Dog No. 6 is in the position where his forefeet are adding their thrust to that of the hindquarters, and the hind feet are about to take the ground. Dog No. 8 shows that the hindquarters have taken their ground in front and have propelled the body of the dog forward while his front legs have moved right forward and are preparing to take their ground to repeat the operation all over again. Study the whole of the illustration carefully: first, Dog No. 7, then dog No. 4, then No. 2, then No. 6 and, finally, No. 8. You will then have a perfect picture of what is required in a galloping dog.

A great many of our present-day 'experts' know little about anatomy and take no trouble to learn, with the result that we often have well-laid-back shoulder-blades, well muscled, mistaken for 'loadedness'. What then is a 'loaded' shoulder? It is a fault of the bone which almost invariably goes with an upright shoulder-blade, and if accompanied, as it so often is, by the two-legs-coming-out-one-hole type of front, the corresponding narrow chest and the flat ribs (they all go to together, as a general rule), it is the hall-mark of the 'weed'. A well-placed shoulder, slanted well back, is a joy to behold, and if there is great breadth in the blade you have an animal of great merit. Such a shoulder is almost invariably well clothed in muscle, and to mistake such conformation and term it a 'loaded' shoulder is a judging crime.

It is true that excessive work such as racing will over-develop the shoulder muscles for the 'beauty show'. It will also 'spread' the shoulder, but this is not an 'overloaded' shoulder in the true sense. After all, a man will develop his muscles in accordance with the type of work he may do, but what results is not malformation of the bone structure. I make no apology for reproducing a photograph of my own Ch. Wingedfoot Marksman of Allways which illustrates quite clearly what a perfectly well-laid-back shoulder should be like.

The *back*. This must of necessity be strong and broad, fairly long and with a firm strong loin, because this acts as the coupling between the fore-end and the hindquarters. To function properly,

C. M. Cooke

Ch. Wingedfoot Marksman of Allways

Ch. Wingedfoot Claire de Lune

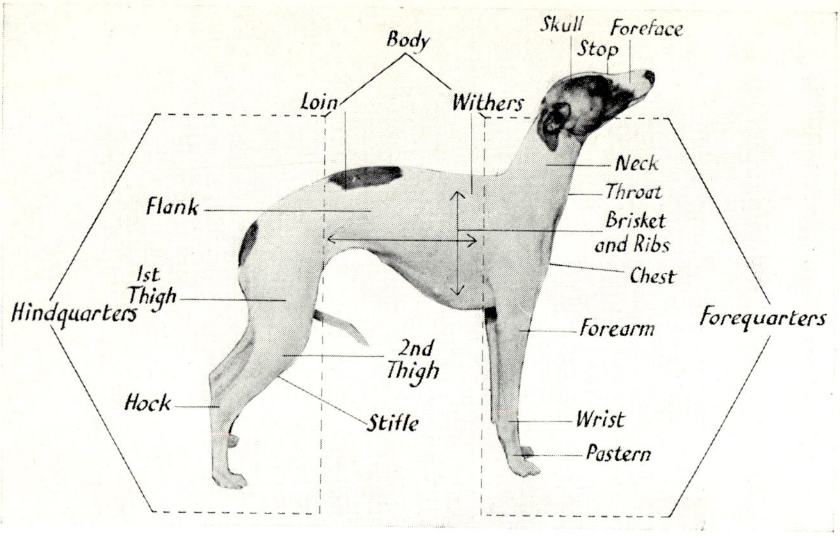

Points of an Exhibition Whippet

Museo Nazionale, Naples

'Wild boar attacked by two dogs'
A statuette found at Pompeii

Ch. Will o' the Wisp of Mimosaland

Puppies twelve days old
(Int. Ch. Wingedfoot Hildegarde and litter)

Forward movement of Wingedfoot Hildebrand

The importance of front legs at speed

and with full power, the loin should be slightly arched, be exceedingly strong and most intricately muscled. Few things detract more from an otherwise lovely Whippet than a flat-back, which becomes apparent when it moves. It denotes the weak loin. If the loin and/or the back is weak, there is no real link-up with the driving power—in other words the Whippet does not function properly and all sorts of troubles result. While on the subject of the back, one is often asked about a 'saw-backed' dog and what can be done about it. That is, how can one get the spine covered if it shows up through the backline? This is largely a matter of development. Some dogs do not fully 'cover their backs' until they are two years old—they are the 'late furnishers'—but they mostly do, and in the meantime 'strapping', i.e. hand massage, will help a lot. Each dog must be considered individually for there is no general rule. Its condition, general condition, should be carefully considered. Its feeding may call for attention —a well-conditioned dog will never have a 'spiney' back—but it is nothing to worry about, for it can generally be overcome with patience.

The *front legs.* These are the props to resist the hind propelling power and to stop a dog from falling. They should be placed

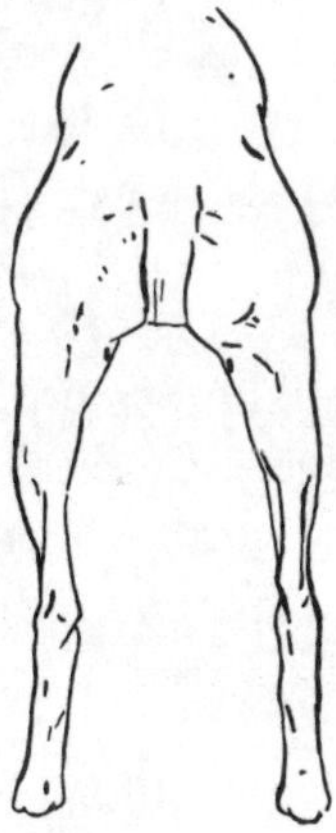

Correct hind formation in a young puppy

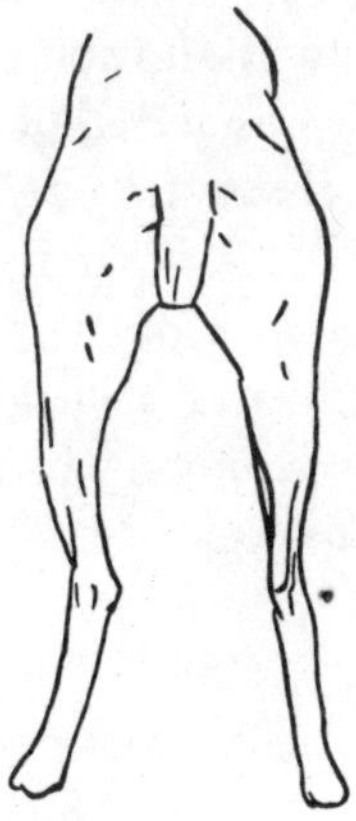

Cow hocks

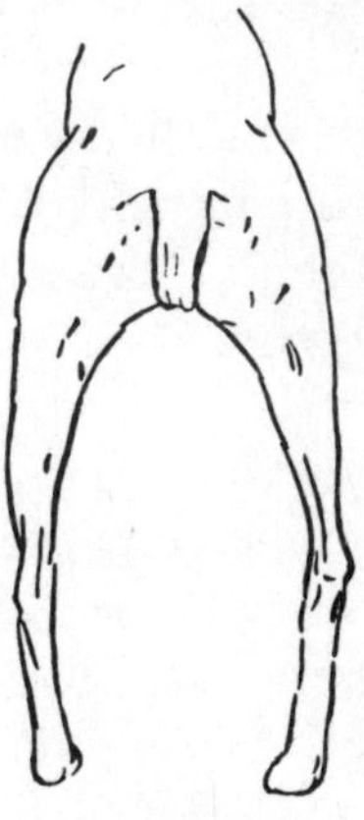

Bow hocks

well back, with elbows close to the body, but not so close under the body that they can be termed 'tied in', as happens in a too narrow-fronted specimen. The points of the elbows in a good dog should point neither in nor out, but straight back. The best way to judge a front, is paradoxically from the *back*. Have your dog 'stood up' and then, while it is held in that position, go round to the rear and have a look at its elbows and note how they fit in with the general conformation. You will then see, for it cannot be hidden from any eye that has even an elementary knowledge of conformation.

The *chest* and *brisket*. The chest must be fairly broad, in conformation with the general build of the dog, to allow for heart room and breathing, while the brisket must be deep and roomy for the same reasons. The heart and lungs *must* be able to function freely and easily when working under great strain and exertion. This will be readily understood and does not call for further comment, except perhaps to say that if you own a dog whose brisket comes down to his elbows and 'cuts up' well under the loin, you have a pearl of great price.

The *pasterns*. These connect the feet to the legs, of course, and should be slightly 'sprung' in order to allow the necessary 'give', which cushions the dog when galloping over hard going, and saves him from jarring on the ground. The pasterns allow for great flexibility in movement, and 'dead upright' pasterns denote the poor mover. An apt illustration is that great racehorse The Tetrarch, which, because of short, straight pasterns, did not stand up to training as a three-year-old.

The *feet*. In this department I have no hesitation in saying that the Whippet has improved out of all knowledge over the last twenty years. Feet have always been a 'something' with me, and one who to some extent acted as my mentor in Whippets, that great judge the late W. J. (Billy) Nichols, always used to say 'No feet—no Whippet' and he was right. Feet are the cushions and they must fulfil that capacity. Thick pads with well 'cut up' toes (the springs again, you see) are called for, with the toes, in addition, being well arched to allow the dog to grip the ground when turning. The round 'walnut foot' sets off a good dog as a frame sets off a picture. But when we come to discuss feet, I have often pondered over the strange fact that the hare, while being the recognized 'game' of the Greyhound, has a completely different type of foot. The hare has no 'ball' to its foot, whereas the Greyhound has a very definite one. Why? It always seems to me that it is like someone having ballet shoes or running pumps, whilst the pursuer is fitted with hobnailed boots in order to catch the speediest thing of its size on earth.

3

Housing, Feeding and Welfare

Housing. Whippets as a breed are able to adjust themselves more or less to any living conditions and are possibly never more happy than when living in the homes of their owner as part of the family. Sharing the comforts of the house, they become the most devoted companions, and because of their sweet natures, handy size and gentleness are the absolute ideal 'first pet' for a child. The question of a child's first dog is something to which I often think insufficient attention is paid. A Peke, for instance, might suggest itself, but I am firmly convinced that it does not come within that category; Toy breed though it is, it is most definitely not every child's 'first pet'. It can too easily be damaged by rough handling, such as a child might give it, and a Peke's eyes are most vulnerable. A Whippet, generally speaking, can take care of itself when with children—average children, that is.

If only one or two Whippets are kept, the purchase of a basket or suitable dog-bed, of which there are several excellent types on the market, together with the addition of a cushion or a small blanket or two, will provide the dogs with everything they require for comfort. If this bed is always kept in one place in the house the dogs soon come to accept it as their own special domain and will keep off the furniture with the smallest amount of training. Brekin Bisque (facing page 65) reclining in perfect comfort in his bed illustrates the use of an excellent idea invented and marketed by Mrs Ena Ford, a one-time keen Whippet exhibitor. One should never spurn the ordinary tea-chest, which may be had even now for a few new pence; Whippets love to snuggle up into them. Completely draught-proof, if they are raised about

3 in. off the floor on blocks of wood nailed under each corner, with a board about 4 in. deep nailed across the bottom of the open front, to retain the bedding, they make as good an indoor kennel as one can find anywhere. Not elaborate or ornamental, they can nevertheless be made most attractive by painting the top and sides, and fixing beading, painted in a contrasting colour, round the edges. If brass-headed nails are also used to good effect, the over-all result is most pleasing. At all events, 'dollied up' or not, a tea-chest makes a most effective indoor kennel.

It does not matter how many dogs are kept, be it a single house-pet or a whole kennel of, say, fifty dogs or more, there are certain general rules which must be observed to ensure that the health and happiness of the Whippet is assured.

Assuming that a large kennel is being started we will devote the rest of this chapter to that aspect. In my experience, the ideal kennel is a converted stable or barn. Not everyone has buildings of this sort available but, for those who have, my advice is to use them to the fullest extent.

I am firmly of the opinion that three things are essential in kennels, namely, freedom from draughts and damp, full and free circulating air, and plenty of light. Dark, draughty, damp kennels will spell disaster from whichever angle they are viewed—so avoid them.

My own kennels are converted barn buildings, planned on the corridor system, and I would never have any other if I could help it. It is a great joy to have kennels one can be proud of and adds much to the enjoyment of owning and looking after dogs; but at the same time it does not necessarily follow that ornate and luxurious fittings are at all necessary or indeed desirable. What is required is plenty of head-room for the attendant, cover under which to work in all weathers, and the general arrangement such that it will save a lot of unnecessary duplication of work and running about; that is, it must incorporate the feed-house, the grooming room, and the room—call it the office if you will—where all the 'paper work' relating to the dogs may be carried out. All this, very grand though it may sound, should not be beyond the ability of anyone to plan provided they have the necessary shell of the building on which to work. However, if this is not available I suggest buying a second-hand hut (the initial outlay will be speedily recovered from the results of your kennel) which can be laid out on the corridor system. A local builder will give advice, help in buying the portable building and probably do much of the work of adapting it. Do get, and this is important, a building which can be made cosy and warm, free from draughts and yet of sufficient height to allow a free passage of air to flow over and through the entire kennel.

Having planned your departments, see that when they are erected there are no struts across the bottom of the doorway leading into the corridor. Unless this is kept in mind it will necessitate using a shovel to pick up the 'sweepings' and preclude your brushing each compartment straight out into the corridor passage. Attention to this simple point will save much back-bending and time.

Much has been written concerning the best type of flooring for kennels. Some advocate brick, others say wood cannot be improved upon. For my part I would say that the old type of stable Blue Bricks makes the perfect flooring, although I appreciate fully that even if they could be obtained today—and have no idea if they are still available or not—their cost would be prohibitive. I think that, taking it all round, a good cement floor, kept well covered with sawdust, is as good as anything. I have used floorings of this nature for many years and have always found them satisfactory in every way. Such a floor must be kept scrupulously clean and dry, and if brushed daily and a dusting of a good powdered disinfectant sprinkled down prior to the sawdust, will be found perfectly satisfactory. The operative word is 'cleanliness', and cleaning and periodical disinfecting of the kennel must become automatic.

The next thing is to attend to the interior furnishing of each compartment. I am not a believer in too much artificial heating. At the same time, I carefully check the temperatures in my kennels and have a thermometer hanging on at least two walls. A fair-sized bench, with a front board to keep the bedding in, is admirable in summer, and if, in winter, a wooden canopy is made to fit over the bench, thus turning it into a kind of box with a smallish means of ingress, and warmly bedded in deep straw, the dogs will generate their own heat and lie cosy and snug. The use of tea-chests as previously suggested for the house-pet will be found entirely satisfactory if installed in the large compartment kennel. I consider them as good as anything; they are exceedingly cheap and can easily be replaced when worn.

When I was in America I inspected several of the kennels which are planned on an entirely different system from any that I have seen in this country, all of them being most beautifully, even elaborately, built, and most, to my mind, along questionable lines. I thought the central heating arrangements were excessive, indeed I consider the Americans themselves make far too much fuss in general about the cold atmosphere.

The most comfortable stay I made was at a house where my charming hostess was most perturbed owing to the fact that the central heating in the Guests' Wing had broken down. She was most disturbed; I was highly delighted and thoroughly enjoyed my stay there.

Regarding the kennels in the States my opinion is that many of the troubles they seem to experience and accept as being a natural course of events could be traced to their excessive heating. A properly groomed, well-fed and well-exercised healthy adult dog does *not* require any artificial heat, always provided he is kennelled and bedded correctly. I am fully aware that large kennels of Greyhounds usually have the inmates 'rugged up' at night, and for dogs employed in coursing, and indeed for racing dogs, where muscular power is such a determining factor, there is much in its favour. I have tried this with my Whippets but have never found a dog with its night rug on when I have opened the kennels the next morning. A rug a night per dog is rather more than my pocket can afford, even if clean sacking is used instead of a blanket. As regards bedding, I incline above all things to the wood-wool type of bedding. This is, as most people will know, a sort of shredded wood that comes in bales, often being used by manufacturers and suppliers of glass-ware and breakable articles as a packing medium. Bedding of this kind is advertised in the canine journals and is quite easily obtainable. A good, clean, long wheat straw makes an excellent bedding and is a good substitute, but the short stuff we get in bales today is only a very second best. Hay? Well, in winter it may have its uses and I should not entirely condemn it, although there are those who do because it is supposed to encourage fleas and is too heating. My chief criticism of hay is that it gets too easily broken up and becomes dusty and messy. A good wood-wool will last for a long time; in addition, it has the merit of being a non-harbourer of vermin and does not get messy or mixed up in the food. On the other hand, wood-wool should be used with the utmost care with puppies because there is the danger of its getting entwined round their necks, with disastrous results. Therefore, the whelping bitch should never be provided with wood-wool bedding in any circumstances.

While on the subject of bedding, which is an important one, I noticed that, in America, newspapers were universally used, sawdust seemed to be unknown, and the suggestion of using it was roundly condemned as being the cause of puppies being blinded and so on. Admiring our American cousins as I wholeheartedly do I must admit that I just could not understand some of their practices in the matter of kennelling their dogs—and yet they nearly all adopt the same system.

Another fitting which should have the closest attention is the water bowl and holder. I am fussy about always having a constant supply of fresh drinking water available for each dog. We all know, however, that many dogs will insist on tipping the water bowl over when they have drunk their fill. This can be overcome if the bowl fits into an iron ring—and the local blacksmith will make one for a very small charge—which is nailed inside the kennel compartment about a foot from the ground. This fitment should be arranged so that it can be re-filled from outside the compartment. It is an easy method of 'watering the dogs' and a great time and trouble saver.

The treatment of all interior woodwork with creosote will act as a deterrent to the dogs chewing gates and posts. If this does not stop them from gnawing it, a completely satisfactory protection is to nail narrow strips of zinc or other metal along the edges of the gates, benches and so on. These strips of metal can be obtained from any metal-working establishment and are usually known as 'off-cuts'. They cost very little and are sometimes even given away. Your local ironmonger will probably be able to tell you where 'off-cuts' can be obtained locally.

It is essential that Whippets should be provided with large and roomy runs. Without these the task of maintaining a sizeable kennel creates work and worry to such an extent that the whole thing becomes hardly worth while. It doesn't matter what the geographical position is, unless you have spacious runs, you will never be free from worry and trouble. I speak from bitter experience.

If you intend to breed Whippets, please don't make the mistake of thinking that a bitch will whelp and rear her puppies successfully if she merely has a compartment to herself in the general kennel. A bitch requires a nursery all to herself and her puppies, preferably out of range of sound from the others—and this should be planned. A small well-built shed will do very well, and it too should have its sizeable run where the puppies can play and grow until they are of an age to be introduced into the main kennel.

A completely separate 'hospital' should also be planned; at some time or another there will be a dog that should be segregated if only for observation. Visiting bitches always require such a kennel. So don't forget your isolation kennel in your lay-out. All this may sound alarming and elaborate at the outset, but it isn't really, and kennels of the type I have outlined are more often than not the outcome of years of development and experience.

I have mentioned earlier that Whippets live happily in the house and do well under such conditions, but I think it will be found that those which appear in the show-ring very 'tucked up' and fussy, and so on, are rarely those which live in a well-managed outside kennel. Whippets are sporting dogs and do better when they are kept and treated in a manner fitting to their calling. In conclusion, one word in regard to kennel management. Do, if at all possible, work to the clock. Dogs get very systemetized and get to know when it is kennel-opening time, feeding time, grooming time, cleaning time, exercising time and closing-up time. Get them into a system and a lot of the work of running a kennel is done. I *know* I am right, for experience has taught me the sense of it.

Feeding. The feeding of human beings and stock animals is of such importance in our modern world that the aid of science has been invoked. In every community, the mother can take her children to clinics where she will receive the best available advice on the care and feeding of her offspring. The farmer, in his turn, has learned that to get the best results from his dairy herd, each cow must be fed on what is termed 'a balanced ration'. As with the mother and the farmer, the dog-owner must also approach feeding matters more or less scientifically, and that holds good whether it is just one dog living with him in the house, or a sizeable kennel of dogs. From my own observations I believe that the dogs put up at shows today are benefiting from up-to-date methods of feeding, for those I have seen at shows are much healthier than those shown twenty-five years ago. The general level of health and fitness in the canine world has never been so high as it is today.

A dog is a meat-eating animal, i.e. carnivorous, and his long and strong canine teeth were made to tear flesh. Throw a dog a tough piece of meat such as a bullock's cheek, and he will stand on it with his front paws, and tear it with his teeth, chewing the pieces he pulls off. This is Nature's way, and it should be introduced to puppies by pegging a large piece of flesh to the ground with, say, an ordinary garden fork. I think, at one time, dogs were exclusively meat-eaters, and the puppies, as soon as they were able, ate meat brought to the nest by their mother, who tore it into small pieces for them. In fact, I *know* this to be so, because I have actually watched a nest of wild dogs being fed in this way. It happened when I was stationed in Central India, my Bearer reporting to me that he had found a nest of wild dogs in a burrow like a fox-earth, in the jungle. Keep this point, about the natural feeding of puppies, in mind when I come, later, to the question of feeding puppies.

At various times I have had quite a large kennel of dogs of different breeds, including several varieties of Toy breeds, and from the experience I have gained on the practical side I have become convinced that meat is the best possible feeding for condition, stamina and general health. By 'meat' I do not mean only the best cut from the joint, but everything. For instance, if a hound catches a rabbit, what does he do with it? He devours every part of his catch; flesh, intestines, bones and skin and the fur coat too! In this way he obtains his natural balanced ration, just as the wild dog did and does, as Nature intended him to. In order to get his food, the wild dog has to hunt for it and, in consequence, takes much more exercise than we can normally give a domestic dog. As a result, the domestic dog has lost much of his hardness. Today, science has proved, because of that fact, that we have to provide certain other foods to counterbalance what he has lost through not living the wild existence his ancestors once enjoyed. His wild way of life enabled the dog to obtain the substances he needed for growth, for the energy that would enable him to hunt to live and protect him from sickness and disease.

It is now accepted that proteins, carbohydrates and fats are the three classifications of food necessary to animal life, plus certain minerals and vitamins. Proteins promote growth. They are the body builders. Carbohydrates and fats create energy and heat and minerals and vitamins cause them so to act that they create life itself and provide the power to reproduce that life. This is perhaps an over-simplified and non-scientific explanation of this most important subject but it gives a rough and ready idea of the principles. Do not overlook the fact that everything discussed here affects the 'one dog owner' just as much as the owner of a large kennel.

What do we classify as proteins? They are, roughly, meat, fish, eggs and milk. Carbohydrates we can say are, in the main, found in certain vegetables, cereals and so on—in other words sugars and starches. Fats of any sort fill in the third section—meat-fats, fish-fats (cod-liver oil, etc.), milk, butter and so on. Vitamins and minerals are found in most raw foods, but I have found that I can get excellent results from using a branded compound called Vivomin. The foregoing is, again, only a rough and ready guide to what is required, and I have not mentioned the whole range of foods suitable for dogs.

In recommending that a dog should be fed on meat, it is necessary to emphasize that there are two kinds of meat: the actual 'body' and 'joint' meat, and with the 'inside' meat, that is, the offals, namely liver, kidneys, heart, tripe and so on. By feeding both kinds of meat the necessary vitamins are then provided. I think the best way to feed the 'outside' meat is in the raw state; the offals I consider should be cooked. Meat cooked for dogs should be simmered slowly, and the fat should be fed as well as the cooked flesh. If the gravy is used, as it should be, of course, with cereals, do not strain off the fat unless it is excessive, as when fat breast of mutton, etc., is used. Even then, do not strain it *all* off. I am strongly of the opinion, based again on long experience, that dogs kept short of fat are more prone to hysteria than those given a fair supply. Fish is exceptionally good for dogs, and they are, in the main, very fond of it. Cooked herrings are extremely good, so are sprats and cods' heads boiled down so that they can be pulped. Fish and liver are excellent for dogs because both contain iodine and phosphorous. Milk is a grand food for dogs of all ages and should be given to them daily. Eggs beaten up in milk make an excellent food for the racing dog. Milk should be given *with* the cream, not skimmed. A half-pint of milk beaten up with one egg makes an excellent breakfast for a Whippet, and if given, in addition to the excellent rusk-biscuits supplied under the branded name of Laughing Dog, at midday, plus a full meat and cereal meal at night, any Whippet will do very well indeed.

Although one must admit that fresh meat is the finest of all foods for dogs, in these days great difficulty is experienced in obtaining regular supplies. For my part I will *not* use, neither do I recommend, 'knacker's meat'. I cannot get away from the thought of the dead animal having been pumped full of various antibiotics and so on. I am also no enthusiast for horse flesh as I do not take kindly to the thought of horses being slaughtered. This used to present a serious difficulty—and, most certainly, an expense.

However, through my friendship with a famous greyhound trainer I was put on to a good thing—Lowe's Granulated Meat, manufactured by the famous Kentish firm of such high repute.

I have used this meat with great success. It is cheap, and is guaranteed to be prepared from pure butcher's meat which has been passed as fit for human consumption. A certain proportion of the fat is removed in the course of manufacture, but sufficient of the marrow fat content is left to provide a food which has been proved by nutritional experts to be both sustaining and satisfying.

I think every kennel of any size would be well advised to have a supply of this preparation standing by at the very least. For my part, my dogs have it served three times a week, and they love it.

I always feed the main meal at night and, as far as possible, always at the same time *after* letting the dogs out for exercise. Naturally a variation of food helps a lot, but I think it is advisable to keep to the same cereal or biscuit meal, once you have found one that suits your dogs. The selecting of a good biscuit meal should be considered carefully. Some years ago, when I was experiencing persistent trouble in my kennel, my vet took up with me the question of biscuit meal and baked brown wholemeal bread slices. What he told me, and later showed me, convinced me that he was right, especially in regard to weevils and so on, which can, and do, get into biscuit meal bought haphazardly from any source. I always use one brand, Laughing Dog brand Wheatmeal, and have found it excellent. I have tested it in many ways and it has always passed the test. The Milkwheat biscuits I find to be outstanding, and it is a joy to see the dogs waiting to get their fair share of their 'elevenses' of this product. It may be found that excessive use of Milkwheat, together with the biscuit meal made by the same firm, may tend to cause Whippets to put on a little extra weight, but this is a matter which can easily be adjusted. In Whippets which somehow seem to resist attempts to put on a little 'condition', I have found these products invaluable. I also recommend the same firm's Milk Food product, from the use of which I have obtained excellent results. This is not surprising when one comes to consider the added content of this preparation. I strongly recommend it.

Food should be varied. On Sundays, for example, I generally feed raw fresh meat only as the main meal, and when this is fed care must be taken to see that each dog gets his full and fair share. Despite what may be said to the contrary, when I feed raw meat only I base my dogs' requirements, that is the adults, on 1 lb. per dog, and I see that each gets it. In order to make certain of this, I use the scales and carefully weigh each ration and feed separately. If this is not done a lot of trouble may ensue if some of the dogs go short. It should be noted that while starch is necessary for promoting energy it should never be fed alone as a main meal. Oatmeal is fattening and is often used extensively in hound kennels and by the shepherds in Scotland. It is claimed that some working sheepdogs live solely on oatmeal throughout their lives. Flaked maize is often spoken of very highly, and I have used it upon occasion in place of biscuit meal. On the other hand, there are those who aver that excessive feeding of maize flakes promotes skin trouble. Flaked maize is quite cheap and easy to obtain. When all is said and done, a careful eye on the dogs to note how they are doing is the real barometer. Incidentally, orange juice is excellent for preventing scurf and is good for coats. Linseed, boiled into a mash, if used in moderation, is also an excellent coat conditioner, but should be used sparingly as it is very heating.

If a good-sized mincer is purchased—and this should be a 'must' in any fair-sized kennel—carrots, greens and other vegetables may be run through it and mixed with the food. The dogs will take it with relish. Onions used in this way are beneficial but they should not be given in excess.

Biscuit meal should be soaked in cold water and should be prepared early each morning to be ready for using for the main meal at night. Cold water should be used—I must emphasize this—in preparing Laughing Dog Wheatmeal meals, as the use of boiling water, or very hot water even, draws out and impairs the vitamin content. Cold water does not have this effect. Meat should be mixed with the soaked meal just prior to feeding and, as I always prefer to serve a warm meal, use the hot gravy in which the meat has been cooked, and see that the whole is well mixed and made appetizing. The consistency of the food when ready to serve should be crumbly moist, which means that if you take a handful and squeeze it, it should remain bound together. Never feed sloppy meals to normally healthy dogs. There is nothing to recommend it as it causes looseness of the bowels and so on. The *only* dry biscuit I feed is Laughing Dog brand Milkwheat biscuits (rusks).

Most dog-owners often refer to the fact that their dogs will eat grass, especially in the Spring of the year, which they either 'throw up'—when it may be seen to be coated with yellow bile—or pass through their bodies undigested, as can be seen by their motions. This is, obviously, Nature's way of providing the dog with something necessary for his constitution, or a means of cleansing himself internally, and a dog should never be stopped from 'grazing' if he wants to do it. On the other hand, I have found that if bullocks' tripes are fed occasionally, or sheep's paunches, a dog will rarely resort to eating grass. This shows that the tripes and the paunches, which should be fed *raw* and not be bleached after they have been hosed down at the abbatoir, as is customary, are an effective substitute for grass.

The following may interest many readers who give considerable thought to their feeding of dogs. I have often pondered over the fact that dogs will 'go barmy' over fresh raw bullocks' tripe or sheep's paunch. I have known them literally to snatch it from one's hand even after they have enjoyed a full main meal. This particularly applies to Greyhounds. *All* of them seem able to find room at any time for a good feed of this type of offal. I set a test one day to see what would happen, and I was so interested in the results that I repeated it again and again, and always with the same result. I took six adult dogs and placed before them, in a straight line, six dishes, each containing: (*a*) cooked oxtails, (*b*) boiled chicken, (*c*) fresh raw red meat—cut up, (*d*) biscuit meal soaked in tasty gravy, (*e*) cooked liver and, finally, (*f*) cut raw bullocks' tripe. In every case the dogs cleared the tripe first. They ran their noses right along the whole line of dishes, and in every case the six dogs at once 'woofed' the tripe. Afterwards they worked their way back along the other dishes, but there was no possible doubt concerning the dogs' passion for fresh raw tripe. For that reason I feed it regularly, twice or three times a week as a main meal, mixed with the biscuit meal or sometimes alone. Finally, and I think this emphasizes the point more than any other, the only time I have known dogs to over-feed themselves to the extent that they have had to 'throw up' to ease their overladen stomachs was when, as an experiment, I fed raw tripe *ad lib*. This is, indeed, the only food on which I have known dogs, literally, to gorge themselves.

I hope the foregoing will give a fairly general idea of how to feed, at least in my judgement, Whippets, to keep them in good health and sparkling condition. Let us, however, sum up on the vitamins. These are necessary to protect a dog from ailments and to promote growth. Vitamins A, B, C and D are found in the foods I have mentioned, but from time to time a toning up with calcium and phosphorous may be beneficial. This is where you will find the benefits of the preparation I have mentioned, Vivomin. Lack of calcium is a serious doggy deficiency and that is when vitamin D becomes very important. Calcium is necessary for bone and teeth promotion and is found in milk. Phosphorous is necessary for gland functions and is found in fish. Iron, which is found in liver and wheat, is necessary to guard against anaemia.

Lastly, never make the mistake of neglecting supplies of pure clean water for drinking—this must always be available.

Welfare. In the general treatment of the Whippet, apart from housing and feeding, exercising and grooming play an important part. Whippets, being single-coated dogs, feel the cold winds, so it is necessary to provide each dog with a warm coat to wear when out on walks. Deva Dog Ware Ltd specialize in Whippet requirements and have a most suitable coat on the market. This can be obtained at their stand which is usually prominent at all the big shows. If any of my readers do not visit many shows the address of this firm is Deva Dog Ware Ltd., Pontycrynfe, Llangodog, Carms. When obtaining a Whippet coat make sure that you get one which fits well and does not chafe at any point, otherwise it will wear away the dog's hair.

Most Whippet owners plan exercising time to suit their circumstances, and the time available. Two miles a day is ample to keep any Whippet reasonably well muscled up and in good general condition. I like to see my dogs go out regularly, and weather permitting, at about the same time each day. I like them to have two miles road-work daily, but if for some reason this is not always possible I like them to have about half an hour's scamper in a safe field. This, in addition to their having full use of their large runs all day, I regard as sufficient exercise. I know there are those who may not agree and will possibly claim that Whippets need much more daily exercise than I have suggested, but I do not think it is so. The Whippet is by nature a very active dog and if he has a good-sized run he will take almost all the exercise he needs without going on the road. Whatever you do, never exercise dogs on leads while riding a bicycle. I have known of some nasty accidents arising from this practice, which is a lazy one when all is said and done. Never allow your dogs to go out with anyone riding a pony either, as the latter can be very quick in the use of its hoof and often is—without warning.

Grooming is something that calls for serious attention. Many people think that because of its naturally short, tight coat a Whippet needs very little attention. This may be true to some extent but to expect your dog to look its best if it is rarely brushed, and then at odd times, is wishful thinking. A Whippet to look really well needs regular grooming, but little bathing. I have found that a systemized method of regular grooming is much the best way to ensure that a dog's coat carries that sleek and satiny look. Of course, inner cleanliness is essential if a dog is to carry a first-class coat, but we will assume that this point has been seen to. I have a grooming outfit which I use regularly and in rotation. This outfit comprises a 'dandy' brush (the kind used in stables) a smaller and softer bristle brush, a rubber spiked brush, a fine-tooth comb, a hound glove and a soft, polishing cloth. The manner in which I groom a dog is as follows: first, a thorough and general brushing over with the 'dandy' brush, this will loosen and remove any mud that may be caked on the dog's coat, and, being stiff, will act as a comb to some degree. Next I use the tooth-comb to ensure that the dog is free from parasites. Following this, I give a thorough over-all brushing with the softer brush. This is followed by a good going-over with the rubber spiked brush, which is very useful and has a certain massaging effect as well as being the correct thing to use when doing the more tender parts of the dog, the face, the underparts and inside the thighs. Next the dog is very thoroughly 'gone over' with the hound glove, and this is followed by a complete 'polishing off' with the soft cloth.

I like grooming a dog and, therefore, it is a pleasure rather than a chore to me, and fifteen minutes spent daily on each dog is really worth the effort. A grooming table, fitted with a small drawer in which to keep the brushes, etc., will be found to be very useful in the grooming room. At the back of the table, on the wall will do, a large mirror should be fixed. Such a mirror can usually be bought for a few shillings from any second-hand furniture dealer. This mirror will prove most useful in helping you to see how your dog appears when 'stacked' for showing. I have always regarded this fitment as another kennel 'must'.

Teeth call for regular inspection. To remove any signs of tartar is a simple matter and should have attention. If the tartar deposit is really bad, one should obtain the small scaling tool made for the purpose and use it to hook the deposit off the teeth in the manner in which your dentist attends to your own. In its early stages tartar can be easily removed by the gentle application of a cloth which has been dipped in hydrogen-peroxide diluted with water. Peroxide should not be used undiluted as it may cause irritation to the gums. The ears should receive regular attention and be inspected from time to time to check against canker. When this is apparent, a light dusting with one of the well-known branded preparations should be carried out. If you should ever have a dog in your kennel so badly affected with canker of the ear that it calls for the use of a syringe, you should call the vet, as damage can easily be done to the ear-drum and may cause permanent deafness, not to mention very great pain. Whippets very often get their ears into their food dishes causing dust and dirt to adhere to the edges. This causes, in time, a thickening of the hair along the edges of the ears and then little clots come away when being groomed, leaving an untidy ragged-looking ear. It is very unsightly and is caused by sheer neglect. If any dog is inclined to mess up his ears in this way the use of a small sponge and a little warm soapy water will speedily put matters right, and in the daily grooming the ears should be carefully brushed, being laid flat on the palm of the attendant's hand, to prevent a reoccurrence.

4

Breeding

We come now to a most absorbing part of our Whippet activities—breeding. Anything I may have to say in this chapter does not mean that I consider my system to be the only one that should be employed, for no one can be dogmatic in regard to the breeding and rearing of puppies. Also, any hints or suggestions I may give as we go along will merely be a recording of what I have found suits me and my dogs, nothing more.

First, the selection of the brood bitch. When I first set about breeding dogs seriously for show I was taught, in fact it was constantly dinned into me, that if I thought first in terms of brood bitches I would soon be thinking in terms of champions. I was assured that this was the only policy to pursue if I wished to become successful. It was sound advice, which I have faithfully followed, and to it I attribute any measure of success my dogs have attained. But what do we require in our brood bitch? Do we know? Have we an ideal or are we just 'waffling around' following this, that and the other as the 'stars' rise and pass over the exhibition horizon? Obviously we must, after careful study, make up our minds what we want to do before we set about it. We will presume, however, that we have given time and thought to the question and that each reader has determined the objective of 'Operation Breeding'.

At this stage perhaps I can illustrate how vitally important it is to know what you want to achieve, by recording how I found the ideal mate for Ch. Wingedfoot Marksman. Marksman at that time was just approaching his full stature as a show-dog.

I decided that, as he continued the line from my first champion of the early 'thirties (a pure Willes-bred dog), Ch. Will o' the Wisp of Mimosaland (that being my wife's prefix), I must find the right bitch if I were to succeed in my plan. For a whole year I went to shows, looking all the time for the right type of bitch for what I had in mind. I did not want pedigree so much—I was looking for *type* first. I knew what I wanted, but for the life of me I just couldn't find what I wanted. Lewis Renwick was also on the look-out for me and he was meeting with the same difficulties as I was.

Then one day, at a London Championship Show, I saw Mrs K. Chapman in the ring handling a bitch which was by no means up to the Benachi standard of fitness or presentation on the day, but which, I saw, had that elusive 'something' that I felt was what I wanted. The more I studied this bitch from the ringside the more firmly I was convinced that she was what I wanted, and I decided that by hook or by crook she *must* become mine. As I was waiting for Mrs Chapman to come out of the ring Lewis Renwick wandered up in that casual way so typical of him and said, 'Douglas, *there* is the bitch you want—that one Mrs Chapman is showing now.' If I had needed confirmation of my own impression of the bitch I could not have had it from a better authority, for if ever a man lived who could size up the potentials of a Whippet, that man was the late Lewis Renwick. To cut a long story short the bitch, through the kindness of Mrs Chapman, became my property and a most devoted and lovable creature she was too. Always one of the 'lean kine' she was rarely shown, but she wasn't required as a show bitch, but as a brood bitch. That bitch was the lovely Wingedfoot Lannette, and a scrutiny of her picture (facing page 64) will convey a complete appreciation of the necessary qualities a successful brood bitch should possess. From the alliance of Marksman and Lannette came no less than five full champions. Today, as I write, Lannette lives in happy retirement back again in the kennel from which she came—Mrs Chapman's—and while she is still registered as being mine, the affection Mrs Chapman has for her is equal to my own, and there she will live out the rest of her days.

We will assume that you know what you want to produce, and we will now look for your bitch. In the first place, because she is required as a matron, she need not necessarily have strong show points; in fact, it is better that she shouldn't have, but there are some essentials she must have. She must certainly not be undersized or weedy. Again, no matter how beautiful she may be over-all, if she has no spring of ribs, a gun-barrel front and so on —in other words inclined to weediness no matter how slightly she shows it—do *not* regard her as a foundation brood bitch for your kennel, not even if she is a champion ten times over. Challenge Certificate winners do not, in turn, produce winners automatically. No, you need, coupled with a decent pedigree, the real matron, the same kind of happy, healthy creature as the jolly, happy laughing-type farmer's wife of Olde England. I know of no better way of expressing it than by saying: a bitch of the obviously matron type.

How do we assess that? Well, first of all I would rather have one a little oversize—I would look for a sound front, good feet, a reachy neck, deep brisket and a good spring of ribs. A little long in the body would not deter me, in fact I should prefer it, and one with definitely strong quarters. Overall she might be a trifle heavy. She may be over-strong throughout for the ring, but so long as she is sound, both in movement and in health and temperament, that would be the one for me to accept as a brood bitch.

The faults for which I would discard a brood bitch would be one bred from a stud dog I knew to have a strong streak of the mon- or cryptorchid in his lineage. I would not 'touch' such a bitch if I knew of this background. Neither would I entertain one with open and thin feet, nor with flat ribs or the other fault, 'barrel-ribs', nor one with too narrow a front. I should cock a questioning eye at one with too short a neck. A bandy-legged mover or a 'weaver' or a 'plaiter' would never be acceptable to me as a brood bitch.

Finally, I should go to a kennel whose exhibits approached my ideal and I would place myself entirely in the hands of the owner, telling him exactly what I wanted and listening very carefully to all he had to tell me. I think no one should experience undue difficulty in obtaining a brood bitch to produce a reasonably good litter at the first attempt. Price? Well, a dog is worth what? 'What the seller can get' the cynic will say, which is about right, but experience has taught me that there are many in the breed who are usually able to supply what you want, and they are very fair and reasonable people. So I should trust them and keep in mind the fact that, all being well, I should recover any initial outlay, and more, in my first litter. Whippets as a rule are extremely easy whelpers and invariably excellent mothers. I should say a ceiling price for a really good type of brood bitch would not be excessive at around £35 but, on the other hand, many a grand bitch has changed hands for under a 'tenner'. Age? If I wanted to begin breeding as early as possible one about two years old would be ideal, but if she had already produced a litter and had been well proved I would not turn one down if it happened to be a year older. It is well to remember, when thinking of brood bitches, that it is a generally accepted fact that the early litters are usually the best, so that if you are offered one which has already had, say, three litters, I would not feel inclined to take her on unless the price was very attractive.

One word of warning. If you are one of those who think that by buying the 'throw-out' bitch puppy of an otherwise excellent litter at a 'give-away' price you are going to establish a top-line kennel, I assure you that you are preparing to take a long and difficult road which may, or may not, have a very sticky ending. I would certainly accept the exact type of brood bitch for which I was seeking in preference to the most brilliant show-type bitch which did not possess the qualifications I consider are so vitally necessary in a brood bitch.

The Stud Dog. It is not necessary to run a stud dog when starting to found a kennel; in fact it is far better not to at the outset. The careful selection of the stud dog must, however, be regarded as step number two. Having secured your brood bitch you have 'something to march on' as it were. You know her breeding, and you should by now have some idea of the various dogs standing at stud, and what they have produced when mated to bitches carrying similar blood-lines to your own bitch. I always think the Terrier folk give most of us a lead in this respect, for they always aver that in a stud dog you *must* have a dog which 'has plenty give'. Avoid a bitchy 'pretty-pretty dog' no matter how brilliant his show record may be. The fact that a dog is a Champion in the show-ring by no means guarantees that he will be a success at stud, as I have remarked already regarding a brood bitch.

Another thing, when you get your brood bitch do not, with your meagre knowledge, immediately start to think in terms of an 'out-cross'. I am convinced that the production of poor dogs of all breeds is the result of experimental indulging in the craze for 'out-crossing'. I often think the most apt analogy in connection with 'out-crossing' is that of a chef who spends hours and hours adding a little of this and a little of that, simmering and tasting and so on until he produces the perfect soup. It is served at the table to a man who, before he has even tasted it, stretches out his hand for the most pungent sauce he can get and dollops in a great spoonful, thus ruining all the care and thought the chef has put into the soup's making. This is just what the experimenter in out-crossing does when he decides to found a 'new blood-line'. So think what you are doing when looking for the sire of your first litter. I would most strongly advise that when you buy your brood bitch you obtain all the details you can of her breeding, and take up with the seller what he would recommend as a suitable mate for her in her next season. Nine times out of ten he will give you some excellent advice, and if he suggests one of his own stud dogs don't immediately jump to wrong conclusions. The seller is probably giving you the very best advice you could possibly have and, possibly, had you not brought her, he would have carried out that same mating with excellent results. Gain all the knowledge you can, therefore, but before finally acting upon it have a look round and see what you can find out from the show catalogues and so on, and what results the dog suggested to you by your 'seller friend' has got. You will be surprised what can be found out in this way and it is exceedingly interesting too, to seek out these details.

Later on, as you gain in experience, you may consider 'adding a little of this and a little of that' in the nature of a little mild 'out-crossing'. But, whatever you do don't plunge in 'at the deep end' at the very outset when you are fired with a laudable ambition but weighed down by lack of experience, for very many high hopes have been dashed in that way. Another pitfall to be avoided is using some local dog just because he is handy to get to. *Use the very best dog for your bitch that you can find*, and don't regard the few extra shillings that may be asked for his service. Also, consider very carefully before agreeing to any suggestion that a puppy should be given in lieu of a stud fee. You may find yourself parting with the 'flyer of the litter', and if your bitch is a really likely proposition as a brood bitch, and the dog is a top-liner and a proved sire of outstanding stock to such a bitch as yours is, the possibilities are distinctly in favour of your being called upon to do so. It is *always* better to pay the stud fee and be done with it—you know where you are then. You will, of course, come to an arrangement with the owner of the stud dog that, in the event of the bitch not producing puppies—a somewhat rare event in the case of Whippets—he will allow your bitch a free service on a subsequent 'season.' This is the general rule and I have never known a stud-dog owner to quibble at it, because naturally he is as keen for his dog to sire something outstanding to your bitch as you are; but it is as well to get the point clear at the time of the first mating.

We are agreed, then, that we need a really masculine type of dog as a stud—one with substance, remembering that what he lacks he cannot be expected to produce—and don't listen to those who may tell you of the wonderful results some little 'weed' who was classically bred produced. It may sound very thrilling but, take it from me, it very rarely happens if, indeed, it ever does. Play safe. Choose a stud dog with an undeniable record and if his fee is a little higher than some other don't let that influence you if you really feel that *he* is the best proposition for your bitch. Remember, there is a great difference between investment and expense, and when you are using a stud dog's services you are investing.

In addition to substance, what else is an essential in the stud dog to look for? Movement. Avoid using a stud dog which is in any way suspect in movement. Bad movers invariably produce bad movers. Never allow anyone to convince you otherwise.

To sum up: you need a stud dog that is strong and masculine, a good mover, as sound as a bell and with quarters and body properties as near perfection as possible. What is more, you need one with an undeniable production record if he has been standing at stud for any time, and, in the case of a younger dog not so much used and whose progeny is not yet either numerous or matured, one whose breeding conforms with your programme, in addition to his physical make-up.

When your bitch is just about ready for mating don't *then* start negotiations for your stud dog, for your mind should have been made up weeks previously and all the details settled long before. The owner of the stud dog likes to have his bookings well in advance, and if his dog has been booked to your bitch and all plans made, it is better to *know* that the dog has not been used, say the day before, than to *hope* he has not, when you arrive with your bitch. It *might* be all right if he has, but you don't want any *might* about it—you need to *know*. So plan well ahead.

Now a few thoughts on in-breeding, without getting too technical. A lot is written on this subject, most of which does no more than hopelessly confuse the novice. I have found, as others have found, that a lot of theory does not work out in actual practice. It is amazing how 'near' one can go without in any way impairing the breed, any breed. For instance, father to daughter more often than not gives very good results, whereas son to mother invariably very poor. Brother and sister matings are fraught with danger and not to be recommended, while grand-father to grand-daughter can be, and often is, brilliantly successful. There is no royal road, but I would ever incline to father to daughter or to grand-daughter as being the most likely inter-family alliance to produce outstanding results. Cousins are more or less normal matings and so on. I and the late Stanley Wilkin, of the famous Tiptree strain of Whippets, had many an argument about close in-breeding which became acrimonious at times, to say the least. I always considered that he indulged in in-breeding to a very dangerous degree. Wilkin ran his dogs on the colony system, as near as makes no difference. When challenged, his reply was always the same: 'There is nothing biologically wrong with it—consider the partridges of the fields. . . .' There seemed to be no answer to that. There is no doubt that Wilkin did much to improve the breed. Fronts and feet he most certainly improved, even if he did flatten out ribs to some extent. Size he seemed to have completely mastered, and one thing about the Tiptrees was that they were certainly a level lot. One strange thing about Stanley Wilkin was that he detested having to attend to a dogs presentation prior to showing it, for he contended that any judge worth his salt should be able to see through 'tittivating up', as he called it, and he was content to leave it at that. That he suffered in the matter of awards goes without saying. Nevertheless he was a grand supporter of the breed.

Whelping is possibly the most nerve-racking experience the novice can have at the outset yet, here again, a little common sense will make this a very simple task, provided there are no complications, which, in Whippets, seldom arise. First, it is always as well to inform your vet and have him 'standing by' in case of emergency. I have always found that veterinary surgeons are invariably most helpful and often as keen and enthusiastic to get results as the owner. I am most fortunate in my own vet, and for this I am most grateful as are, I am sure, many breeders. Be sure that you have the whelping day well in mind, and for a day or so before the happy event takes place put your bitch on her own in her whelping quarters. Watch her carefully and note how she is getting on. The bitch should be allowed the use of her whelping box when she is put on her own, and those who do not allow this make a great mistake, in my opinion.

Assuming that the reader has made all these arrangements, a few hints regarding the care of the matron in whelp will not be out of place. Building up the bitch should receive special care even before the mating. For a period of about five weeks after mating her usual daily routine may be continued, but after that period a check should be put upon her taking any form of violent exercise: high jumping, falls and the possibility of her getting bruised. Good walks, however, and free use of a large run should be encouraged even during the week just prior to whelping. One word of warning here—if you are taking the 'in-whelp' bitch out for walks with a few others, and they are all on leads as you go through a gate, do take care that, in their eagerness to get out, the mated bitch does not get crushed against the sides of the gate-way. I have known more than one instance where puppies have been lost through just this very thing happening. Dogs normally burst through gate-ways, and it is never noticed that they bump themselves against the posts. Normally it doesn't matter much, but with a bitch in whelp it becomes a very different matter. If there is any doubt about the presence of worms the bitch should be wormed within three weeks following her service, but *not* later. Any doubt about her skin condition should call for its immediate clearing, for a whelping bitch needs to be absolutely healthy in every respect. It is of the utmost importance, too, to ensure that the brood bitch is not allowed to become over-fat before service because a bitch in such a condition can suffer very greatly.

Generous feeding of raw meat and fish (because of its iodine content) during pregnancy should be the rule. A teaspoonful of bicarbonate of soda may be added to the drinking water occasionally during this period. The giving of wheat-germ oil, because of its high vitamin-E content, will tend to avoid sterility and miscarriage. Cod-liver oil is also a valuable addition to the diet at this time. As a precaution against acid milk, calcium gluconate should be included as a contributor of bone-calcium to the dam. Milk of magnesia every third day or so will act as an intestinal cleanser in a mild way.

About or before the fifth week it can generally be determined whether the bitch is carrying or not; but the less one probes and messes the bitch about the better.

Usually the gestation period is about sixty-three days, but the whelping may occur as early as the fifty-eighth day or as late as the sixty-seventh day—outside these rather wide margins survival of the puppies is doubtful, although there are plenty of exceptions. Almost all bitches will whelp their puppies without assistance, and indeed many owners tend to be over-solicitous and constantly in attendance upon a whelping bitch. True she will need careful watching, but don't interfere with her too much. She knows a great deal more about whelping puppies than either you or I do. Keep an eye on her then; but don't worry her unduly, for she will be in a high state of nervous tension, so 'quietly does it'.

Items that may be placed handy are as follows: a supply of newspapers for bedding (unless you prefer to use, as I do, clean sheets of sacking), paper tissues for drying the puppies, scissors (blunt-ended), petroleum jelly, brandy (a small drop of which may be necessary to keep a puppy alive), an eye-dropper for the emergency feeding of a puppy, wash basin and towel for the attendant's hands and a waste-paper basket or receptacle for the many things to be thrown away.

A few hours before she whelps the bitch may become very restless and wander round gathering paper or pieces of anything and trying to build a nest. This is quite a natural thing for her to do, so don't become alarmed. If she is long doing this a little walk on a lead may help to bring on the labour pains, when she may be taken back to her bed again. A slight discharge at this time may be noticed—indicating that her 'time' is near at hand—and should give no occasion for panic, for nothing has gone wrong.

When labour pains begin the bitch may be observed contracting and relaxing her abdomen muscles and stretching out and relaxing her legs. The bitch is now undergoing physical and mental strain, so don't worry her. The first puppy should arrive within an hour or two hours after labour pains start, and if they are prolonged beyond this time your vet should be called in immediately. When the first puppy arrives, watch the mother carefully because it will be enclosed in a membrane bag. Unless the dam frees it immediately—and nearly every time she will—this must be done for her without loss of time, otherwise the puppy will be lost. The placenta, or after-birth, may come either with the puppy or afterwards. If it does not come with the puppy *never pull on the cord in an effort to hasten its arrival*. The dam will usually bite through the umbilical cord, the connecting tube in the womb for nourishment between the foetus and mother, but I always sever this cord about two inches from the puppy's navel. It is advisable to tie the cord with a piece of silk near the navel in order to avoid haemorrhage. Any small length of the cord from the navel will soon shrivel up, generally within a day or two. If the bitch wishes to eat the afterbirth, which is Nature's way, let her, although I know there are some who will shudder at this advice. It is, I repeat, Nature's way on these occasions and, I say, interfere with Nature as little as possible.

Sometimes a puppy will be assumed to be dead soon after birth. If the bitch is licking it and drying it or even just tumbling it about, do not be too quick to presume its demise. If another arrives when the first is still silent and seemingly dead, take the first one away in a warm blanket, keep it very warm, and, if you are not nervous about doing it, gently massage it, after opening its mouth and breathing sharply into its lungs. My wife, whom I always regarded as being something of a 'wizard' in the whelping of puppies, has saved many and many a puppy by this means. It never fails to give me cause for great wonder when I see life started by this action.

Whatever you do, don't try to use instruments to help in the birth of a puppy. If you are in any doubt at all, call your vet. If the bitch wishes to relieve herself during whelping don't stop her, but see that she gets back into her box without delay.

Don't feed the bitch with anything for at least an hour after whelping, but if during whelping she appears exhausted offer her a little water and, if you think fit, add a few drops of brandy to some water, which should be offered in a spoon. Whelping bitches always move me very deeply—a feeling I never get over—the tenderness of the mother together with her amazing knowledge is something I never cease to marvel at. I like to be near the bitch at this time, and a few quiet words are, I find, always appreciated, sometimes by that extraordinary soft look in her eyes which all bitches seem to have when whelping, and a faint wag of her tail. While the bitch is cleaning her latest arrival it is better to gently remove the earlier ones and place them in a warm, softly blanketed box unless she gets distressed by your taking them from her. I always think that one at a time is enough for a bitch to attend to at this stage. After the last one has arrived they may all be gently given back to her, after her bedding has been changed, and she will then settle down comfortably with them. Normal puppies will, after being dried, start to suckle within an hour of being born—some indeed will begin almost at once. It is well before leaving her to see that each puppy *is* suckling and, if necessary, to open its mouth gently and put it on the actual breast. Misshapen or crippled puppies (which will be exceedingly rare in a litter of Whippets) should be 'put down' at once, but make quite sure first that they *are* crippled or deformed.

When you are quite satisfied that the bitch has settled down comfortably, and you can see she is attending to her puppies, licking them and generally tending them, leave her alone in the quiet for some hours with just occasional visits to let her know that you are still at hand. She will understand, but don't worry her, and don't be too inquisitive in regard to her puppies.

A few hours after her whelping, if all is well, the bitch may be offered a little milk or warm milk food, and you will soon note if she wants it or not. If she refuses it, don't become alarmed, try again later. When she takes it, offer it to her every two or three hours. Later she may take a little finely minced cooked fish or *lean* meat and so gradually get on to her food. Here again, don't worry if she will not take any solid food for a bit, and don't try to force her. Taught as she is by a thousand generations of the instincts of her kind, she will give the puppies all the attention they need and she knows what she wants for herself. After the first five or six days all danger of milk fever will have passed and she may now be fed as she requires. A nursing mother bringing along a healthy strong litter of five or more puppies can hardly be over-fed and from now on she should be given the most nourishing food you can afford. The puppies from this time on will be at the breast almost all the time, for at this stage it is true to say that they live to eat and eat to live. The strain on the bitch is great and perhaps a little detail in regard to her feeding which will be necessary throughout the six weeks or so nursing period, may be helpful to the novice breeder. Feed her three or, preferably four times a day. Include plenty of raw meat, such as minced raw lean beef, milk, cod-liver oil and a conditioner (such as Vivomin) strong in mineral elements, especially calcium lactate. The mother needs plenty of calcium for bone building in the puppies. If she lacks it, the drain on her may bring on eclampsia or nursing fits. If this comes about, then you *are* in trouble—so go all out to avoid it. If the bitch has a tendency to loose bowels feed cooked meat in place of raw. A daily raw egg beaten up in milk is of great benefit to both the mother and the puppies, and this is something which should never be omitted from the daily diet of a nursing mother.

At about three or four days, provided the puppies are strong and healthy, remove the dew claws. This is done with a curved pair of sharp scissors. When carrying out this simple operation, gently—I emphasize gently—press the blades of the scissors into the leg to ensure that the dewclaw is taken off properly and that it will not grow again, in which event it will call for the attention of your vet, otherwise the dog will go through life marred by a nasty blemish—a badly severed dewclaw. If you are nervous of doing this little operation ask your vet to attend to it or call in the most experienced doggy friend you have. It is a very simple operation when all is said and done. Whatever else you do, don't delay the operation too long, otherwise excessive loss of blood will occur and so take a heavy toll of the puppy's stamina. After removing the dewclaws dab the little wound gently with bicarbonate of soda or some other gentle preparation which will stop any small amount of bleeding.

At about twelve days onwards the puppies' eyes will begin to open. (If they are a milky-blue don't immediately jump to the conclusion that they have been born blind.) For three weeks the puppies should be kept in a subdued light. During this time wash the mother's breasts with a little warm water using clean tissues—*do not use any form of disinfectant.*

If there is a little 'runt puppy' in the litter which your kindly instincts make you feel you *must* rear, since every litter contains a strong little bully, see that the little one gets the most productive teat of his mother—usually at the rear—and see that he does not get pushed out and so starved that he gradually fades out. He may not always be the 'runt', you know, so give him a chance.

At about three to four weeks, weaning may start. Your puppies are now getting along on their life's highway. You may have had an exhausting time, but now comes what I think is the 'prettiest' time of all.

Rearing the Puppies. Every stage of a dog's life is exciting but the most thrilling is when the little 'time-wasters' have arrived. I call them that because, as with most people I suppose, puppies cause me to spend more and more time watching them and playing with them when I know full well that I should be engaged in doing something of much more importance in the kennels. Still, I love my little 'time-wasters' and I am sure my readers do too—so what?

Puppies, you should bear in mind, may be born with worms or may pick up the eggs immediately after birth. If they are badly infected they should be wormed as early as five weeks of age, for such puppies stand a very good chance of succumbing to the first serious illness. It is as well to consult your vet when thinking of very early worming for more puppies die from 'worming' than by suffering from the worms themselves.

At the age of about three months puppies should have their vaccination against distemper and hard pad. Again consult your vet on this matter and *don't delay it.*

When the time for weaning comes, the change from the mother's milk to a solid diet and other milk foods must not be abrupt. From the age of three to four weeks, puppies can be taught to take a little scraped fresh lean raw meat. It may be found necessary to get them to do this at first by offering it on the finger, when they will start by sucking it off rather than by chewing it. However, they learn quickly, but to get them to take it in the first instance is the main operation—usually there is not the slightest difficulty. They should also be taught to lap broth, milk-food and so on. Gradually increase the amount of meat daily and they will soon get into the swing of things. There is

C. M. Cooke

Int. Ch. Wingedfoot Hildegarde

Ch. Robmaywin Stargazer of Allways

C. M. Cooke

Wingedfoot Lannette

C. M. Cooke

Ch. Wingedfoot Wild Goose

A. E. Baker

Brekin Bisque

Diane Pearce

Ch. Dondelayo Duette

Rolf Kristensson

Mme Donath-Seeuwen's kennels in Den Dolder, Holland

Henk Busma

Whippet racing at Amsterdam track

little danger of their over-feeding at this stage although common sense plays its part here too. Cod-liver oil may be given in small quantities daily almost from the beginning of the weaning.

After the weaning on to solid foods proper has ended puppies should be fed five times every twenty-four hours until the age of ten to twelve weeks. Always remember that if in winter the last feed is given, say about six o'clock, owing to the long winter's night it is far too long for them to go without food until, say, about eight o'clock the following morning. So do bear this in mind and feed, if you can possibly manage it, the last meal of the day quite late at night. Actually I like all my puppies to have their last meal of the day between ten and eleven o'clock at night. Then, if they are fed quite early next morning they will not drop back at all. It seems a superficial thing to mention this 'long night' break in the feeding of young puppies but so many people overlook this very important factor. 'Little and often' should be the golden rule rather than a less number of heavier meals, for excessive pot-bellies can, and often do, cause weak hocks and loose shoulders. So, with a number of smaller meals, let the puppies stuff themselves, for they need all the body-building food and nourishment they can get.

Through the months of puppyhood the daily growth is almost visible to the eye, and the properly fed, healthy, well nourished puppy is a joy to behold. The time has now come, say at the age of five months or so, when we can seriously get down to the final stage of the puppy's life, and we are now getting along to the serious side of the show business.

The Selection of the Show Puppy. In this connection, since it was so well received when it was published, and with the kind permission of the Editor of *Our Dogs*, I will reproduce here an article I wrote recently on this subject:

If I were asked what particular phase of my doggy activities gave me the greatest thrill I think I should say 'choosing the pick of the litter'.

I think there is nothing quite so interesting as to take a litter and quietly examine each puppy, thinking ahead all the time what it is likely to achieve when it is fully matured. Will it bring you yet another Champion to your kennel? Will it 'breed you one' if you are thinking in terms of building up a strong kennel? Or will it be a 'likely one' to have a bit of fun with around the local shows? And so on.

Competition in Whippets today is so keen that most topline decisions by really first-rate judges of the breed are of a knife-edge variety—so we must approach our task of selection very carefully.

First of all, make up your mind *what* you want—stick to it—and don't be 'talked out' of your original intentions. It is of the greatest assistance to anyone going over a litter if they have a full knowledge of the sire and/or the dam, and, maybe, even a passing knowledge of those farther back in the pedigree. So study the puppies' pedigree carefully before you even have a look at the dogs themselves.

For the purpose of these few hints let us assume that the would-be buyers of a puppy know little or nothing about the breed, but that they have assured themselves that the youngsters are 'bred right'.

It is quite true to say that Whippets breed exceedingly true to type and here is where a knowledge of their pedigree will be of the greatest importance. It is no less true, however, to say that whilst the majority who have a passing knowledge of the breed invariably claim that they are an 'easy breed' and that the selection of a puppy is a simple matter. Nothing could be further from the truth in actual fact.

What *is* true is that it is the easiest thing in the world to pick a 'flat catcher' at the age of, say, three months, which will eventually turn out to be not worth his keep as a show-dog. Nearly all young Whippets are, to the uninitiated, like cats in the dark in so far as they all look alike at the first glance.

Having pondered well and truly on these things, let us approach our litter. First of all, and this is important, have a good look at the place where the puppies are housed. Size up the breeder and try to get some idea regarding his feeding methods and so on. Having satisfied yourself that the puppies have been sensibly and comfortably reared to date, turn your attention to the puppies themselves. Not forgetting that the pedigree *must* play a big part in their ultimate development you will go into details regarding how they are bred. I am no believer in the 'chance puppy' but that 'like comes from like' nine times out of ten.

In the 'old days'—that is to say back in the ''twenties'—the main bugbear of the breed was size. One had always to keep that thought in mind of how big the puppies were likely to grow when they finished up. Today that is, happily, not the main problem. It may well be said 'they come too small' these days rather than otherwise. Another predominant old-time fault—now happily no longer with us—was weak pasterns. Thin feet used to be regularly noticed and I am sorry to record all too often too readily passed over in the ring. Fronts were not up to the standard they have reached today, whilst 'wheel backs' were the rule rather than the exception. Make no mistake about it—the breed today is definitely *not slipping*. It is undoubtedly far better than ever it has been as a show proposition, and has a much wider appeal than it has hitherto enjoyed. Anyone who claims the opposite to be the case simply labels himself as being either prejudiced or very ignorant of the modern-day Whippet. If the breed has a main fault today I would say it is in movement, so, when bearing the sire and dam in mind, think also upon how they moved in the ring, for action is terribly hereditary.

Now to our litter. What have we got? Six nice level sound puppies, say, at twelve weeks of age (and don't buy one under that age for your first puppy or you'll probably regret it if you do). My great friend the late Capt. Lewis Renwick, probably one of the greatest judges of the breed that ever lived, always used to say when looking over a litter with me, 'If in doubt and all else is equal, choose the one with the longest neck.' A rough and ready guide but how right he was! So first of all we'll have a look at their necks then as a main point.

Here is one which, as we stand it up (and it is amazing how a three months' old puppy can be made to stand up) shows definite signs of a deep brisket. It has neat little feet, a nice front and sweet little head—slim and intelligent looking. It has, however, a shortish and thickish neck with definitely narrow thighs. Discard it. The next, whilst very attractive, shows a decided tendency to being weak behind, for its hocks are very cow-like even at this age. Forget it.

Now here is your 'flat catcher' in puppy No. 3. A bitch say, flashily marked, with a lengthy neck, a deep brisket well cut up and possessing fine broad thighs. Standing on the neatest of feet she has her 'wonderful front' pointed out to you with great pride. Now this 'wonderful front' is one which is like a gun-barrel. It certainly is wonderful—wonderful that the dog can keep its balance on it, especially when running. Don't look any farther, for a Whippet with one of those fronts, with its elbows so tucked under its body that they almost touch, is a 'pain in the neck' to any good judge of the breed when it enters the ring.

Puppy No. 4 is another of similar type. *Not* so narrow in front but it stands with its feet at 'ten to two'. Drop that one back into the nest also—you don't want it. Puppy No. 5 appears to be exceptionally good all over at first glance. It has a beautiful deep brisket. In fact it is almost down to its elbows already. Study this puppy's length of back very carefully and check it for 'liberty' (i.e. the space between the last rib and hip bone—its couplings). Should it have a tendency towards a short back you may do a lot of winning with it as a youngster, but when it reaches maturity, because of excessively deep brisket and short back—having no liberty—it may give the impression of cutting off too sharply over the loins—a point which few judges will forgive in the fierce competition of today. A puppy of this type is always a bit of a gamble and considerable thought should be given to every aspect of it. Beware the extra deep brisket when it comes with a shortish back—no matter how attractive it is otherwise.

Now our last one, puppy No. 6. This is *it*! What do we find? A bright eye. A slim, long head, surmounted by the neatest of well-folded ears set on a long graceful tapering neck. Slim, graceful, elegant—all the essentials are there. The neck moulds beautifully into well-laid-back shoulders. The back is strong and broad with no sign of spine bones showing. The length between the last rib and the hip bone is ample and, when viewed from above, the ribs have a definite spring with no flat-sided appearance. The tail is lengthy and hangs well between the legs with an elegant curve. When stood up he comes on straight slim legs, the front ones having straight flat-sided bone with no bulge at the elbows. His hindquarters are broad across the thigh and have a grand bend of stifle, denoting strong quarters to come. His brisket is deepish, not too deep at this age and is nicely cut up under his loin which, with his obvious liberty, definitely stamps him as 'a real 'un'. The little knee knobs are of sufficient size to denote that he will not become a mere 'little pretty-pretty one' but an upstanding true dog when he finishes. His feet are small, neat, round and well knuckled up, the sort that will never go wrong. As we look at this promising youngster from behind we note how true he stands, how his hocks are in dead straight line and how when a slight pressure is put on his back, they neither turn in nor out but gently sag like a well-balanced spring.

This then is your treasure—*buy him* and you will have a dog which will beat far more in the ring than will ever beat him.

Some questions might well be asked at this stage. I will anticipate a few of them. For instance—colour. As it is said that no good horse can be a bad colour so in the same way can it be said of Whippets. Parti-colours are most attractive in the ring and they have a strong appeal to the judge in Variety classes. To breed for colour in Whippets, however, can be a very disappointing experiment, although there are kennels which give considerable thought and time towards this end. Fawn, in its many attractive shades, is the predominating colour of the breed to all intents and purposes.

Movement—how does one estimate movement when it is obvious that a young puppy cannot be taken on a lead and seen to advantage? True—therefore this is where knowledge of the sire and the dam comes in for one thing. A good plan is to let your puppy—your selected puppy—run free and to watch him in play. Faulty movement will soon be detected, likewise sound movement plainly seen.

Finally, having decided upon your puppy, check up its general condition and details. For instance, ask if it has been 'wormed' and what resulted. Note the texture of the coat. Does it shine or is it open and inclined to be staring? Take into consideration if it has been wormed or not in such a case. If the coat is coarse, or thickish, recall the colour of the sire and/or the dam. If either was a white, the great probability is that with the shedding of the puppy coat the adult coat will be of the finest texture. It is an undoubted fact that, with whites, the puppies often come with a very thick, almost Smooth Terrier-like texture coat. This need not disturb you if you know the pedigree.

Now to show the opposite side of the picture, may I refer to what a great judge (and again I refer to Capt. Renwick) opined was one of the best three bitches bred during the last fifty years—to wit Ch. Wingedfoot Hildegarde. This bitch, now famous, was an only one. She was the ugliest, fattest, laziest, coarsest Whippet puppy I have ever seen. In fact, I make no secret about it, had she not been the only one in that litter I should probably have disregarded her. Never was there such an ugly little puppy. Her coat was as thick as a doormat. She was too idle to walk and literally sprawled for weeks and weeks. Eating and sleeping was all she did! A lazy little horror! Yet her pedigree said she could *not* be what she appeared to be. Her sire was a very elegant champion and her dam was the sister of a champion and a lovely bitch—up to size—in herself. Her grandsire was a champion of great renown and her great-grandsire was a champion also. She came from a grand line of well-known winners and she was bred according to plan and 'in the purple'. I felt that she must be the real ugly duckling and that her development must be towards the 'swan beautiful'. Her record is too well known to need recalling here—her picture (facing page 29) shows her as she is today—the ugly duckling story in real truth.

The moral of the above is to emphasize the importance of never disregarding the pedigree and to remember always that, as I have said, at the beginning of this article, Whippets breed exceedingly true to type. Keep that in mind and what I have tried to outline and you will not go far wrong. In fact you won't go wrong at all.

DIET SHEET FOR WHIPPETS

Puppies

From 6 *weeks to* 12 *weeks of age* (Ages are approximate)

8 a.m. Egg and milk, warm, to which a few drops of cod-liver oil and ¼ teaspoonful of calcium phosphate has been added, *or* a bowl of Laughing Dog Milk Food mixed as instructions.

11 a.m. 3 to 4 oz. each finely minced, or scraped at first, lean, fresh raw meat. *Not* 'knacker' meat—but butchers' meat which is sold for human consumption.

2 p.m. Egg and milk—or plain warm, unskimmed milk or Laughing Dog Milk Food if they prefer it.

5 p.m. Bowl of Laughing Dog Puppy Meal soaked in meat gravy to which must be added minced cooked meat (rabbit if possible once a week and fish once a week) the whole being well mixed.

10 p.m. Baked brown bread, preferably which has been spread with good beef dripping prior to baking *or* cereals *or* wholemeal bread *or* Laughing Dog Milk Rusks, in warm milk.

From 12 *weeks of age*

8 a.m. As at 8 weeks but increase the quantities.

11 a.m. 4–6 oz. *minced* (not scraped at this age) fresh raw meat mixed with a little Laughing Dog Puppy Meal—the whole being well soaked in cooked meat gravy.

4 p.m. As given at 5 p.m. to puppies of 6 weeks to 12 weeks, but increase the quantities.

10 p.m. Laughing Dog Milk Food *or* egg and milk if preferred.

From 6 months of age

8 a.m. As before but do *not* increase the quantities of cod-liver oil and calcium, but substitute in their place Vivomin, given according to the instructions.

2 p.m. Egg and milk—warm plus a bowl of Laughing Dog Rusks.

6 p.m. 8–10 oz. minced (not too fine) fresh raw red meat, mixed with Laughing Dog Puppy Meal. Minced fresh vegetables, such as spinach, carrots or small quantity of onions may be added to this meal—the whole being soaked in warm meat gravy.

Adult stage—12 months

9 a.m. Warm egg and milk—nothing added.

11 a.m. Laughing Dog Milk Rusks—*ad lib.*

5 p.m. The equivalent of 1 lb fresh raw minced red meat. Mix with Laughing Wheatmeal and add Vivomin according to instructions.
This 'main meal' may be varied by giving cooked meat of various kinds—rabbit, oxtail—boned breast of mutton—well cooked, with chopped or minced fresh raw vegetables added from time to time.

Reviser's Note: The foregoing diet sheet is excellent and would be difficult to improve upon. However, in this expensive era many breeders have found that their dogs will thrive on one of the 'complete diet' foods now on the market, such as Purina or Wuffitmix. We have fed one such food to our stock over the past two years with admirable results and with considerable saving of outlay. The dogs of all ages and various breeds relish it, whether fed dry or with a little added meat or gravy, and all are in improved condition. Many breeders, of course, may disagree with this policy and the pet-dog owner may not wish to experiment on these lines; but it is worth a trial. A word of warning, however, to all Whippet owners: should you consider making a change to a 'complete diet', do make this change very gradually, adding a small amount of the new food on the first day and increasing the quantity daily until the complete change has been made in, say, a week to ten days. Feeding in this manner has the added advantages of ease of handling of food and of speeding up the process of feeding in the larger kennels.—K.S.

Served	Due Whelp	Served	Due Whelp	Served	Due Whelp	Served	Due Whelp	Served	Due Whelp	Served	Due Whelp	Served	Due Whelp	Served	Due Whelp	Served	Due Whelp	Served	Due Whelp	Served	Due Whelp	Served	Due Whelp
Jan.	*March*	*Feb.*	*April*	*March*	*May*	*April*	*June*	*May*	*July*	*June*	*Aug.*	*July*	*Sept.*	*Aug.*	*Oct.*	*Sept.*	*Nov.*	*Oct.*	*Dec.*	*Nov.*	*Jan.*	*Dec.*	*Feb.*
1	5	1	5	1	3	1	3	1	3	1	3	1	2	1	3	1	3	1	3	1	3	1	2
2	6	2	6	2	4	2	4	2	4	2	4	2	3	2	4	2	4	2	4	2	4	2	3
3	7	3	7	3	5	3	5	3	5	3	5	3	4	3	5	3	5	3	5	3	5	3	4
4	8	4	8	4	6	4	6	4	6	4	6	4	5	4	6	4	6	4	6	4	6	4	5
5	9	5	9	5	7	5	7	5	7	5	7	5	6	5	7	5	7	5	7	5	7	5	6
6	10	6	10	6	8	6	8	6	8	6	8	6	7	6	8	6	8	6	8	6	8	6	7
7	11	7	11	7	9	7	9	7	9	7	9	7	8	7	9	7	9	7	9	7	9	7	8
8	12	8	12	8	10	8	10	8	10	8	10	8	9	8	10	8	10	8	10	8	10	8	9
9	13	9	13	9	11	9	11	9	11	9	11	9	10	9	11	9	11	9	11	9	11	9	10
10	14	10	14	10	12	10	12	10	12	10	12	10	11	10	12	10	12	10	12	10	12	10	11
11	15	11	15	11	13	11	13	11	13	11	13	11	12	11	13	11	13	11	13	11	13	11	12
12	16	12	16	12	14	12	14	12	14	12	14	12	13	12	14	12	14	12	14	12	14	12	13
13	17	13	17	13	15	13	15	13	15	13	15	13	14	13	15	13	15	13	15	13	15	13	14
14	18	14	18	14	16	14	16	14	16	14	16	14	15	14	16	14	16	14	16	14	16	14	15
15	19	15	19	15	17	15	17	15	17	15	17	15	16	15	17	15	17	15	17	15	17	15	16
16	20	16	20	16	18	16	18	16	18	16	18	16	17	16	18	16	18	16	18	16	18	16	17
17	21	17	21	17	19	17	19	17	19	17	19	17	18	17	19	17	19	17	19	17	19	17	18
18	22	18	22	18	20	18	20	18	20	18	20	18	19	18	20	18	20	18	20	18	20	18	19
19	23	19	23	19	21	19	21	19	21	19	21	19	20	19	21	19	21	19	21	19	21	19	20
20	24	20	24	20	22	20	22	20	22	20	22	20	21	20	22	20	22	20	22	20	22	20	21
21	25	21	25	21	23	21	23	21	23	21	23	21	22	21	23	21	23	21	23	21	23	21	22
22	26	22	26	22	24	22	24	22	24	22	24	22	23	22	24	22	24	22	24	22	24	22	23
23	27	23	27	23	25	23	25	23	25	23	25	23	24	23	25	23	25	23	25	23	25	23	24
24	28	24	28	24	26	24	26	24	26	24	26	24	25	24	26	24	26	24	26	24	26	24	25
25	29	25	29	25	27	25	27	25	27	25	27	25	26	25	27	25	27	25	27	25	27	25	26
26	30	26	30	26	28	26	28	26	28	26	28	26	27	26	28	26	28	26	28	26	28	26	27
27	31	27	MAY 1	27	29	27	29	27	29	27	29	27	28	27	29	27	29	27	29	27	29	27	28
28	APR. 1	28	2	28	30	28	30	28	30	28	30	28	29	28	30	28	30	28	30	28	30	28	MAR. 1
29	2			29	31	29	JULY 1	29	31	29	31	29	30	29	31	29	DEC. 1	29	31	29	31	29	2
30	3			30	JUNE 1	30	2	30	AUG. 1	30	SEPT. 1	30	OCT. 1	30	NOV. 1	30	2	30	JAN. 1	30	FEB. 1	30	3
31	4			31	2			31	2			31	2	31	2			31	2			31	4

Note. The normal period of gestation in bitches is sixty-three days from the date of service, but must not be accepted that this period may not be anticipated or exceeded. A day or tw grace either way should always be allowed for.

5

Showing

WE HAVE discussed how best to house our Whippets and feed them, we have bred and reared our first litter and selected our best puppy, and so we come to its training, preparing it for show and actually handling it in the ring.

These matters often scare the novice at the outset; but there is no cause for alarm, for common sense is the keynote to all the so-called mysteries of showing and handling and preparing the dog for the ring. It is really all quite simple, as is evidenced by the fact that many novices who have set about the task sensibly, without fuss and undue excitement have walked away with the highest honours.

A puppy must be six months of age before it can be entered for any show (unless it is shown in a litter class) and if you will take my advice you will, as a general rule, take nine months as a more suitable minimum age for a Whippet to be shown with much chance of success. But, of course, some puppies are more forward than others. A lot will naturally depend upon the puppy, but nine months is a fair age to 'think around' when you are contemplating showing.

Training. Obviously, if it is going to stand much chance of winning, the puppy must be well trained to go on a lead. It is in this early 'lead training' that so many novices go wrong and often ruin a puppy for life as a show-dog. I do not like to see a young puppy, perhaps quite frantic, trying to escape from his first introduction to his lead. When you come to consider, it must be quite a terrifying ordeal for a puppy until he gets used to it. The wise thing to do is to put a light little collar on your puppy a couple of days before you attempt to put him on a lead and let him run loose in the normal way with the others, free and untrammelled. He will probably try to get it off at first but he will soon forget it and run around normally. That is step number one. Next, attach a lead to the little collar he is wearing. He will probably jump around for a bit, or stand stock still and refuse to move, or he may trot along, as I have had them, like an old veteran. Watch him, talk to him gently to encourage him, and whatever he does, get him to move along with you. I never take them far from their run in the first instance; often I train them to the lead for the first time actually round their run, because the more they are 'at home' the quicker they settle down, having no new world to attract or scare them as well as the restraint of the lead. Study your puppy, and proceed along these lines, and you will find that, in the course of one or two lessons, he will trot along quite happily wherever you want him to go.

When he accepts the lead, take him, together with an older dog that he knows well, out on the highway—in safety of course—and get him used to traffic and cars and street noises. After a week of this quiet training, I think you will find that he behaves for all the world as if he has been 'to the manner born', as indeed he has. Actually before we start to train the puppy to go on the lead, his very early training to stand should have begun at about the age of six weeks—then, paradoxical as it may sound, the training for stance in the ring becomes no training at all. If you take your puppy at a very early age and stand him up, say daily, on a table to have a look at him for a few moments, by the time he is going on a lead he knows how you want him to stand and does it quite naturally. Little Whippets are very quick to learn.

Handling. How *do* we want him to stand in the ring in order to show himself to the best advantage? Some may well ask that question, judging from some of the positions one sees dogs placed in from time to time. Let me say here and now that I detest seeing the product of the type of handler who makes his dog—as *he* claims—'stand like a rock', by which he means stand stiff and immovable, without any lead or hand on him. Let those who like it, do it if they wish, but for my part I dislike it because nine times out of ten the relaxed beauty has gone out of the dog. I see no merit in a show-dog trained like this. In fact I see very much against it.

To 'stand a dog up' or, as some say, to 'stack him', there are certain fundamental points to observe. Get these into the right position and all the rest will fall into line. First, the hocks, i.e. the hind legs. These are the anchor, as it were, and must at all times be absolutely perpendicular to the ground—they must form a right angle, neither leaning forward nor backwards. Get the hocks into position first. Then drop your dog's front legs so that they come down straight under him with his elbows close to his brisket. See that his back is not stretched out too flat (although in a puppy you may find that this may be flatter than in an adult dog, which has naturally muscled up) and you will have your dog covering his natural ground with all four legs in the right position. Place your hand under his muzzle and get the feeling that you are 'shaking his neck out' to its full length, that is, without making it appear as if you were trying to pull his head off in an endeavour to give him a long shapely neck. Just keep your eye on his backline, to avoid that 'too flat' appearance, and you will find that you have your dog looking as well as it is possible to make him. His front legs will be straight from his shoulder, giving him his natural front, and, if his hocks are in the right position—and this is the *key point* in showing a Whippet, no matter what anyone may say—you are doing everything you can for him.

Some handlers in the breed are excellent, others very poor, and the following 'dont's' may be helpful. It does not matter whether you prefer to show your dog by standing in front of him, at the back (the old-fashioned way, as I call it), or whether you prefer to kneel at his side. I myself prefer to show most dogs from the front. By doing so, I always feel I have more control over him, and I am able to see the whole of him with very little effort. What is more important I can get a good view of his top.

In addition, the dog can see me, he knows me in this position and he has confidence and relaxes and *that* is the whole secret.

I hold definite views regarding dogs. For instance I always *talk* to my dogs through my hands. I will not go into a lot of detail here, but I am convinced, through many years of experience, that is is quite possible, and indeed desirable, to be able to communicate one's thoughts to a dog through touch. Actually, although they may not realize this nearly everyone *knows* it, even if they have never seriously thought about it. For instance, suppose you were hiding from, say, a friend, in some bushes or in a wood, and as he approached, your dog, which was crouched by your side, showed signs of barking—what would you do? I'll guarantee you would lay your hand on his head and he would immediately refrain. You would be talking to your dog through your touch. I have long realized this, and a little while ago I had a sceptical friend in my kennel and was able to prove my contention to him. It is quite possible to make a dog apprehensive, that is, nervous and almost fearful as though anticipating a sharp rebuke, merely through the touch of the hand. It is no less easy immediately to change that feeling to one of great pleasure, which the dog will show by a wagging tail or even by getting excited. I have long since satisfied myself that this is quite normal, because dogs are keen and sensitive to reactions of all our moods. Every good horseman knows how his mount will react to him—there is nothing new or extraordinary about it. What I am leading up to is that a nervous handler does *not* help his dog to be confident, and I wish more exhibitors would realize this simple fact. When I am 'showing' a dog my hands are never still on him for a moment. All the while he is being 'shown' he is being gently caressed and 'talked to' and he is quite 'at home', for that is how he is treated daily in his kennel at grooming time. He is relaxed and 'easy', thereby showing himself to the best advantage. Every 'handling time' should become fixed in your dog's mind as being 'petting time', and if you can get your dog to understand that, you will never have any trouble with him in the show-ring. What is more, he will do his very best for you, and himself.

A great fault so many make in handling their Whippet is

'tucking it up' too much. By this I mean that they over-do tapping him under tummy in order to make him, as they think, arch his back nicely. Actually, this constant 'tucking a dog up' gets him into the habit of standing with a humped back that makes him almost resemble a miniature camel, and it certainly prevents him from covering his ground, as he should. In addition it gives the impression of a 'wheel back'. It is altogether wrong. Another very common fault is covering the muzzle with the whole of the hand when holding his head out to show the length of neck. I've seen some of our best handlers making this mistake, and I can never understand why it is they seem unable to appreciate that when they hide—as they certainly do—the whole of a dog's muzzle from the judge, they are deliberately spoiling the symmetry of the dog as a whole. It is quite easy to get your dog to stretch his neck out to its full length by just a little light touching *under* the jaw, and most certainly *not* by covering the whole of his face, from his eyes to his nose, with the hand. Watch this point because it is quite important.

Movement in the breed is very much commented upon in these days. When getting the puppy to go on the lead you will obviously have taken every opportunity to watch his movement, both fore and aft. You will no doubt have had him 'walked up' for you by someone else while you watched him from behind, in front, and from the side. There is nothing you can do about improving movement—it's either there or it isn't—but when, in the ring, you *are* moving your dog, never get between your exhibit and the judge. Few things are more annoying to a judge who is trying to see the best in your dog if you keep getting between him and your exhibit, thus preventing him from arriving at a correct decision. I remember once, in my youth, stewarding for a famous judge who got so annoyed with a fussy woman handler who kept getting between the judge and her dog that he said to her in acid tones: 'Madam, when you have finished your performance do you mind if I see how your dog moves?' The exhibitor looked somewhat taken aback—I could only hope she learned a lesson from it.

So much then for handling. There is nothing very much in it

if, as I say, common sense is used. Just observe the few hints I have given you and I am sure that you will find that all goes well. Don't get flustered and remember any judge *does* like a calm exhibitor who quietly and quickly carries out what is required. This too remember, any judge worthy of the name will always allow an obvious novice all the time in the world to get settled and relaxed in the ring.

Preparing for Show. We come next to the all important preparation of the dog for the great day when he enters the ring. Here again, common sense is the keynote. Let's have a look at your puppy and see what we shall find. Nails? Yes, they need shortening to allow his feet to look their best. So get a good nail file, and in this connection I am pleased to be able to tell you that there is a new one on the market, made and supplied by Deva Dog Ware Ltd, which will, I am quite sure, prove to be a boon and a blessing to everyone. Hold the dog's foot up to the light and note where the 'pink', inside the nail, ends, and mark it with the file on top of the nail, because we must avoid cutting that 'pink' which, if we do, will give the dog pain and cause bleeding. There is *no* excuse for paining a dog when trimming the nails, never forget that. I have witnessed some very nasty things when dogs have been having their nails cut, and I have had many high words about it, for I will *not* tolerate anyone giving unnecessary pain to any dog. Having marked a ring round the nail denoting the limit to which it needs to be cut, go on filing round the ring until the nail bends. Then you may either snip it off with nail cutters or carry on with the file until it drops off. Round off the end of the cut nail and the simple job is done. That's all there is to it; a simple operation which need give no one any concern at all. A square-cut nail left ragged at the end, or an excessively long nail, denotes bad kennel management and bad presentation.

What about the dog's neck? Is there a long ridge of fur down the side of the neck, on both the right and left sides? If so, it needs to be thinned out and is quite a simple matter to do. It is best done by careful use of thinning scissors—those with serrated edges. *Never* use a razor-blade in any circumstances, and don't use ordinary scissors or try to rasp it down with a knife. In the old days, singeing was employed and that can be carried out quite well, but I do not think dogs like it much and a heavy hand can cause an unsightly mess. It is a simple operation but should not be overdone. Excessive barbering has nothing good about it, but a little tidying up is necessary at times. The same remarks apply to the feathering on the thighs if they are becoming ragged and too profuse, but don't overdo this either. The same with the tail—use the serrated scissors again—but be *very* careful, and above all things with the tail—avoid the razor-blade or a sharp-cutting instrument. In regard to the whiskers on the face. This is a matter of taste. I know there are some judges who prefer to see them left on—others like to see the face tidied up. But as Nature intended these 'feelers' to be of use I see no reason why they should be removed. If you do wish to remove them, a blunt-ended pair of scissors should be used. Did you know that Whippets move these 'feelers'? Some people think they do not, but they do, as you will see if you carefully watch a dog when it is excited or alarmed. It is said, by those who should know, that they are Nature's 'measuring stick'; when an animal approaches a space through which it wishes to pass, it relies upon the 'feelers' to indicate if it can do so without getting into difficulties. I don't know whether this is so or not—but it's a nice thought. So we'll leave them on, shall we?

The foregoing in my opinion is about all that is necessary to do to a Whippet, from the barbering point of view, to prepare it for the show-ring. So we come to the final touches—shampooing.

Some exhibitors claim that they never wash their Whippets for show. I can only say that they never need tell anyone that, because it will be plain for all to see. No dog can look its best if it is shown with a dull lack-lustre coat which it *must* have if a Whippet is brushed only at odd times and *never* washed. Let there be *no* misunderstanding about that. An unwashed white dog for instance, no matter how much it is powdered, can never look other than dingy, and the same applies to a dog of any other colour. Therefore, most certainly bath your exhibit, at the latest two days before the show. I consider it advisable to bath the dog forty-eight hours before a show and to keep it so that it cannot get messed up before the show day, especially if it is a white one or parti-coloured. There are all sorts of shampoos on the market but the ones I recommend are supplied by Messrs Deva Dog Ware Ltd. Some are especially put up for white dogs, containing a 'blue' addition, others for fawns, containing egg and lemon, which I find is particularly good, and yet another, specially prepared for Greyhounds and Whippets, which is very quick in its action and requires no rinsing. (It will be noticed that I have made several references to Deva Dog Ware Ltd, and I do so simply because I know these people are specializing in equipment for Whippets and have made quite a study of the requirements of the breed.) If, however, you have a special preference for some other kind of shampoo there can be nothing against its use—these things are a matter of choice and preference. I would warn novices against using ordinary washing detergents, for they were not made for washing dogs. The great thing to remember when shampooing a single-coated dog, such as the Whippet, is to ensure that the animal is thoroughly rinsed after washing. For this reason it is essential to use a large sponge, and I recommend one of those large-type sponges which may be bought very cheaply, and are primarily used for washing motor-cars. It is also necessary to have three baths, or three changes of water if the dog is bathed in a sink, and to see that every vestige of soap is removed from the coat. I recommend two shampoos actually, as the first application of the mixture will remove only the grease in the coat, and if the dog is then rinsed and dried there will still be a lot of scum remaining in the coat. So, in order to get the best result, shampoo twice and rinse three times, and use the sponge all the while. After the final rinse, dry the dog and place him in a warm room, but not too near a fire otherwise his coat will curl and may persist so for days before getting back to its natural state. Furthermore, remember that it takes some hours before the natural oil comes back into the coat, so don't wash a dog a few hours before you exhibit it or it won't look its best. As I keep repeating, common sense comes into everything connected with the exhibition of dogs.

Well now, you and your dog are ready to go to the show, but before we do so there is one other thing to which we must give some attention, namely, the show-bag.

I consider it to be a 'must' for every exhibitor to set up, and keep ready for use, a properly equipped show-bag. This should be of sufficient size, without being cumbersome, to contain everything that will or will be likely to be required while at a show. If laid out and always kept handy it saves much time and annoyance. If the items which should be taken to a show have to be assembled and packed every time you exhibit, as sure as Fate something will get left behind, and that will most certainly be the item you will have a special use for during the day. Let us have a look at what we are likely to require. First, your blankets for your dog while it is on the bench. Two small ones will be better than one large one; three is even better than two, especially if it is an open-air event and inclined to be cold. That extra blanket *over* the dog will be a great boon. So three blankets then, and let them be gay and cheerful and not these drab affairs so many use —or used to use. After all, your dog is 'on parade' at a show and a bright bench often means a sale of a puppy to an attracted visitor to the show. Then there is the coat your dog will wear. In summer, he should have a light linen one to keep him clean—this seems to be one of the neglected items in these days I notice—in winter a well-cut warm one. Here again, as so many ask where coats can be bought, Messrs Deva Dog Ware Ltd are specializing in Whippet coats from now on. Let the dog's coat be attractive and it should have some colour to it. Uniform colours for all the dogs from a kennel always make an attractive picture. After all, gay colours do not cost any more, or any less, so why be drab?

A bench chain and collar you will need, your brushes—a heavy one (dandy brush) for your first brushing, a light one for your second brushing, and a rubber one for the final brushing—a hound glove and a 'polishing cloth'—an old silk scarf is excellent for this purpose. You will also need a bottle of spirit shampoo (in case your dog gets soiled on the way to the show as so often happens), a sponge for use if you have to 'touch him up' with the spirit shampoo, and of course you will need a good thick towel. Include also in your pre-packed show-bag the following items—because 'you never know'—a small roll of bandage, a small bottle of mild antiseptic (many a dog-bite at a show can be minimized if one comes prepared), a pair of good blunt-nosed scissors, a nail file, a small pair of tweezers (I was once very sorry I had none when my exhibit was stung in the face by a bee) and finally, I think, a roll of cotton-wool. Oh yes, one more item, a small pack of paper tissues which are *most* useful for a dozen things.

If you are one who likes to feed and water your dogs while at shows, a small water-bowl and a food dish should also be added to the show-bag. Incidentally, I find that the preparation Full-o-Pep is a 'feed' most dogs will take at shows, even when they turn their noses up at most other things. This preparation has the merit of being very clean to handle and is packed in a convenient size. Some exhibitors prefer to give their dogs milk while at shows, if so, add a milk bottle to your show-bag, and in any case it is always a good idea to take water with you. With a bag packed as I have outlined you should be well equipped for anything, but remember to add the 'schedule' of the show to remind you of the classes in which you are entered. Your 'Early Removal Permit' should also be kept in the show-bag. It may sound quite a chore to lay out a bag as I have suggested, but believe me it will be a boon and a blessing if you will only take the trouble to organize it.

Entering Your Dog. It may be as well at this point to comment on the making of entries when you receive the schedule. First of all you should always watch the advertisement columns of the dog journals which carry forthcoming show announcements. The hon secretary of any show sends out schedules automatically to exhibitors who have previously entered at his show, but until you have entered, or until you have become a recognized exhibitor, you should not feel that you are bound to receive one without applying for it. So write off as early as possible for a schedule, directly you read the announcement. When you get it, study it carefully.

This is most necessary, because it is easy to enter a dog in a class for which it is not eligible. For instance, a puppy winning a Challenge Certificate is not eligible for any class, except those governed by age, such as Puppy or Junior up to and including Post-Graduate. Don't take it for granted that your dog is available for anything until you have read the Definition of Classes, which will be found at the heading of every schedule. You already understand, of course, that every dog entered at any show must be registered with the Kennel Club. If you have a dog which has not been registered, or you have bought one which has not been transferred to your name through the Kennel Club, and you wish to show it, send on details of registration or transfer, as the case may be, to the Kennel Club, using the appropriate forms, and if you do not receive the official certificate back from the Kennel Club by the time the entries close for the show you wish to attend, it is in order for you to enter your dog, giving the name for which you have applied, and add the initials N.A.F. (name applied for) after it. In a similar case arising from a transfer, the initials T.A.F. (transfer applied for) are not now required. You are quite in order to enter in this manner. When you send on your entries, make a note to remind you to mark your schedule so that you know which dog has been entered in which class, because it is only too easy to forget in which classes you have entered and to, as I have been guilty of doing on one occasion, take the wrong dog to the show. Also, make a note of the show date. It may sound silly to stress this point, but many an experienced exhibitor has suffered from a mild mental aberration and arrived at the venue a day too soon or a day too late. So make notes of all you have done, to be on the safe side.

Obviously the competition you meet at any show will be largely governed by the status of the show, and it may be as well to have a word with an experienced 'old hand' who will be able to guide you in such matters. Don't fly too high, and always bear in mind that even though you have entered modestly in the Puppy class only, it can be that your exhibit may impress the judge so much that you may eventually win Best of Breed, in addition to the Challenge Certificate. This actually happened to me once when showing at Cruft's, and it has happened to others more than once. The soundest policy is to enter the dog in the class or classes where it would seem to have a reasonable chance of success rather than to 'shoot at the moon' and be content if you manage to stick on the kitchen ceiling. Set your sights on the target you wish to hit and proceed little by little, for in this way you will build up your dog's reputation much more soundly than by achieving a spectacular win here and there and getting a severe 'bumping down' the next time he comes out.

So, with a well-schooled, well-presented dog, and satisfied that our entries have been made out correctly, and carrying our complete show-bag we arrive at the show venue. Have a one-track mind at this stage, namely to get your dog inside the building, through the vet's examination and then on to his bench at the earliest possible moment. Greetings to friends may be warm and friendly, but let them be short, for their sake and for yours, for general 'chit-chat' can wait until later in the day. Directly you arrive at your bench get the blankets down and your dog installed comfortably. Buy a catalogue and find out when you are likely to be required in the ring; note the competition and generally satisfy yourself that all is in order regarding your own entries. Note your ring number, also the number of the ring in which you will be judged. Check also on its position and how far it is from your bench. Then start to get your dog ready. It may well be that you will not be required in the ring for a couple of hours, but never mind, have the dog brushed and ready, except perhaps for the final touches, and then you may relax if you wish. When the judge is ready to begin work, be at the ringside, unflustered and with everything 'ship-shape and Bristol fashion'.

When you enter the ring keep your wits about you. Don't indulge in chatting to your neighbouring competitor if you cannot give the fullest attention to your dog. Know your ring number when asked by the ring steward, and when the judge takes over the class keep your eye on him and follow his method of working. When he comes to your exhibit just answer any question he may ask, what the dog's age is for instance, with a plain short answer. Don't try to engage him in conversation, no matter how well you may know him. It can easily give a wrong impression and sully any award your dog may win. What is worse is, it may irritate the judge who is concentrating on his task. When asked to move your dog, take it easy, be calm—remember you communicate your feelings to your dog very easily—and move straight away from the judge, turn smartly, pause to 'collect' your dog, and then come straight back to the judge. If he asks you to go again, don't jump to the conclusion that you have done something wrong. It may well be that the judge is so impressed by your dog's movement that he wants to see its action again. Just calmly repeat the exercise and, when the judge indicates that he is satisfied with what he has seen, go quietly back to your place in the line.

When the last exhibit is being judged for movement, start to 'stack' your dog so that when the judge looks along the line you are ready and your dog is showing for all he is worth. When the judge has finished his movement examination don't *relax*. Keep your dog 'well up to the mark' no matter if the judge is occupied at the other end of the line with some other exhibit or not. Many a 'red' has been lost because the judge, having been very impressed with an exhibit earlier in the class, comes across another farther down the line, which takes his eye. He remembers yours and, when he has finished with the one he is also impressed with, he may glance down the line at yours. If you are gossiping, and your dog is standing like a concertina, bang goes the good impression, and you may be lucky to get into second place. I am fully aware there are those who say, 'Rest your dog—don't tire him out', but that is nonsense in a normal class. In a huge Group class it may well be different, but if any dog worth his salt can't stand being 'shown' for a quarter of an hour it is not much of a dog and, maybe, shouldn't be there at all. No! When you are showing, *show* all the time.

Finally, I will pass on a little advice given to me as a young man—too many years ago now, I am sorry to say—namely 'Win with a smile—lose with a laugh', for this is a very censorious world and our best-intended actions are often very much misconstrued, especially by those who are always ready to see some ulterior motive in the most innocuous thing you may do or say. You may come across these people, and you will find that, as a rule, those who always 'know' what is 'behind everything', according to them, are those whose winnings are not particularly outstanding. If your show career is star-studded, as I hope it will be, always remember that 'The tallest trees draw the most wind' and the envious are always with us.

6

Judging the Breed

TO ALMOST every keen and ambitious exhibitor there one day comes the desire to act in a judging capacity. This is quite understandable, as few experiences can be more enjoyable than in running the rule over a good entry of first-class specimens of the breed when they are brought together. I read a somewhat scathing article recently which started off by saying 'If the judicially able were as numerous as the judicially ambitious what a happier and more peaceful atmosphere dogdom would enjoy.' I think that was rather sweeping, although one does find at times that, with some, ambition gets ahead of ability—but not, I think, to any serious degree. I am all for new judges entering the lists, and I do all I can to support them, as I think we all should. Some of the more ambitious often become quite bitter if their being appointed as a judge of the breed is not as readily sanctioned by the Kennel Club as they feel it should. A lot of these heart-burnings would subside, and some of the thoughtless expressions would never be made, if only the disgruntled ones did but know the detailed records of exhibitors and minor judges of small shows, which the Kennel Club keep and refer to. I have checked this and you may take it from me that no case is ever submitted to the ruling body who nominate a new judge for the breed—any breed of course—without the file of the person concerned being very carefully scrutinized at Clarges Street.

There must be many people in the dog world who have not seen the questionnaire which has to be completed and sent to the Kennel Club when a judge is put forward to award Challenge

Certificates in a breed for the first time. On the front page the judge has to sign a declaration that the information he has given is correct, and that if at any time altered circumstances render his replies no longer accurate he will inform the Kennel Club immediately. In the body of the questionnaire, the judge is required to give the registered names and Stud Book numbers of all dogs of the breed owned or bred by him and entered in the Kennel Club Stud Book by reason of their wins. Below this, there is a second section for the names and registered numbers of other dogs of the breed owned or bred by him.

In the third section, the judge has to give the names and dates of shows at which he has judged classes of the breed or variety. He is also required in each case to state the type of show and the number of classes he judged. The section below this is for the names and dates of shows at which he has judged classes of any breed.

On the back of the questionnaire there are five questions to be answered. The first of these is 'Are you on a list of judges compiled by a club for this breed? If so, please state the title of the club.' The next question is 'Have you, at any time, received any reward or expenses for preparing dogs for exhibition? If yes, please supply full particulars for consideration.' The following question refers to the handling of other people's dogs at shows, and reads 'Have you at any time handled a dog or dogs other than your own at a show? If yes, give the registered names of these dogs and say if you received any reward or expenses for so doing.' In reply to this question a judge might give the names of several well-known dogs he has handled for other people and for which he has not received any reward or expenses. The Committee might think it advisable that he should not judge the breed under these circumstances since the competition for Challenge Certificates might be reduced by these well-known dogs not being entered. This is followed by the question 'Are you at present employed in any kennel? If yes, please supply particulars.' And the final question is 'Are you the proprietor of or do you assist in the management of a dog shop? If yes, please supply full particulars.'

Each of these questionnaires—and there are many of them—is considered in detail by the Shows Regulation Committee at its regular meetings.

Obviously the first thing necessary for any judge to have is a full and comprehensive knowledge of the breed and the Standard laid down by the Kennel Club for that breed. Often it is claimed that, if a judge has never been a breeder of the dogs he sets out to judge, he cannot be a sound judge of them. In the main, I would say there may be something in that claim, but it does not always follow, and I recall the late Mr Holland Buckley, Senr, at a Kennel Club banquet in the 'thirties touching on that very subject in an after-dinner speech, when he rocked the whole of dogdom in mirth by stating that when this was put to him by a lady exhibitor, his reply was 'Madam, I have never laid an egg, but I do assure you I know a good one when I see it.' I think it is much more to the point—and I have made my views on this very clear for years—to suggest that one may easily assess the ability of a judge if one takes into consideration the type and quality of that breed which he, or she, has in his or her kennel. *That* is the test, I think, and far above any other consideration. However, by and large, I do not think we have much to complain about in regard to the judges who regularly officiate at the bigger shows.

Widely diverging views are taken from time to time regarding judges who hail from other countries officiating over here. I think this is often over-stressed, because a different point of view is always interesting, and it is well to remember that an adverse opinion regarding a well-known winning dog does not necessarily do that dog any serious harm—it still remains the same animal. So many tend to overlook this simple fact. So, in the same way, if any exhibit suddenly gets exalted far higher than its usual rating by other tested and proved judges, it by no means follows that the animal has suddenly changed for the better. I always recall the comment attributed to the late Jack Holgate, one of the most famous Whippet judges in the history of the breed, who is reported to have said, and it would be typical of the man as I knew him, 'Don't tell me what it has won, tell me what it has beaten and who judged it.' There is a world of wisdom in that remark, whether it was Jack Holgate who made it or anyone else. Likewise, the famous comment attributed to the late Jimmy Garrow, when confronted by an angry exhibitor who stated in no uncertain terms that his dog had been very unfairly and very badly judged, and went on to discuss in great detail its breeding. Garrow listened very carefully and very patiently and, when the angry exhibitor paused for breath, quietly remarked, 'Ah well, I'll tell you what, lad, next time you show under me, leave the dog at home and bring the pedigree instead!' I am sure no further comment is necessary.

When discussing the judging of the breed one cannot do other than express a personal opinion, and that is all that I set out to do, for most of us who have been acting in a judging capacity for long each adopt, I suppose, a style of our own. For my part, one of the most important things I have in mind is the fact that for weeks and weeks the competitors, who by bringing their dog along for my opinion are paying me a compliment, have been carefully tending and preparing their dogs, they have paid fairly high entry fees and have gone to considerable expense in travelling to the show. It is, as I see it, up to me, since they have gone to all that trouble and expense to have my opinion of their exhibit, to give the animal the most careful examination, to extend them every courtesy, and to banish from my mind any personal feelings I may have either in regard to the exhibit or the exhibitor. No prejudice should influence any judge, either for or against, in regard to colour, breeding or anything which is not covered by the Standard. For instance, I knew of a judge who said to me that Standard or not, he would never put a dog up which had a 'butterfly nose'. He was wrong, entirely wrong, and if he had taken the trouble to read his Standard more carefully he would have realized the fact. Like most judges, I suppose, I dislike a 'butterfly nose', but it is permissible in a parti-colour, as the Standard plainly states, therefore a personal opinion should not be allowed to sway a judge's placing.

In my opinion, unless anyone acting as a judge can honestly say that he sinks all personal views, then I say he is not a fit person to be a judge. I have no two thoughts in this connection, and never will have. I think most judges feel this way about things, and I think every exhibitor should accept this as a fact. At times, when one puts up the dog of an exhibitor who is not, perchance, one's closest friend—I'll put it no higher than that—one experiences a feeling of satisfaction that one has done the job right. This may be construed as personal vanity, but be that as it may, I—and I know there are many more like me—I am one who places his opinion of himself as a judge far higher than the one I may hold of myself as an individual. In this respect I will quote Mr J. B Priestley who said recently: 'I am a vain man, a vain man but not a conceited one, in so far as I place a high value upon my ability to do my job.' I think if everyone felt that way we should see some very fine expositions of judging.

Don't ever forget there is something in 'Judge not that ye be not judged' and this was brought home to me when I was a somewhat new judge of Championship Shows. Glancing round the ring I saw a lovely row of grinning faces obviously enjoying some joke at my expense. Just as a matter of interest sitting in that row were Lewis Renwick, Major Harry Gunn, Alf Rose, Ernest Sobey and one or two more very experienced judges of the old school. It shook me a little and I began to wonder what I had done, or was about to do wrong. I subsequently learned it was because they were having small wagers on various dogs lined up before me and that I had no less than five C.C. winners together in one class and one was standing—at that moment—at the bottom of the line. From what was said later, I gathered that I passed muster by that very knowledgeable and critical audience that day. In pleasing myself, apparently I had pleased them also, which was very nice to know.

I always think a judge should remember his ringside in so far as he should line his dogs up so that a clear view may be enjoyed by the onlookers. He should make it possible for the ringsiders to see, and if possible to follow, what he is doing. This can be done in several ways, but some judges do not seem to consider the ringsiders at all, which I think is a pity. If the dogs are lined up in the same way each time the final placings are made, the onlookers quickly 'catch on' and the judge's work becomes much more interesting to them. If, for example, the judge places his winner at one end of the line-up in one class and works from the opposite end in another, ringsiders find it hard to follow his judging. A little thought along these lines makes watching a judge at work much more interesting, and ringsiders *are* entitled to consideration.

As regards consideration for the nervous exhibitor, although no judge wants to start lengthy conversations in the ring, how pleasing and heartening, and how relaxing too, it is to an exhibitor if the judge has a kindly word to say about his or her exhibit. A gentle pat on the dog's head or a smile to the handler will do much to make that judge register well. These little gestures, small in themselves, mean so much to a new exhibitor and they cost the judge nothing. Personally, I prefer the friendly, smiling judge, even the 'chatty' judge, to the one who 'puts the wind up' exhibitor and dog alike by appearing so terribly important. As someone once said: 'The trouble with some judges is that when they are appointed they think they have been anointed'—a very silly view to take indeed.

As I have said, I am all for the introduction of 'new blood' into the lists of judges, and now that the Kennel Club has relaxed their rule concerning those who have boarding kennels, I hope we shall see several new faces as 'head man' in the ring, always provided they are *au fait* with what is required of them.

I make no bones about it, I *like* judging, although I must admit that it can be very tiring at times, as I experienced when judging Cruft's large entry in 1958. The trips abroad, which sometimes follow after one has been judging for some time here at home, are most interesting experiences. From time to time one hears certain criticisms regarding methods employed by some judges in the ring. For instance, the late Bernard Fitter used to scare some people when he entered the ring carrying his measuring stick. Actually, although I saw him with his stick in the ring on many occasions, I saw him use it only on one occasion. It is often said that if a judge cannot estimate the height of a dog by looking at it he should never be asked to judge. That is utter nonsense, and many a judge would silence some of the 'know alls' who speak so loudly about size from the ringside, if he 'ran the rule' over one or two of his exhibits in the ring, just to let the 'know alls' understand that he did *not* overlook the size angle when making his placings. A ringside is no vantage point from which to judge a class of dogs, that is why the critiques from the ringside are hardly worth the paper they are written on at times. The judge's report on the dogs which came under him are the only reports that amount to anything on that day.

Then there are the criticisms levelled at the use of the table, which some judges use to stand their dogs on for examination. I neither advocate it nor condemn it. Against it is the undoubted fact that most dogs do *not* look their best when standing on a table. On the other hand, standing them in this way is only a matter of training from the time they are puppies. What is true, is that some judges are not getting any younger, and they may find it very tiring to keep constantly bending down to examine dozens of exhibits, especially after lunch. I think from the ring-siders' point of view the use of the table has much to recommend it. One thing I think should be borne in mind in this connection, by all judges, is that the table should not be so near the ringside that spectators can sit almost over-hanging the table. It gives a bad impression, and when audible comments are made, which the judge can plainly hear, it is not to be wondered at if some 'wise-acre' claims that the ringsiders are doing the judging! I have heard it said on more than one occasion, and the judge should look to this point. I think, on the whole, however, that the Whippet, because he is a sporting breed, should be judged where he belongs, on the ground, unless the judge is suffering from a disability which makes it painful for him to do much bending.

Recently we have been hearing a lot about movement; how bad it is generally in the breed today. I often wonder what allowances many judges make when they are judging movement. On the other hand, many exhibitors ask for trouble by not using their heads before taking their dogs into the ring; for instance, when showing a bitch in, or just out of, season. Not only is this an undesirable practice from whichever angle it is viewed, but it is a highly risky thing to do when thinking in terms of winning, owing to the almost certain fact that she will move 'all over the place', most certainly by 'going close behind'. The same thing applies when a dog wishes to relieve itself—that will always affect movement. Young dogs and puppies of both sexes can move differently from day to day, according to their temperament, and this brings to mind the query as to whether all judges do judge puppies *as* puppies or as adult dogs. To liken a puppy to a mature dog is just as stupid as trying to compare a young boy or girl to an adult of the same sex. I don't think this is taken into consideration as it should be at times. For instance, one often reads a critique on a young dog which goes something like this: 'Lacks brisket and needs to body up.' Now there's a thing! Of course a young dog puppy lacks brisket and needs to body up—he would be a very strange puppy if he didn't. What the judge *should* have said was: 'Gives small indication of maturing in either depth of brisket or body properties,' *then* one would know that he *had* judged the exhibit as a puppy and still found it lacking. Still on the subject of judges' critiques, I make no apology for saying that some are not worth the space they take up in the canine journals. This is because a judge who takes no notes merely goes home and writes what he thinks will sound clever and smart, yet, if he were to be truthful, he would have to admit that that he could not recall what most of the dogs looked like because he had almost forgotten them since he judged them. I realized long ago that to give a true critique a judge must make full notes while he has the dogs before him and before they leave the ring. So, if I keep exhibitors waiting in the ring while I record the impressions I gained while actually judging, it is because I wish my critique to be in accordance with the details that influenced my placings as I saw them, and not merely some 'clever clap-trap' which has no relation to the actual dogs I had before me.

Referring again to movement, I think it essential to appreciate action correctly, to see the dog in motion from the side as well as from the front and rear. It should at least be moved round the ring even if it is not 'run up' and judged from the side. One hopes indeed that this fact will be borne in mind rather more than it is at present.

All in all, in judging Whippets the golden rule should be: 'Check for soundness and symmetry and balance.' An exaggerated dog is not necessarily a good dog. An unbalanced dog is a poor dog. Cloddiness should never outweigh raciness, and there are far too many cloddy-type dogs winning today, in my opinion. The Whippet is a 'speed king', not a 'shire horse' or a hunter. So my advice to the new judge is to bank on soundness, symmetry and balance and he will not go far wrong; in fact he will soon build up a reputation as sound as the dogs he will put up.

7

The Specialist Breed Clubs

WE NOW have no less than five specialist clubs* solely concerned with Whippets, namely the Whippet Club, the National Whippet Association, the Midland Whippet Club, the Northern Counties Whippet Club and the Whippet Club of Scotland.

The Whippet Club. This is the senior club. It has been in existence since 1899 and has such an interesting history that it will not be out of place to give a résumé of it here.

So far as is known, before 1899 there were no clubs whose objects were for the betterment of the Whippet, which was the reason for the Whippet Club's inception, and it was recognized and registered by the Kennel Club in that year. Previous to this date many Whippet enthusiasts no doubt met and discussed breed matters, and it may well be that there were actually in existence at that time clubs devoted entirely to the racing side of Whippets; but there seem to be no records in existence today.

We know, however, that at a meeting of the Kennel Club Committee, held at the Agricultural Hall on April 16th, 1890, a letter was read from Mr Herbert Viccars requesting a class to be provided in the Register of Names for Whippets. It was decided that such a class be provided and numbered 57 (*vide* extracts from the *Kennel Gazette* for May, 1890). So Whippets have been recognized at the Kennel Club as a breed since that date. Mr Herbert Viccars was a pioneer and actually owned some well-known dogs.

* In 1972 there are eight. See Appendix B.—K.S.

Another point of interest may be found in the *Kennel Gazette* for August, 1898, which states that Mr E. T. Cox applied for registration of the title 'The Whippet Club'. This was granted by the Committee at a meeting held on October 3rd, 1898.

A further point of interest is contained in the report in the October, 1900, issue of the *Kennel Gazette* which states that 'The Whippet Handicap' promoted by the Whippet Club was held at the Crystal Palace.

The original Minute Book of the Whippet Club beginning in 1899 is now missing and, therefore, the earliest existing record of the Whippet Club's proceedings is contained in a Minute Book of the Club Meeting which was held at Richmond Show on June 21st, 1907. At that time the Chairman was Mr Fred Bottomley and a Mr C. B. Payne was the hon. secretary. In 1910, the late Lewis Renwick was appointed as hon. secretary and the late Bernard Fitter installed as hon. treasurer. Right up to the time of Renwick's death he held, in conjunction with Fitter, one or other of these offices, excepting the short time he was living in Australia during the 'thirties. To mark his great services to the breed, although at that time he did not hold office owing to advancing years, Bernard Fitter was made an honorary life member in 1957, together with another great stalwart of the breed since the Whippet Club's inception, and a founder member, the late Mr Ernest Sobey.

The work the Whippet Club has done for the breed over the years can never be denied, and it will be difficult for those who have newly come into the breed to appreciate that in the early days, even almost into the mid 'thirties, there was hardly a class put on for the breed without the show executive concerned requiring a very liberal guarantee for the various classes, unless it happened to be one of the big Championship Shows, and even they regarded Whippets as one of the lesser breeds.

Guaranteeing a class meant that, should the entry fees not aggregate enough to pay prize money on offer, the guarantor (usually the Whippet Club) became responsible for the difference. Thus it was that, when the breed was struggling, through the help given by the Whippet Club and its members individually, the great shows up and down the country were encouraged to schedule classes which they most certainly would not have done without safeguards against financial loss. While guarantees are generously offered by all the clubs today, the popularity of the breed is such that it is rare indeed that such guarantors are called upon to meet any deficiency. By keeping a careful check on the panel of recognized breed judges the Whippet Club in the old days kept a careful check on the breed being judged according to the breed requirements. It would seem that the Whippet Club did much in recommending suitable judges, from their approved panel, to the Committees of the bigger shows, a system which appeared to work quite well in keeping the breed true to type. It would also seem to have become a recognized procedure for the secretaries to call on the Whippet Club for that service. Today, of course, the final approval of a judge is in the hands of the Kennel Club who keep the breed lists of judges. A perusal of the old-time records of the Whippet Club brings to light many items of interest. One such is provided by a recording of the fact that at a meeting held at the Kennel Club Show in 1908 it was resolved to ask the Kennel Club 'if the name of Whippet could be altered to Miniature Greyhound'. No doubt the Kennel Club refused to accede to this, for no mention is made recording any reply to this approach, and the name of Whippet still stands.

A pleasant feature of the old-time minutes of the Whippet Club is noted by the unusual practice of passing votes of thanks to the judges after they had officiated at shows. I suppose that, as the club selected the judges, they felt it was only right and proper, and indeed their place, to thank them. This I think shows how influential the Whippet Club was in the early days and how important its function. It might be of interest also to record an actual extract at this stage, which indicates how things went in those days. In the minutes of the meeting held at the Crystal Palace on October 18th, 1910, the following is recorded: 'The following judges were appointed for the undermentioned shows to be held in 1911—Birmingham, Mr Lewis Renwick; Cruft's, Mr W. J. Roland; Manchester, Mr Will Hally; L.K.A., Mr E. J. Sobey; Taunton, Mr C. B. Payne, and then followed the suggested classification, which was for six classes at each show. A further point of interest in connection with the foregoing extract is that there is a record that, at the 1911 L.K.A. Show there were sixty-three entries which was noted as being a record entry; Mr E. J. Sobey being the judge. In 1912, the Whippet Club was forced, owing to a serious strain upon its financial resources and owing to the poor entries received, to withdraw guaranteed cash support from the Northern and Midland shows, and only the Southern counties were supported. Finally, in 1913, the Whippet Club held its first postal ballot for judges for the following year. For those who may be interested to know the result of that ballot, the following names came out top of the poll: Messrs Fred H. Bottomley, W. Lewis Renwick, Bernard S. Fitter, E. J. Sobey, F. W. Botterill and Sir Edmund Chaytor, Bart. One outstanding item in this list of the then popular judges, is the fact that the postal ballot held for 1951 contained three of the names which appeared in the 1913 ballot!

During World War I the Whippet Club did not function, and a General Meeting was called for November, 1919, at the Queen's Hotel, Leicester Square, London. This meeting was presided over by Sir Edmund Chaytor, when it was decided to recommence activities. A further point of interest is shown in the recorded fact that, owing to an outbreak of rabies in the country, it was decided to defer the discussion as to whether a Club Show should be held or not. I think this was the last rabies epidemic in Great Britain and was, I have always understood, confined to South Wales. Lewis Renwick once told me that the Glamorgan Hounds were all destroyed by order of the Government and, he always added, he was never likely to forget it because that was the pack with which he always hunted. This pack was re-established by public subscription and through the generosity of other Hunts.

To resume, a milestone in the annals of the breed was when, in 1921, the Kennel Club asked what shows the Whippet Club recommended for the allocation of Challenge Certificates. The following were put forward: Cruft's, Birmingham, Cardiff, Taunton, Bristol and Reading.

The financial side of the Whippet Club in the 'twenties is interesting for, at the 25th Anniversary Meeting, held at the Alexandra Palace on October 1st, 1924, with Mr Fred Bottomley in the chair, it was considered a very satisfactory position when the hon. treasurer produced his balance sheet showing that the club's bank balance was £22 12*s.* 1*d.* in spite of the fact that £15 12*s.* had been paid out to shows for guarantees.

So one reads interesting details from the old records still in existence, proving over and over again what a wonderful job for the breed the Whippet Club has done. That this good yeoman service will be carried on to bigger and even better things is assured when one comes to realize that in the present hon. secretary, Mrs M. R. Jones, we have one of the hardest working, most enthusiastic and experienced of Whippeteers, who neither spares herself nor her time in any endeavour to make the Whippet Club better and better. For my part, having been hon. treasurer of the Whippet Club for several years now, I regard anything I may be called upon to do personally a great pleasure, and, quite frankly, I admit to a very sentimental attachment to the grand old Whippet Club.

It was after World War II that the 'boom' in Whippets began to show, for at the first show put on at the London Scottish Drill Hall, with the late J. E. Barker 'on the woolsack', for thirteen classes, fifty-seven dogs paraded, making an entry of 180. At the same venue a second show was staged and judged by the late Lewis Renwick, when in fourteen classes, sixty-five dogs made up an entry of 167. Cardiff, under the late H. G. Sanders, drew an entry of 117 in ten classes. Capt H. Price-Jones, judging at the Lime Grove Baths in 1947, and deputizing for E. J. Sobey, who was indisposed, drew an entry of 164 made up of thirty-three dogs in fourteen classes. New faces were being seen among the exhibitors, and on March 11th, 1950, the club held a Jubilee Show at the Horticultural Hall, London. This show was to celebrate the 50th Anniversary of the Whippet Club, and it is pleasing to record that unstinted support was given by the National Whippet Association and the Midland Whippet Club. Both these latter clubs recognized the good work done by the

Whippet Club, and their co-operation with the senior club's effort is very praiseworthy. The cost was high and, from what I saw of things after the show, it was not fully appreciated at the time of its inception how right royally the party held after the judging would be attended. However, 'a good time was enjoyed by all'. The judges at this show were Mr H. B. Evans and Mr Leo C. Wilson. A record entry paraded, totalling 233, and the whole effort was voted a huge success. It was easily the biggest thing of its kind that had been attempted in the breed up to that time.

The fact that there are now no less than three of the recognized clubs holding Championship status, shows how Whippets have gone from strength to strength, and some excellent events have been staged by all three. The 1959 Whippet Club Championship Show held at the Seymour Hall, Marylebone, London, probably reached the high-water mark in the way of show organization under the management of Mr John Kidd, when some deft touches of showmanship were in evidence, my most amusing recollection being of the strains of the 'Entry of the Gladiators' march which was played as the exhibits entered the hall. A wonderful parade of champions was warmly received and a noble sight they made. The present President, the Hon. Allan Mackay, presented the club with a beautiful perpetual trophy—the Enterkine Silver Tray for Best in Show, surely one of the most valuable and beautiful club trophies offered by any club in dogdom. I was honoured by winning this with Ch. Wingedfoot Claire de Lune who was awarded Best of Breed by the two judges, Mrs Dorothy Lewis and Mrs Peggy Stancomb. The club trophies were graciously presented at the close of the show by the very charming wife of the President.

Each year that the Whippet Club has held a Championship Show it has drawn better and better entries.

The National Whippet Association. This very go-ahead club, whose title, I remember, was suggested by me at the inaugural meeting, was formed in 1936. A get-together was arranged by the veteran exhibitor of the breed, Mrs Edith Conway-Evans, at a show held by the Muswell Hill Canine Society, and was attended by all those exhibiting the breed that day—a total of six! The N.W.A. was pluckily launched on a capital of £2, but Mrs Conway-Evans, supported by those of us who attended her meeting, got busy canvassing new members and getting trophies offered and so gradually the N.W.A. became established. Whippets owe much to 'The Grand Old Lady of the Breed', Mrs Conway-Evans, especially for the manner in which she kept the interest in the breed alive during the war years. In pre-war days the trophies offered by the N.W.A. were almost confined for competition to the old Met and Essex Championship Shows, Cruft's and the W.E.L.K.S.

Immediately after the war, the N.W.A. was granted Championship status and held their first Championship Show at the Scottish Drill Hall, London, on May 4th, 1946, at which I judged. In October, 1945, however, the N.W.A. had already put on an Open Benched Show, at which the late J. Emlyn Owen officiated. With sixteen classes scheduled, the entry totalled no less than 271, a record which, for the breed, I do not think has yet been surpassed. As the present hon. secretary so rightly says, in pre-war days an entry of even seventy-one would have shaken most people rigid, which indicates how the interest in the breed had developed. Actually my own entry at the Championship Show which was put on early in the following year totalled 239, a further indication that the development of the interest was obviously no mere flash in the pan. Further shows, all well supported, were put on by the indefatigable hon. secretary, Mrs Conway-Evans, but, after her Open Show at Leeds in February, 1947, which, incidentally, she organized and ran while suffering from a broken leg, the position of hon. secretary passed to Mrs S. Elizabeth Evans who has most worthily, and indeed most successfully, held that exacting post ever since. If great credit is due to Mrs Conway-Evans, and it most certainly is, equal acknowledgements must be accorded to her successor Mrs S. E. Evans. Both ladies have given great and unstinted service to the N.W.A. and the club has prospered accordingly. Having a keen eye for the social side of the club, the N.W.A., through the efforts of its very keen hon. secretary, held the first of their now famous Members' Lunches at the W.E.L.K.S. Championship Show in 1948. This was a joint effort on the part of the members, and proved to be an excellent innovation thoroughly enjoyed by all who participated in it, so it is easy to understand why the 'N.W.A. Lunch', as it is known now to one and all, became an annual, and deservedly popular, fixture. Mrs Evans, however, is nothing if not a very shrewd person, and she felt that a summer show would prove to be a better fixture with which to link up these lunch gatherings. With her eye on the correct setting for a picnic-type Members' Lunch, which the club by this time was well able to afford for its members, a tie-up with Windsor was made. C.C.'s not being available for the breed at that time at this show, Mrs Evans boldly went right to the heart of things, the Kennel Club Headquarters, and begged for an allocation of certificates for Windsor. This was granted the following year. Thus it came about that Windsor Championship Show has become the home of the N.W.A. Summer Show and is now quite an event in the social calendar of the club.

The go-ahead N.W.A. has no less than twenty-six trophies for competition among its members, all of which, with only one exception, are perpetual.

The Midland Whippet Club. This is a most enthusiastic club, having as its hon. secretary the dynamic Mrs Dorothy Lewis, who devotes a great deal of her time to its affairs. Few 'hon. secs.' work harder, or even as hard as Mrs Lewis does in the interests of her 'baby'—the Midland Whippet Club.

When the club was originally formed in 1949 the first hon. secretary was Mr Spiers. I remember his coming to me at the W.E.L.K.S. that year and complaining that he was not getting the full support from some quarters that he felt was necessary to get things moving, and asked for my help and for some publicity for the efforts being made to form the club. In my canine Press 'breed notes' I wrote that I was strongly in favour of this club being formed, and even if what I then said brought 'coals of fire' down on my head—which I expected—the fact remains that the Midland Whippet Club came into existence and has done a remarkably good job of work in its own sphere ever since.

After a shaky start, and after a year had passed, Mrs Dorothy Lewis took over the secretaryship and from that time the club has steadily gone ahead. The club is exceedingly fortunate in having as its Patron the Chairman of the Kennel Club, Air Commodore J. A. C. Cecil-Wright, A.F.C., T.D., D.L., and, for its President, Mrs J. L. Wingate. The Chairman of the club is Mr Fred Jones, and this team has been together for a period approaching a decade. It is reasonably safe to say that under such guidance the affairs and the progress of the Midland Whippet Club are assured.

The club puts up for competition eleven very fine cups and trophies. It has a sound bank balance and a very wide and representative membership. I always think the badge of this club is perhaps the prettiest of all, being enamelled in white and blue, and it is very proudly worn by most of its members at the shows. The Midland Whippet Club is very generous in the 'cash specials' it offers at most shows featuring the breed, also in the matter of its guarantees.

A Club Show is held annually in the Midlands and one in conjunction with the Handsworth Park Show in Birmingham, during which event the club provides an excellent free lunch for the executives of the club. A pleasant innovation is the holding of the annual raffle which is drawn at Bingley Hall, Birmingham Championship Show, each year, when some excellent prizes are distributed to the fortunate winners. The club pays out well over £25 each year in 'cash special awards' at Open and Championship Shows, and often quite a lot more.

This club gives a very helpful and instructive service to Midland followers of the breed and it is well worth considering from a point of view of enrolling.

The Northern Counties Whippet Club. This very go-ahead club last but one to be formed of the five existing clubs, and an excellent job of work it is doing. Great credit is due to the enthusiasts who rallied round and got together and who are doing so much now to boost the breed in the North.

The N.C.W.C. was actually founded in 1955 with twenty-nine Founder Members. At the first General Meeting held in March, 1956, Mrs D. F. Whitwell was elected President of the club and has held that office continuously. Mr and Mrs R. Hodgson were the mainsprings in getting the club started and have been Chairman and hon. secretary respectively since the club was formed. The membership has steadily mounted each year until, at the time of writing (1960), no less than 140 fully paid-up members are enrolled. The club since its inception has held eight Limited Shows, two each year, and was granted Championship status by the Kennel Club in recognition of the good work done for the breed. It held its first full-scale Championship Show in Leeds, in July, 1959, an event which was highly successful, and was judged by the American, Mr Anton Rost, the entry being 201, made up of eighty-nine dogs. The Kennel Club has again granted this club Championship status for 1960 and it is reasonable to assume that this will become a permanent grant.

In May, 1958, the club was honoured by the patronage of the Right Hon. the Viscountess Leverhulme.

One outstanding innovation of the Northern Club is their yearly issue to all members of a Year Book, covering the activities of the club over the previous year, at a price of 5*s*. 6*d*. The amount of work that this entails is cheerfully borne by the hon. secretary who is nothing if not unsparing in her efforts for the club's welfare. Contained in this Year Book are interesting and instructive articles by various members, all of which are calculated to be of help to the beginner in the breed. Another worthwhile effort was the organizing of a rally which was held in the garden of the President, from all accounts an event that was enjoyed by all. Over fifty members attended this 'get-together', bringing with them twenty-four Whippets.

The spirit of goodwill engendered in, and by, this club cannot possibly do other than foster good relations far and wide, and do much to popularize the breed and raise its standard in the North. Every right-thinking person connected with Whippets will express the hope that the Northern Counties Whippet Club will go on from strength to strength as I am certain that it will.

The Whippet Club of Scotland. In the late summer of 1959 Whippet owners in Scotland felt that as the breed was making such satisfactory progress the time had come to consider the formation of a club of their own. That indefatigable person Mrs Constance Crawford, wrote all known owners north o' the Border and to those resident in the north of England. In addition the proposed club was made known to many of the leading kennels in the South. The response to her approach was very enthusiastic and Mrs Crawford speaks very warmly of the encouragement she received from all the existing breed clubs. Support was promised on all sides. A meeting of the Scottish enthusiasts was arranged and held at the Edinburgh Championship Show on October 3rd, 1959. The Northern Counties Whippet Club agreed to sponsor the Scots; the Scottish Kennel Club was approached and approved the formation of the club. Finally the Kennel Club granted the application in April, 1960. Thus came into being the Whippet Club of Scotland, and it carried the good wishes of all.

Miss Amanda Selway was elected hon. secretary and Mrs Pat Selway hon. treasurer, but, owing to the fact that Air Vice-Marshal Selway was posted abroad much earlier than was expected at the time, Mrs Constance Crawford took over the post of hon. secretary and Mr Neil M. Crawford that of hon. treasurer.

One feels that a grand job of work for the breed is being done, and will continue to be done, in Scotland—and it is pleasing to me personally to see so many of the southern enthusiasts wearing at shows the most attractive badge of the Whippet Club of Scotland.

8

The Kennel Club

THIS chapter is written especially for the novice but, as so many experienced breeders and exhibitors seem to be singularly misinformed, or even uninformed, in regard to our ruling body perhaps they will not be entirely wasting their time by glancing through the following lines.

First, it must be recognized at the very outset that we breeders and exhibitors owe everything to the Kennel Club, for without the guidance and control of that body there would definitely be no dog shows held today, at least not in a manner which would appeal to most of us. It is true to say, although I have never attended any, that there are a few shows held in various parts of the country which are not licensed by the Kennel Club and therefore not conducted under their control. These shows must *not* be attended by anyone either as an exhibitor or a judge unless they are prepared to be 'warned off' from exhibiting or officiating at any show which is held under Kennel Club licence. I hope that this is fully understood, for if anyone *is* 'warned off' by the ruling body it means that their whole future as an exhibitor, breeder or judge is definitely and completely ended. This is as it should be, but it cannot be too strongly emphasized.

I have the greatest respect and regard for the Kennel Club in every way. I have found that, when approached, the various officials are always very fair, very firm and at the same time very friendly and helpful. Frankly, there have been occasions when I have been very pleasantly surprised to have been accorded such courteous help and guidance in response to some small request.

Everyone should place complete confidence in the Kennel Club and be very thankful that we have such experienced men who are prepared to give so much of their time, quite freely, in order to see that our doggy interests are protected. I use the word 'men' advisedly, as this is correct, for, although there is an overwhelming number of women in 'the dog game' today, far outnumbering the men, full membership to the Kennel Club is confined to men only. This is regarded by some as being very autocratic, but there is no doubt that the affairs of dogdom are very capably handled under the present arrangement.

There is a Ladies' Branch of the Kennel Club which is purely a social arrangement, but both men and women are eligible as Associate Members of the Kennel Club.

Responsibility for the registration and transfer of all dogs before entry in Shows, Field Trials, Working Trials and Obedience Tests, allocation of Championship status and of Challenge Certificates to various Shows and Trials, the licensing of all Shows and Matches, the recording of all registered Societies, the forming of all rules governing dogdom as a whole, and the watchful supervision over all who digress from these rules, is wholly and solely that of the Kennel Club.

Kennel Club Publications. Three regular publications emanate from the Kennel Club, the *Kennel Gazette* (monthly) and the *Kennel Club Stud Book* and the *Kennel Club Year Book* (annually). These 'dog-man's bibles' are available to everyone at a small cost and may be obtained from the Kennel Club.

The Kennel Club Liaison Council. This Council, more commonly known as the K.C.L.C., is a body elected by the clubs which are registered with the Kennel Club. The country is divided into areas and the clubs in those areas nominate and vote for their representatives. The number depends upon the number of the clubs in the area. The Championship Show Societies have separate representatives, and each breed council may nominate one representative (eighty-two breeds represented in 1970/71). These representatives receive and place on the agenda of the K.C.L.C. for consideration any suggestions or complaints they may receive from the clubs throughout the country. After full consideration is given to such items by the Council they are either rejected or passed for the consideration of the Kennel Club. Four delegates from the K.C.L.C. sit on the Committee of the Kennel Club. In this way it is assured that the deliberations of the Council go to the Kennel Club for examination and final ruling, not only in written form but also supported by the backing of the delegates. The Secretary of the Kennel Club is also the Secretary of the K.C.L.C., which completes the tie-up in a very satisfactory manner.

Registrations. Every dog, before it can be shown, must be registered with the K.C. The appropriate form, which is supplied free, is obtainable from the Kennel Club. This, when completed, must be returned with the necessary fee. If the dog has been registered by the breeder, or the vendor from whom it was bought, the new owner must apply to the K.C. for a 'Transfer of a Registered Dog' form if he or she wishes to register it in his or her name. The return of this form together with the appropriate fee will result in a Transfer Certificate being received in due course from the Kennel Club. If you buy a dog which has already been registered with the K.C. his registration certificate should be handed to you together with the pedigree of the animal. If, for some reason, an applicant wishes to register a dog, precluding it from being exhibited or bred from, they can ensure the required restrictions are recorded by advising the Kennel Club of their wishes at the time of registration. When a dog has already been registered, and later it is decided to restrict it, the registration certificate should be sent to the Kennel Club intimating what is required, when it will be returned in due course marked 'Not eligible for Exhibition' or 'Progeny not eligible for registration' or both, according to what is required. In certain instances there are many advantages arising from this form of registration, and the service is given free by the Kennel Club.

Prefixes and Affixes. Most breeders reach a stage when they feel they would like to register a prefix or an affix which will always denote their dogs in the future; a trade-mark, as it were. The Kennel Club should be advised when an application form will be forthcoming. Considerable thought should be given to the selection of a name for a prefix as there are many such applications already granted and a duplication of names will never be sanctioned from Clarges Street.

Export Details. The time may come when you will receive an order which asks for a dog to be exported abroad. Several points have to be observed before the dog can go. First, you will require the Kennel Club's official 'Export Pedigree' as, without this, the dog will not be accepted by the ruling body of the country to which he is going. This pedigree is issued at a fee of £2·50 at the present time (1972), and is applied for when making application for the transfer of the dog to its new owner. If a mated bitch is to be exported, enquiry should be made to the Kennel Club regarding the necessity, or not, of sending a 'Stud Service Certificate' and an official pedigree of the sire. The Kennel Club will advise on this matter. It is now necessary for every exporter to complete an official Kennel Club form which is called 'Certificate re Monorchidism and Cryptorchidism' in respect of all male dogs going abroad. Unless this form is duly completed and submitted to the Kennel Club at the time of applying for an export pedigree the latter document will not be issued. This is a fairly recent regulation and a very important one which must be observed. The form is very simple and self explanatory. A veterinary surgeon must be asked to sign this form when completing the necessary Certificate of Health. An export pedigree is required to accompany a dog only when it is going to the U.S.A. For a dog going to any other country this document may follow later by mail. The Kennel Club will mail this for you if requested at the time of submitting the completed document for their acceptance.

Challenge Certificates. There are three main awards over and above the ordinary prize cards, regarding which the novice may wish to have some further information. The main award is the Kennel Club Challenge Certificate. This is the top award any dog or bitch can win, and they are on offer at Championship Shows only, but not always granted by the Kennel Club to every breed scheduled at a Championship Show, so it is as well to make sure of this before entering. A Challenge Certificate is only awarded at the discretion of the judge, and he may be of the opinion that a dog which won in a lower class is a better dog than the one to which he awarded first place in the Open class. This will result in the winner of the lower class being called into the ring for comparison with the winner of the Open class since, because they are in different classes, they have not previously met in competition, and it may well be that the winning dog of the lower class will be awarded the Challenge Certificate. (It is now common practice to call the Challenge Certificate the 'C.C.'.) The large, and very much prized, green and white card is *not* the official certificate, but the 'bench card' to be affixed over the winning dog on his bench at the show. The official Certificate is forwarded to the winning owner by post from the Kennel Club after the show. The awarding of three C.C.'s by three different judges to the same dog entitles that dog to carry the proud title of Champion. The dog may go on winning as many C.C.'s at subsequent shows as he is capable of doing, and he may be shown under any judge whether he has awarded him a C.C. previously or not. This is not a practice which brings much popularity to the dog's owner, but it is a moot point whether a top-line champion should be withheld from any show in order to give another dog a chance. In my view, although I rarely if ever show a dog under the same Championship Show judge who has awarded the dog a C.C previously, I would say that one of the worst things that could happen would be for a spate of second-class champions to appear through lack of competition. At all Championship Shows an award which is much sought is that of 'Best of Breed'. This large red and white card is awarded by the judge to whichever is the better of the C.C. winning dog and the C.C. winning bitch and entitles the winner to go forward to compete for Best in Show against all the other breeds. There is no further certificate issued by the Kennel Club in regard to a 'Best of Breed' award. Another much-prized award is granted by the Kennel Club, the Breeders' Diploma. This is awarded, I think, as a graceful, complimentary gesture by the ruling body to the breeder, whether or not he or she actually owns the dog at the time it becomes a champion. It is a recognition to the breeder, who may or may not be able to attend shows and yet contributes so much by breeding the best stock and passing it on to others to show. Application for this Diploma must be made by the breeder of the dog to the Kennel Club, as the award is not automatic. Application for the Diploma must be made by letter only; there is no official form of application. The award of Junior Warrant is one which is, and rightly so, keenly sought. It is the recognition of an outstanding *young* dog of undoubted quality far above the average. The qualification necessary to entitle a dog to receive this award is the winning of twenty-five points between the age of six months and eighteen months of age, and they are estimated as follows: three points for winning a 1st at a Championship Show; one point for a 1st at an Open Show. Each win to be in Breed classes and not in Variety classes. Applications must be made to the Kennel Club for this award when the dog has completed his total of points, as, again, it is not automatic.

Breeding Terms. The Kennel Club issues an official form of agreement in respect of Breeding Terms arrangements, whether 'part' or 'full' and, if taken advantage of by the parties concerned, the loan is officially recorded at Headquarters, Clarges Street. This form is known as the 'Loan or use of Bitches' form and is issued for a fee of £1. In the event of a dispute arising, the Kennel Club acts as adjudicator. Many breeders prefer to make their own terms but, for my part, I am inclined to advise those who may at any time consider this form of breeding by arrangement to think twice before they venture. There are too many 'ifs' and 'buts' about the whole thing to make it worth while in the majority of cases. While that is my opinion, not everyone will agree, but one can only speak from personal experience.

The Kennel Club Stud Book. This is a yearly publication in which is recorded the results of all Championship Shows; it is a wonderful reference book. The dogs qualified for entry in the Stud Book are those which win Challenge Certificates, Reserve Best of Sex or First, Second or Third prizes in the major classes of Championship Shows. Entry in the Stud Book is also obtained by wins at Field Trials, Working Trials and Obedience Tests. A dog may also be admitted to the Stud Book 'by nomination'. An application form furnished by the K.C. must be completed and returned, with the appropriate fee, for a dog which is the sire or dam of winners entered, and entitled to be entered in the Stud Book, or one which is the son or daughter of winners entered, or entitled to be entered, in the Stud Book.

SHOWS IN GENERAL

Now for a few words on shows in general. There are four types of shows: Championship, Open, Limited and Sanction.

Championship Shows are those where anyone may exhibit provided the dog is registered with the Kennel Club, and where Challenge Certificates are offered by the Kennel Club. These may be general shows or Specialist Club one-breed Championship Shows; for example, the Whippet Club Championship Show. It naturally follows that it is only by winning a C.C. at this type of show that a dog starts his climb towards the title of champion.

Open Shows. These are similar to Championship Shows with the exception that C.C.'s are not offered by the Kennel Club.

Limited Shows. These are shows where the entry is confined to members of the club or society promoting the show and are restricted to a minimum number of classes—hence the title Limited Show.

Sanction Shows. These come lower in the scale and are those which are restricted to a maximum of twenty classes, to medium-grade dogs and to members of the society promoting the show only.

There is, however, another type of show termed the *Exemption Show.* These are usually run in connection with fêtes and so on, the proceeds of which are generally donated to some charity. The Kennel Club sanctions these shows provided they do not schedule more than four classes for Kennel Club-registered dogs. Other types of classes are usually scheduled but are of a type not put on by Kennel Club-authorized shows in the usual way. All dogs, whether registered with the Kennel Club or not, may compete in these 'comic' classes (which are exceedingly good fun and all help a worthy cause financially) and entries are usually accepted up to, and including, the day of the show. These shows can be most amusing and they are usually regarded as a 'day out' by most regular exhibitors. There is much to recommend them.

Matches. This is another form of exhibiting dogs, and the meetings, usually held in some local hall in the evenings, are arranged in such a way that two dogs only are in competition at the same time. Each dog is allotted a number when it is entered, and two numbers are drawn 'from the hat', which results in the dogs bearing those numbers being called together for competition. By a process of elimination the numbers are whittled down until only two remain and these meet in the final. Each dog must be the property of a member of the society or club promoting the Match or of the members of the opposing club or society, as these Matches are often arranged between nearby clubs or societies. There is much to be said for these Matches from the novice's point of view. They can be educational as well as enjoyable and the would-be aspirant to higher honours in dogdom is well advised to visit a Match if one is held in his or her neighbourhood.

9

Famous Whippet Kennels

IN WRITING on this subject it is difficult to decide what to mention and what to leave out. Obviously it can be possible to mention only a few, and quite impossible to mention all those kennels that qualify under the heading of 'Famous', for that would almost call for a book in itself. I have therefore mentioned those which I feel have had a definite influence on the breed; yet here again I must admit that there are many more of these than I have room to record. Again, I have often heard it said that the present-day Whippeteer does not want to 'live in the past', and in any event much has been written about pre-war kennels in works still available. So, after much deliberation, I have decided to set before my readers a small selection of famous kennels in the hope that my doing so will not cause anyone to feel that either they or their kennel has been in any way slighted.

Although many famous names come to mind: the Bottomley brothers with their famous 'Manorleys', Mrs Barry Adams with her all-conquering 'Of Ynys' Whippets, Mr Emlyn Owen, Mr Harries-Jones, Mr Taylor and his lovely 'Yentocs' dogs—oh! many of the old names come crowding back as I reflect—there is one name which stands out high above them all—Mr W. L. Beara of Appledore, Devon, the owner of the Willes Whippets.

To have met Willie Beara is to be able to boast about it, for he was an outstanding man in many ways. Kindly, helpful, full of fun and good spirits, he was without doubt one of the greatest-hearted doggy men I have ever known. Willie Beara would, and did, help any lame dog over a style. He was a big man in every way, in outlook as well as in physique, and with his amazing blue eyes and his great booming laugh he made everyone who met him feel on good terms with themselves and the world in general. I never heard Willie Beara say an unkind or thoughtless word against anyone, and in these days that is something I feel many in the 'dog game' will be inclined to take leave to doubt. But it is an honest fact. I make no secret about it, I loved the old Maestro, and when I was judging in the West Country only a few years ago I was most touched that Willie Beara had specially made the trip in order to show a dog under me. That I had to place him well down the list quite saddened me, but Willie gave me his usual great grin and I am sure he never gave it a second thought. *That* was the man, and *that* part of his make-up was why I am quite sure that if a ballot could be taken Willie Beara would top the poll as being the best loved and the greatest of *all* Whippeteers. Honest as the day, as he was in all his dealings, I am convinced that not only was he quite incapable of doing a mean action, he was equally as incapable of even thinking of one. His contemporaries had only one little 'grouse' against him: he would never judge the breed in the ring. I am quite sure that it was solely because he was that type of man who could never bring himself to hurt anyone, even by putting their dog out of the prize money. He would never admit to this, but one day I openly challenged him with it. He steadfastly refused to answer beyond saying, 'Well, old friend, you know how they take it to heart—why make them unhappy?' and I knew then the true reason he would never 'take the woolsack'. Incidentally, I was once approached by Charles Cruft to try to get Willie Beara to 'do them' for Cruft's in the days when this event was held at the old Agricultural Hall in Islington, but to no avail.

W. L. Beara seriously started the Willes strain in 1912 after his purchase of the famous bitch Falside Fascination, although the record shows that he won a C.C. with a black dog named Verulam Warbler at the old Crystal Palace in 1903. His best stud dog was probably one that was 'up to size', but proved to be a remarkable sire, Willesberg. His best bitch was probably Ch.

Willesbrenda, who was never beaten in the ring. I always regard the bitch Willesbubbles as being the best bitch he ever bred, which view was shared by J. E. Barker. I bought and re-named her Clevona Chloe. This bitch was not shown to any great extent and never appeared in the honours rolls, as she should have done. She was, incidentally, the litter sister to another dog I bought from Beara, one which eventually became my own Ch. Will o' the Wisp of Mimosaland, after I had passed him on to Mrs. Critchley-Salmonson who was a great supporter of the breed in the early 'thirties. Ch. Wingedfoot Marksman is in direct line from Ch. Will o' the Wisp. Ch. Willesbleina was another 'lovely' bred and shown by Beara—there were many others. Just for the record, the following are some of the champions bred by W. L. Beara: Champions Willesbeaux, Willesblond, Willesbera, Willesbrenda, Willesbleina, Silver Knight, Una, Firebrand, Will o' the Wisp of Mimosaland, Willesblair, Delphine, Willesbelle, Willesbella, Willesbea. A remarkable record by a very remarkable man who, as I have previously said, it was a pleasure and privilege to have known and call a friend.

Yet, great as was the personality of W. L. Beara in the Whippet world before World War II, there was one whose influence was probably even greater. I refer to one who rejoiced in the nickname of 'the novices' friend'—Mr. Bernard S. Fitter. A quiet, unassuming man, his whole interests were bound up in Whippets, and never has the breed had a more loyal adherent nor such lifelong advocate of its virtues. A truly great judge of the breed, he was at all times absolutely fair and just in his decisions. I make no bones about it that when I first became active in showing the breed I felt that Fitter was inclined to be too 'slow' and over-cautious. As I got to know him better with the passing of time I came to understand that his seeming 'slowness' and reluctance to adopt very readily any new idea was typical of the man's natural steadiness and care.

Fitter owned many good dogs, some of which were made Champions, and were famous in their day, among them Chs. Boy Scrounger and Snooker. I feel I would be right in saying that

Fitter's favourite dog was Boy Smuggler to which he was greatly attached.

I look back upon a little thing I arranged in regard to Bernard Fitter and which I shall recall for as long as memory lasts. I had a phone call one Friday night from his charming wife Inez—one of the great bridge players of the 'thirties—who sadly informed me that Bernard was being taken to hospital on the following Sunday and that she feared the worst. She went on to say that the thing that had kept Bernard going for so many weeks was looking forward to his weekly *Our Dogs* (for which journal he was a regular contributor for many many years—right back to the time when the breed notes column was headed Whippet Wireless). His greatest worry was, she told me, that he felt he would never judge the breed again. I felt very touched upon hearing this and arranged with her to hold back his entry to hospital on the Sunday until I arrived, informing her that we would have a dog show and that Bernard should judge! She asked him, as he lay in bed, poor chap, if he felt he could tackle it —and his response, she said, was immediate. 'Come by all means,' she said to me, 'and bless you!' I thereupon telephoned Lewis Renwick and contacted Mrs Dorothy Lewis, and, great troupers that they were, and are, they immediately agreed to co-operate.

So very early on the Sunday morning, we three set out in my car, together with Ch. Wingedfoot Marksman of Allways, Ch. Wingedfoot Wild Goose and Ch. Wingedfoot Hildegarde for Fitter's last judging appointment. We arrived at Fitter's bedside, as I remember, about 11 a.m. and then carefully and solemnly handled all three dogs, for his judgement. Renwick handled Hildegarde, Mrs Lewis handled Wild Goose and I handled Marksman. Never did three handlers take their job more seriously and never was a judge more interested in his job. Fitter, bless him, made Goose 1st, Marksman 2nd and Hildegarde 3rd. That was a great judge's last show and I think that three very quiet and deeply moved handlers left his house that afternoon.

Fitter lived for several weeks after that day, and Mrs Fitter always said that she was convinced that his life was very much prolonged by the happy interlude we provided for him. I hope it was so. Lewis Renwick and I attended his funeral later and then discovered that he was an ardent Spiritualist—as was Stanley Wilkin, I understand—and we were most impressed by what we saw and heard. The breed owes much to Bernard Fitter, whose name will never be forgotten.

It has been said of Captain Lewis Renwick in relation to Whippets that the association was accepted by all who knew him as that of ham and eggs! He was indeed an ardent Whippet lover and had actually owned and showed them as well as bred them, from the age of twelve. His great record in the breed has been discussed too many times to need repetition here. I would rather write of Renwick as the man—the man I came to know and love so well. He was perhaps the greatest authority on the breed in the world; he was most certainly, in my opinion, one of the greatest judges. He was so sound, so clear thinking and, what is more, so utterly impartial.

To illustrate the latter point I would mention that I once had a Pointer bitch with a good show record of which I was inordinately proud. I entered her under Lewis Renwick when he was judging Varieties at an Open show in no less than nine classes. My reward was One Reserve only. Although I lived at his flat for the main part of the week in those days his placing of the bitch was never mentioned by either of us. But one night, over a year later, sitting before his fire, reminiscing on dogs and shows in general, Renwick suddenly laughed and said to his charming wife: 'You know, Douglas has never really forgiven me for putting his Pointer bitch down as I did,' and, turning to me, asked, 'Have you?' My reply was: 'No, I jolly well haven't. Whatever did you find wrong with her?'

Then he told me. It was so truly Renwick. He said he felt that she was a lovely bitch, but also he couldn't get away from the fact that she was certainly a small one. He felt he either had to put a bitch like that, with her many excellent points, right up, or put her right out. There could be no halfway line. He formed his final judgement, he told me, because he suddenly recalled the days when he and his father used to shoot over a certain kale field in South Wales, and he suddenly realized that, had he been shooting over my bitch, she would be useless for her job, because she would never be seen! He quite realized that there is no standard height in Pointers—but that was his decision. And what could be fairer than that?

How many times, I wonder, when I used to get incensed over something which I considered to be very unkind and suggested a reprisal did Renwick say over and over again: 'Never act in anger, Douglas. We must be fair; those people are speaking without knowledge'? So, in his gentle way, he went through life. Although he was careless, according to some, over details which he considered of no consequence, I always regarded him as a 'great old Edwardian' and a gentleman in everything he said or did.

As I write this I find myself pausing, going over again, the many happy times I had in Lewis Renwick's company. Often I have seen him take a firm stand at a time when he could have been readily excused from doing so—but he always stood by his firm principles and he *never* wavered.

With the passing of Lewis Renwick the breed lost perhaps its greatest supporter. I know that I lost my greatest and most respected friend. I can truthfully say this—and I say it with no sense of shame: so great was his influence upon me in matters appertaining to the breed that I never judge without he crosses my mind, and invariably I find myself thinking, when faced with a difficult decision, 'I wonder how Lewis would have placed these two?'—and that, I think, is the greatest compliment anyone can pay another judge.

THE BREKIN KENNELS

Owned by Lady F. M. Danckwerts, this kennel was always famous for the manner in which the inmates were presented. Before she became interested in Whippets Lady Danckwerts had had considerable experience in several breeds, and she was perhaps better known in Dandie Dinmont Terriers in pre-war days than in any other breed.

The first Whippet puppy which brought about the Brekin advent into the breed was one purchased from Mrs. Edith Conway-Evans as a pet, named Crusader of Conevan, and he arrived on D-Day. Crusader was shown and he did some good winning in Graduate and Limit classes, but he never got higher than second place in the Open class for dogs at any Championship Show. His main fault is, as I recall, that he was full measure in size, and at that time size was one of the main points on which the early post-war judges seemed to make the majority of their decisions. Crusader had an exceptionally reachy neck and he was without doubt a grand mover, being as sound as a bell fore and aft. Lady Danckwerts subsequently 'borrowed', to use her own term, a companion from Mrs Conway-Evans to keep Crusader company. This was Crusader's litter sister, none other than the famous (as she later became) White Statue of Conevan, and she was very soon bought outright and began her show career. Lewis Renwick always bracketed White Statue with two contemporary bitches and rated them the best three to be shown during the fifty years he was associated with the breed.

Be that as it may, White Statue soon became a champion and did much for the breed, for from her came in direct descent a line of superlative bitches: Ch. Brekin Spode, Brekin Porcelain, Ch. Brekin Ballet Shoes, Brekin Bitter Sweet and Brekin Willow Pattern. Willow Pattern was in turn the dam of three famous Champions in one litter, namely Ch. Fieldspring Bartsia of Allways, Ch. Fieldspring Betony and Int. Ch. Wingedfoot Fieldspring Bryony. How I found these puppies by candlelight is quite a story in itself. The lovely Lily of Laguna and Laguna Limelight, both full Champions of renown, were out of Brekin Ballet Shoes. Today, Brekin Dorothy Perkins of Test, Brekin Terra Cotta and Tranwells Brekin Sally Lunn are keeping the Brekin prefix to the fore, although Lady Danckwerts herself has given up active exhibiting. Her Ladyship avows that she derived more satisfaction from her wins with Brekin Spode because she was home-bred and did the most spectacular winning, chief of which was winning Best in Show, both days, at Leicester, in 1948, and the Hound Group at the L.K.A.

It is quite possible that Ch. White Statue of Conevan was the outstanding bitch of this kennel, even though she was never enamoured of the show-ring and was a difficult bitch to condition and handle. She also tended to put on too much weight. Lady Danckwerts refers to her as her one-time problem child. The rapid rise of the Brekin Kennel in the breed cannot be said to result from rigid adherance to a preconceived breeding programme, but it does go to show what can be done if careful and intelligent matings are arranged and a set 'line of country', when once determined, is faithfully followed out.

THE LADIESFIELDS

This very keen and enthusiastic kennel, which specializes in 'colour breeding', started in the breed in 1946 with the purchase of a dog which appears in many pedigrees, Snitterfield Cornstalk. As Mrs Margaret Wigg is a stickler for Whippets being regarded first and foremost as sporting and working dogs and being able to stand up to their job, Cornstalk was regarded in that light from the first. Actually Mrs Wigg had been attracted to the breed through coming into contact with a working Whippet during her war-work on the land, and by being impressed with what this dog could, and did, do. Cornstalk, naturally, had to emulate this war-time dog in every way and, from what I gather, right well he did his work. 'Stalky' was an adept at catching his rabbit, but he went much farther, he coursed and retrieved hares, whether alone or accompanied. When 'on his own' he brought his catch home, and if there was no one about the place he sat on the doorstep with his catch and never left it until he 'officially handed it over', and even then, only to a recognized member of the household. This dog, from all reports, must have been 'quite a boy' for he gathered in eggs, rounded up stock and so on.

In 1948, Miranda of Thickthorne, a parti-colour bitch, joined the kennel. Mated to Cornstalk the litter contained an outstanding bitch which, in Mr Fred Barnes's ownership, produced Papyrus

Grass and Silver Moon, which did a lot of winning in top company. White Swan was another of the litter which, in turn, produced the well-known Ch. Ladiesfield Starturn, a black dog. Actually, one of Cornstalk's first litter is still in the kennel at the age of eleven and half years and, being a 'Ladiesfield worker', this fellow was still catching rabbits at the age of ten years! Ladiesfield Bluemoon is an outstanding inmate of this kennel, and the record shows that the present-day Ladiesfield show stock all came from the original 'workers'. Mrs Wigg is firm in her belief that, to develop the true character of a Whippet it must be allowed full scope in following its natural instinct to hunt and work generally. To, as she puts it, 'do the job Nature intended it to'. She set out to breed 'blacks', and her greatest thrills have come from her wins with that colour. Admitting the difficulty of breeding Whippets to colour, which I have mentioned in earlier chapters, Mrs Wigg regards it as a challenge to anyone really interested in breeding, and I agree with her entirely. As this owner has piloted a home-bred black dog right among the 'top-liners' of the breed she may very rightfully regard it as something of an achievement, for the way of the 'colour specialist' is a rough and heart-breaking one indeed.

I must admit that I have every wish personally to see the best of success come to this enthusiastic kennel where the dogs are sincerely loved for themselves, bred along the most carefully thought-out lines for what is required of them, and where, in addition, they must have a rattling good time. Good luck to them, I say, and I wish there were more kept like them.

THE BENACHIE KENNELS

Just after World War II the Benachie Whippets literally 'swept the board', and many and many a lovely dog, most beautifully presented (as all the Benachies invariably are) and expertly handled, has caught my eye at different times whether I happened to be a ringsider or the judge, for they were always quite outstanding.

The kennel was started in 1941, when Mrs Chapman bought a little sister of the then all-conquering Ch. Samema Princess. This was a white bitch by Ch. Manorley Manala out of Oxted Dainty Maid. Wise in her generation, Mrs Chapman mated this bitch to that great dog I always admired so much, Ch. Conquisitor, owned at one time by the late Emlyn Owen, and from this alliance came the first Benachie show-dog, Happy Landings. This dog won a big breed class under Mr Warner Hill the first time out, but his greatest achievement was his siring of the famous Ch. Pilot Officer Prune. How many pedigrees this dog's name appears in, to be sure! Prune's dam was a small silver bitch by Silver Beige of Luss. Prune had a grand career, winning seven C.C.'s under seven different judges and was more than a score of times B.I.S. Ch. Pilot Officer Prune sired no less than nine English Champions. He was retired from the ring quite early to make way for his son Ch. Flying Officer Kite. (In this respect he was followed by my own dog Ch. Wingedfoot Marksman of Allways who was also held back on many an occasion to make way for *his* son, Ch. Wingedfoot Wild Goose. Had this not been so it is quite certain that both Prune and Marksman could, and indeed would, have added many more C.C.'s to their belts!) Ch. Flying Officer Kite won five C.C.'s and sired that grand bitch Ch. En for Nonsense, a great favourite of the late Lewis Renwick, which is, in my opinion, the hall-mark on any dog, for Renwick was a truly great judge. Kite won much as the record shows, particularly his winning the Hound Group at Blackpool under the American all-rounder Captain Will Judy. Unfortunately, Captain Will Judy went a little awry, according to our standards, in writing his critique, but this did not detract one iota from Kite's great win on the day, and it was all received in good humour. I liked Kite, I always liked him, for he was a dog with the real Whippet character. But then that means little because I have always liked all the Benachies. Incidentally, Kite won B.I.S. all Breeds at Bournemouth Championship Show in 1949 under three different judges.

Bitches holding full Championship status followed in quick succession at this time, Ch. Tea for Teresa, the lovely and ever-remembered Ch. Jay for Jewel—and what a gem of a bitch she was—Ch. En for Nonsense, until we come to the present day when we have that elegant fellow Ch. Bouquet. I could go on for hours reporting on the lovely dogs that have been bred in the Benachie Kennels, for I have admired them all. I have only one 'complaint' in regard to their popular owner, and that is that she is adamant in her refusal to judge the breed. Such a pity it is, I think, but there it is, and I suppose, like the late W. L. Beara, she feels she knows best. I must tell one little story about the Benachies. One night when visiting Mrs Chapman, an event I always looked forward to with much pleasure, she and I sat in the sma' hours discussing Whippets when I asked her why she never mated any of her bitches to my own dog Marksman. Her reply was that she would never send them 'boxed' by rail, and I lived so far away. That I understood, knowing the intense feelings she has for her dogs, but when she mentioned that actually in the room with us was Eh for Adorable, *in season*, I told her that Marksman was outside asleep in my car. We immediately agreed upon their marriage, and the result was Int. Ch. Wingedfoot Ringmaster and his sister, the amazing Wingedfoot Tu Whit Tu Whoo who, in the ownership of Mr Joe Fisher of Nottingham, must surely hold the record of the number of Best in Show wins by any Whippet—I believe in the region of no less than forty, in addition to several Reserve C.C.'s., and now holds two C.C.'s won in 1960 when transferred to Mrs. A. Argyle Reverting to Ch. Pilot Officer Prune, the following Champions were sired by him: Ch. Flying Officer Kite, Ch. Tea for Teresa, Ch. Jay for Jewel, Ch. Rosa of Ballymoy, Ch. Peppard Pied Piper, Ch. Seagift Silly Symphony, Ch. Springmere Fanfare, Ch. Bellavista Barrie, and Ch. Seagift Speedlite Mustang. Ch. Pilot Officer Prune died in the summer of 1959 at the age of fourteen years. I think, without doubt, he was Mrs Chapman's favourite, and that I can understand. Be that as it may, I know that his loss even at his advanced years was a sad blow to her. A great pillar of the breed, his name will live always in the annals as it so well deserves.

It is very pleasing to learn that in the young entry waiting to make their début, the Benachies have worthy followers of the great dogs which have carried the kennel to fame, and that there is no sign that the enthusiasm of their owner is other than just as keen as it ever was.

THE PEPPARD KENNELS

Beginning in 1945, this lively kennel has consistently made its presence felt at most of our major shows within striking distance, and, indeed, at times very far afield. 'Presentation' is one of the outstanding features of the Peppards and it was the interest of owners like Mr and Mrs Donald H. L. Gollan that did much, in my opinion, to rocket the breed into popularity. The first inmate of this kennel was the well-known Desperado of Toytown, who was by Ch. Boy Scrounger out of Spider of Sands. Shown at the zoned shows at that time, and before Championship Shows proper were started again, Desperado did very well, but Whippet classes being few and far between it was mainly in Variety classes that his success was attained, and he was awarded B.I.S. on at least two occasions.

In 1946 the bitch Zanza Zita joined the kennel. By Flight Lieutenant out of Zanza Zala, she whelped four puppies, three of which went to the United States, while the remaining bitch became the well-known Ch. Sweet Pepper of Peppard, attaining her full status in December, 1949. In 1948, however, she was mated to Ch. Pilot Officer Prune and in a litter of four produced the well-known Ch. Peppard Pied Piper. This was a remarkable story of quick success, but one which fully endorses all I have written in previous chapters regarding the selection of correct 'blood-lines' and the sensible continuance of them. Both Mr and Mrs Gollan have had experience with horses and I should say that their knowledge in this connection has stood them in good stead. The win of Sweet Pepper's first C.C. at Richmond in July, 1949, is looked back upon by her owners as their most pleasurable ring victory, and this can be readily understood, as it was only the third time she had been entered at a Championship Show because of a serious set-back in contracting a bad attack of distemper, and later on she had her maternal duties to attend to. Ch. Peppard Pied Piper won his first C.C. in April, 1950, and completed his status in October of that year. Moving to their present address, in 1953, the Peppards did not compete in the show-ring for a full year and then bred the first black to be added to the kennel from a litter sister of Pied Piper named Peppard Purple Primrose. This newcomer became Peppard Black Boy and there is a sweet story connected with his birth. When she had whelped what was thought to be her full litter one cold dark evening in October, Primrose insisted upon going out into the garden, which is a very normal thing for a bitch to do in such circumstances. She returned after a few minutes carrying what appeared to be a large black bone which she carefully deposited in the nest with her newly arrived puppies. That 'bone' turned out to be the 'blackest ever', Peppard Black Boy! The Peppards are of course a perfect example of a real amateur kennel, and are by no means commercially minded. Most perfectly housed the dogs have full access to their owners' very pretty house and extensive gardens, and it is a joy to see Whippets living in such circumstances and surroundings and enjoying the loving care of such owners as Mr and Mrs Gollan—all of which I have referred to in print before. To me this means much, for I can well remember when Whippets as a breed were only regarded as 'hole and corner dogs', and so I delight indeed to see them living as the Peppards do.

I had the pleasure of stewarding for Mr Gollan when he first judged and, after watching his method of appraising them for a while, I knew that in him we had a new judge who had definite ideas.

THE ALLWAYS KENNELS

This kennel, owned by Mr and Mrs Fred Jones, needs no introduction from me, as inmates from here are regularly seen at most shows where the breed is featured. Both Mr and Mrs Jones are very experienced 'doggy' people and have had much experience in other breeds, namely Greyhounds (for many years), and later

C. M. Cooke

Whippet Club Championship Show Progeny Class, 1956

Ch. Wingedfoot Marksman of Allways (centre with the author), supported by (*left to right*) Ch. Mistrals Mrs. Miniver, Wingedfoot To Whit To Whoo, Int. Ch. Wingedfoot Ringmaster, Ch. Wingedfoot Wild Goose, Ch. Evening Star of Allways

D. Jones, Riverwood, Stallam

How a Whippet should be handled. With a light touch Kay Douglas-Todd holds Noswal Barbelle of Wingedfoot firm yet relaxed

Thomas Fall

Ch. Shalfleet Starstruck

Newark Advertiser

Ch. Harque The Lark

Int. Ch. Wingedfoot
Ringmaster

C. M. Cooke

Wingedfoot
Shenandoah

C. M. Cooke

Ch. Boughton
Modra

Ch. Allways Wingedfoot
Running Fox

C. M. Cooke

Ch. Laguna Ligonier

C. M. Cooke

Ch. Lily of Laguna

'Daxies' among others. It was largely owing to living in a built-up area at the time which decided Mr and Mrs Jones to take up Whippets.

Strangely enough the Allways were not very successful at the start and experience was gained the hard way—the best in the long run. Fred always claims that 'Bobbie' was the one who 'stuck her toes in' and would not give up, whereas 'Bobbie' always insists that it was Fred's lifelong love of Greyhounds that caused them to 'stick at it' with the Whippets. For my part I would suggest that it was a combination of effort on the part of two sensible, level-headed people who determined to 'get there' and eventually succeeded, as the record proves. Thinking in terms of brood bitches, as every right-thinking person should when building up a kennel, the Allways first Championship came in 1951. The Allways foundation brood bitch was that great matron Bolney Starshine of Allways. The first 'top-liner' from this bitch's second litter went to Australia and took top honours there. In her first litter she bred the 'Great Marksman' (which I was lucky enough to buy from this kennel) who won fifteen C.C.'s. His litter brother Martyn of Allways was a dog very similar in type but a little heavier all over when he finally matured. When I saw him in Germany Martyn had become the undisputed racing champion of the Continent. I had the privilege of being present when he was beaten, for this honour, at Mannheim by his own daughter.

Martyn became an International Champion on the bench as well as a Race Champion, and I had the pleasure when judging on the Continent to award him a C.A.C.I.B., which he richly merited. He has done much for Whippets on both the bench and the track on the Continent. It is quite safe to say that Starshine set the feet of the Allways on the rungs of the ladder of success. She died only recently, at the ripe old age of thirteen years, and it is pleasant to record that right up to the end she was a really grand-looking bitch. It was always a great pleasure to see her.

The next Allways star was one I always have a little joke about and say 'I saw him first', which was when I bought his litter sister

Bryony, Ch. Fieldspring Bartsia of Allways. 'The little gentleman of the breed' I always called him, and this title fitted him like a glove, for he was always, and still is, a dainty, fastidious dog who gives the impression of taking a great pride in his personal appearance. Soon after Bartsia joined the Allways team his sister Betony, who also became a famous Champion, was bought. Between them they 'wiped the eye' of many a dog in shows up and down the country both in their breed, and in Variety classes. One Sunday morning I made a decision which resulted in my parting with a young Marksman dog named Wingedfoot Running Fox. I had not the slightest doubt about his qualities and stated my views emphatically. He is the one and only dog I have ever sold of which I said I was *sure* he would become a champion. What Ch. Allways Wingedfoot Running Fox, now the property of Mr Joe Fisher of Nottingham, has done, both in the ring and as a stud dog, is common knowledge. It is pleasing to record that although Running Fox was bought by Mr Fisher when a fully qualified Champion, he has doubled his C.C. wins in his present ownership.

The mating of Betony to Marksman produced another star in the shape of Ch. Evening Star of Allways. Later Ch. Allways Wingedfoot Running Fox produced another Champion in Ch. Choirmaster of Allways, now in the kennel of Mr Harry Bridge in America. Then Bartsia came into the picture as a sire and produced Ch. Silver Sprite of Allways, a lovely little bitch which was eventually transferred to the ownership of the Hon. Allan Mackay. Followed German Ch. Atoms Flash of Allways, also Int. Ch. Wise Child of Allways, which was by a son of Bartsia. Fred Jones, in his wisdom, then purchased part of a litter sired by Ch. Evening Star of Allways from Mr Robbins which was double in-bred to Marksman, and among these puppies was none other than Ch. Robmaywin Stargazer of Allways. Curiously enough this dog did not impress everyone as a puppy, but Fred Jones never wavered in his faith in the dog, and it fell to my lot eventually to award him his final and qualifying certificate and Best of Breed at Cruft's in 1958. Later that day he won the Hound Group at the same show and has since gone on from success to success and now has seventeen C.C.s to his name, fourteen of which were won under different judges, adding lustre to the breed he so nobly represents.

This, in brief, is the Allways story, from which it will be plainly seen that finding the right line and keeping faithfully to it has yet, once again, proved to be a brilliant success.

THE 'OF TEST' KENNELS

Speaking of personalities among Whippets we most certainly have one who is, happily, still active as a judge, breeder and exhibitor in the first flight. Her remarkable experiences are outstanding both with dogs and horses. I refer to the popular hon. sec. of the Midland Whippet Club, Mrs Dorothy Lewis. Few people make as strong a claim as she to be a life-long dog lover, in so far that at the age of eight years she was helping to look after her parents' Greyhounds and Whippets in the holidays, which, I should imagine, were many, as she had a private governess in the old style.

Mrs Lewis recalls that in that kennel, in addition to coursing Greyhounds, there were three Whippets, Spider, Buzz and Fly. These coursed with the Greyhounds around Badminton, Sheraton and the Malmesbury areas on non-hunting days. Among the regular company, which numbered about twenty, each follower usually turning up with two or three hounds apiece, were the present Duke of Beaufort and his sister Lady Blanche Douglas. Collies were Mrs Lewis's first love as regards show-dogs, and she had considerable success with them. Later, Labradors filled the bill, but she reverted to Collies again at a later date. A win at the L.K.A. in 1924 with this breed is recorded for Best Brace and a pair of silver spoons Mrs Lewis still has among her trophies are highly prized. But it was in connection with Greyhounds that Mrs Lewis was mainly known. She held a Public Trainer's Licence, for which she qualified in the kennels of Mrs Joan Bennet, who at that time trained for such well-known owners as Captain E. A. V. Stanley and Brigadier General Critchley of the White City. Mrs

Lewis's last coursing season was just prior to the war, when her hounds ran forty-eight courses and won forty-two of them.

An interesting item in this sporting lady's career in dogs was the report of 'Leveret' of the *Star* (Mr Leo C. Wilson, of course) on 'Bring Luck of Test', a Greyhound she bred and which, in addition to his show career, had a brilliant track record. He got into the final of the *Daily Mirror* £200 Challenge Trophy and subsequently went on to qualify to run in the Greyhound Derby. 'Leveret', writing in the *Star* evening newspaper, headed his report by saying: 'First Show Dog to Win' and added: 'Bring Luck demonstrates the value of conformation.' He went on to say: 'What pleased me was the striking illustration of my theory as to the value of conformation, which was shown when Bring Luck won and, when I spoke to Mrs Woodcock [which was Mrs Lewis's name at that time], his owner, I found that she had not only bred and reared him but, a short time before at Bath Championship Show, had won three Firsts with him and only entered him at the White City for sport.'

Mrs Lewis won consistently, both in the ring and in the field, with her track hounds, all of which were dual-purpose animals and bred accordingly. It is easy to understand why today Mrs Lewis is a stickler, when judging, for Whippets which give the impression that they can do the job for which they were originally bred. Becoming seriously interested in Whippets from a show angle in 1937, or thereabouts, the 'of Test' entries have always to be reckoned with. Breeding to a consistent programme, there is not much doubt about the future progress of this kennel.

Apart from attaining fame as a doggy enthusiast from many angles, Mrs Lewis was also a well-known figure in horse circles at one time and has many creditable wins to her name in the show-ring. She has often acted in a judging capacity in connection with horses and between the age of twenty and thirty-four Mrs Lewis hunted, on average, three days a week with no less than fifteen different packs in fifteen different counties in England, Ireland, Scotland and Wales during those years. A magnificent and fearless horsewoman, she gained her Institute of Horse Instructor's Certificate in 1930, and many pony clubs up and down the country owe much to her for help and guidance to them in their early days.

And now, may I add a little 'aside' of my own in connection with Mrs Lewis? She will never forgive me for it, I know, but I do happen to know that at one time she was one of our leading sartorial experts in the matter of correct hunting 'turn-out'. I think this early training in the matter of minute detail in 'horsey circles'—if I may use that term—has stood her in good stead in the rearing and showing of her dogs, that allied to her vast practical experience.

THE LAGUNA KENNELS

Owned by the popular Mrs D. U. McKay, the 'Lagunas' are always well to the fore in almost any show within travelling distance of their home. The kennels were founded in 1939, largely, I think, because Mrs McKay had been interested for a considerable time in coursing and hacking. She was usually accompanied on her rides by two Irish Setters and a Greyhound and she felt that a Whippet would strengthen, what she terms, her 'pack'.

The first inmate in Whippets was purchased from Stanley (Tiptree) Wilkin. Kept as a working pet, it was only natural that Mrs McKay's interest in the breed developed and led to her taking over from Tiptree Kennels, about a year after buying her first Whippet, a bitch named Tiptree Joan. She was by Tiptree Monk out of Tiptree Gladys. Joan was the foundation bitch of the Lagunas, and in her first litter by Tiptree Glamour she produced Ch. Tiptree Jay, Tiptree Ray (who won two C.C.s) and a bitch which, incidentally, was a great favourite of mine, Jovial Judy. It will be seen that the two first-mentioned were sold to Stanley Wilkin and sailed under his prefix. Jovial Judy won 150 awards, which included several 'Best in Shows'. Judy was always Mrs McKay's favourite and she lived until 1959, when she died at the age of fourteen years. Judy produced that fine dog Ch. Laguna Liege, and he won his first C.C. and Best of Breed at the Jubilee Show of the Whippet Club. That day, which Mrs McKay regards as her most thrilling win, Ch. Laguna Liege won

Sir Harold Danckwerts' beautiful trophy. Liege won seven C.C.s in all.

The Laguna Kennels have produced ten Champions, all home bred with the exception of Ch. Brekin Ballet Shoes. A famous dog, U.S.A. Ch. Laguna Lucky Lad, was sent from this kennel to that of Mrs Anderson of Long Island, U.S.A., and has had a tremendous run of successes which included winning the Hound Group at the Westchester Show, which is quite an important event in the American calender. I saw Lucky Lad when I was in America and he looked a credit to his breeder and to English Whippets. A flashily marked dog he made a strong appeal 'on the other side'. Ch. Lily of Laguna was a bitch as sweet and as pretty as her name. Always a great favourite of mine, I derived much pleasure in introducing her in the Parade of Champions at the Championship Show held by the Whippet Club in 1959. Lily won eleven C.C.s and many Best in Show awards. She was the dam of Ch. Laguna Leading Lady. The introduction of Brekin Ballet Shoes was an outstanding success, for she produced four Champions: Lily of Laguna, Laguna Limelight, Laguna Lucky Lad and Laguna Lullaby. A wonderful record. I always think that the success of the Lagunas proves what I have always claimed, that if only newcomers to the breed would stick to the proved breeding system of the vendor of their first bitch instead of immediately thinking in terms of 'out-crossing' we should hear of many more successes.

Mrs McKay in her wisdom did that, and after gathering of experience in the right way, then thought about strengthening her kennel—hence Brekin Ballet Shoes and so on—to further successes which I am quite sure will continue for as long as the owner of the Lagunas maintains her interest, which I am very happy to say shows not the slightest indication of waning.

THE BALLAGAN WHIPPETS

A very enthusiastic kennel, which is strictly non-commercial and at present domiciled in Scotland, the Ballagan Whippets and their charming owner probably do more to enhance the popularity of the Whippet abroad than any other kennel. This is owing to the fact that, being the wife of a high-ranking R.A.F. staff officer, Mrs Selway lives from time to time and for varying periods in many parts of the world. Her Whippets always accompany her and they are always shown if it is at all possible. I have had the great pleasure of seeing Mrs Selway win with her Whippet bitch at Madison Square Gardens, New York, when, amid that sparkling company at this American canine social event, Mrs Selway showed what English tweeds, when properly worn, can do against mink coats and diamonds! The 'tweeds' had it by the length of a street, or maybe it was the smile, or the walk, I wouldn't know! What I do know, however, is that I never saw a prettier combination of handler and exhibit than I did that day in Mrs Selway and the Whippet, Ballagan Twinrivers Charlotte.

Mrs Selway's interest in Whippets began at the age of ten years, she tells me, when she attempted to hire a Whippet at a cost of 2*s*. a week in order to join up with the local rabbit catching pack! An irate father who discovered 'the plot' soon put a stop to that. However, the love for the Whippet still remained strong with our Ballagan enthusiast, and so it came about that, in 1949, her husband and daughter returned from a mysterious trip to London carrying a cardboard box and presented it to her, it being her birthday. Anticipating that it was a birthday cake, her delight can be imagined when, on opening the box, she found her 'dream Whippet' cuddling up in the packing, Heathermead Ada, at the ripe old age of six weeks. A silver-fawn with a blue mask, this bitch became an ambassador for the breed very quickly. Shown fearlessly, she collected many 'reds' including wins at Cruft's,and in 1951 she produced her first litter. Hand-reared, no fewer than four of the six puppies born were lost at the age of six weeks. Later, when living in Gloucestershire, a second litter was produced and from this came the well-known Ballagan Lightning, the dam-to-be of Mr John Kidd's Ch. Quicksilver of Allways.

Moving to live in France and taking Ada and a daughter of Ch. Fieldspring Bartsia of Allways, Ballagan Swiftsure, Mrs Selway joined the Whippet Club of France and became a regular exhibitor at the French and Belgian shows. While there she won the C.A.C. and C.A.C.I.B. with Heathermead Ada, and at the Paris Exposition International, Ada became Champion de Beaute. She was then retired. Swiftsure had a very successful show record on the Continent, too, winning three Junior Classes, one C.A.C.I.B. and once was made Best in Hound Group at Le Havre. Posted to America, Mrs Selway travelled in the *Queen Mary*, complete with the Ballagans, and recalls how seasick Swiftsure was during the voyage. In March, 1956, Swiftsure won a 'first' at Washington and, two days later, when chasing squirrels in the garden, he broke a leg and sustained internal injuries from which he subsequently died. This was a great blow to Mrs Selway, who, while she will not altogether agree that she has ever had a favourite Whippet, admits, somewhat wistfully, that probably there can never quite be another Swiftsure, a feeling most of us can appreciate when we lose a dog which was an outstanding 'character', as this Swiftsure most certainly was. However, in due course another twelve-week-old puppy arrived from the Allways Kennels and became Ballagan Twinrivers Charlotte. By Ch. Evening Star of Allways out of Spray of Allways, this young bitch gave Mrs Selway her greatest thrill in dogs by winning in the Open Bitch class at Madison Square Gardens, New York, to which I have already referred. Misfortune, however, seemed to dog the progress of the Ballagans for only three months after the Madison Square triumph Charlotte was run over by a truck in Maine, and although she made a good recovery was never able to be shown again.

Back in England once more, and posted this time to Scotland, with Ada and Charlotte both in quarantine, Venus of Allways joined the kennels to get the Ballagans going again. Thus it was, in 1958, 'reds' and other awards came the way of the Ballagans, both in breed and variety classes 'north o' the Border'. Ballagan Annie Laurie, by Briarcliffe Bing Boy ex Twinriver Charlotte, made her ring début and has had a very successful run, her wins including Best Puppy at Birmingham. Considerable interest is being taken in a litter by Ch. Allways Wingedfoot Running Fox out of Venus of Allways, but it may yet prove to be overseas that their fame will be spread, as Mrs Selway feels that shortly yet another move may have to be made. She suggests that a re-registration of the Ballagan prefix—to carry Romany with it—might be a good idea seeing that they have had no less than nine homes in eleven years. While all who know her will regret her having yet again to leave these shores, no one will need convincing that, wherever they go, the Ballagans and their delightful owner will never do other than carry the torch for the breed high, wide and blazing. Good luck, Ballagans, one wishes there were more kennels run on your honest, cheerful, sporting lines.

One amusing tale about the Ballagans before we leave them. Some time ago whilst sailing on Loch Ness, Mrs Selway's Whippets 'took a purler' overboard and, naturally, swam for the shore. Apparently they were seen by a lorry driver among others, and Mrs Selway's amusement can be imagined when in the following issue of a well-known Scottish newspaper she read of 'a definite and confirmed report' that the Loch Ness Monster had been seen again. One eye-witness had stated that it was a very large animal, with a head like a Greyhound, which travelled at a great pace through the water; another, that it was at least twenty-five feet in length, and so on and so on. There was a lot more on similar lines. Mrs Selway's comments were to the effect that she had sometimes felt that one or two of her dogs were 'just up to size' maybe, but she had never imagined that they were as big as was reported by the 'reliable eye-witnesses'; all of which just goes to show . . . or does it?

THE BRIARCLIFFE KENNELS

This is not one of the oldest kennels in the breed, but it is one that has certainly made its presence felt in a comparatively short time, also one that has done much to popularize the breed in the North of England. Mr and Mrs Hodgson have done yeoman service. Cocker Spaniels were their first love and these started the Briarcliffes in 1942, several good winners being bred and made up to

'Show Champion' status, which is good going indeed in such a popular breed. Never a large kennel numerically, the Briarcliffes are a very good example of the small breeder making good. Whippets had always been regarded by them in a kindly way, and it was not surprising therefore that the many outstanding good points that Whippets possess eventually caused them to oust the 'merry Cocker'.

The first purchase was a shrewd one in 1950, and this eventually became Ch. Flyways Fiery of Briarcliffe. Mrs Hodgson saw this young dog, at one of her local shows, making his début. As often happens with a youngster, Fiery won nothing on that occasion and his ring manners left much to be desired. Mrs Hodgson has an eye for a dog, and so the eleven-month old puppy was transferred to her. Ch. Flyways Fiery of Briarcliffe was a real silver fawn—an attractive colour not very often seen—and he thrilled his new owner indeed when he won his first C.C. under Miss Stevenson at Chester, in 1951. His second C.C. was won under the late Mr Bernard Fitter at Blackpool, in 1952. Then followed a heartbreaking two years when at show after show Fiery just missed the top award, and many a less enthusiastic owner would have given up the struggle. To her everlasting credit Mrs Hodgson did not, and in March, 1954, the third C.C. was won under the late Mr Tom Scott, who also awarded the dog Best of Breed. Fiery was four years of age at that time and seemed to be at his peak. A month or so later he won his fourth C.C. under Lady F. M. Danckwerts at Leeds. Buying a daughter of Fiery out of a bitch named Ballagan Rikki Tikki, which became Briarcliffe Belita, a series of good wins fell to the kennels and three good litters of six in each were reared with ease. Belita turned out to be an excellent coursing dog and killed her hare remarkably quickly. In the first of three litters of Belita's was Briarcliffe Bustle, winner of two C.C.'s, and Briarcliffe Bing Boy, winner of two reserve C.C.s'.

Mrs Hodgson's favourite is perhaps one of her latest acquisitions, Ballagan Prince Charlie of Briarcliffe, and we shall no doubt hear more of him later.

The Briarcliffe is another purely amateur kennel, by which I mean that the dogs are kept solely as a hobby and for themselves alone, and there is no intention to make it numerically large. To have one or two good dogs going the rounds of the shows and maybe another home-bred youngster coming along, plus the pleasure of owning them, fulfils all Mrs Hodgson's amibitions. Good luck, Briarcliffes, you're doing a grand job.

THE POPPY KENNELS

No one could ever sit down to write a few lines about the old-time kennels and overlook the 'Poppies', for there is no doubt that in Mrs Eileen Martin we have a Whippeteer 'dyed in the wool' and probably one of the most loyal and staunch supporters the breed has ever known.

I marvel, at times, when I see this enthusiastic lady exhibiting at shows miles away from her home, and learn that she started in the wee sma' hours and would not be home again until late in the day following the show. Where she gets her energy from I cannot imagine. No one has, I venture to suggest, ever seen Mrs Martin without her happy smile and her cheery word at any time at any show. Win or lose it is all the same to Eileen, and here again I can only stand and gaze in wonder. I suppose she and I have disagreed over Whippets more than anyone, but I don't think either of us has ever lost our friendly regard for each other. I remember some lovely dogs that sailed under the Poppy prefix and, as a judge, Mrs Martin's services are always in demand. But I think it is true to say that it is easier to get the proverbial camel through the eye of the needle than to get her to agree to 'take the woolsack' as a rule.

A great admirer of the late W. L. Beara's dogs, she built her kennel largely upon his strain and lines, being wise in her generation. Coming from a family well known in dog circles for their St Bernards, it was when Mrs Martin, while a schoolgirl in Harrogate, saw her first Whippet that she decided one day she would own and breed them. She made her first purchase of a black dog in 1911, and 'blacks' still stand high in her favour to this day. Willeslie was the first bitch she owned, the only one of that sex in a Ch. Willesbeaux litter. This little bitch, Willesli, was only sixteen inches high and, mated to a dog Mrs Martin owned at that time, whelped two puppies and then died. At her wit's end to know what to do Mrs Martin put both pups in with an old doe rabbit she kept as a pet and which had just had a litter and, to her great joy, this old rabbit accepted them and suckled them. At the age of two weeks Mrs Martin started to hand-feed them but the old rabbit, who lived loose in the house and garden, still came looking for them and cared for them as well. It is a remarkable little story which I think is well worth relating.

That same summer Mrs Martin had produced a magnificent crop of poppies and it was natural that when it came to naming one of the puppies, it became Poppy, and thus the kennel name started! Mrs Martin recalls that Poppy was a good winner, but in those days, as it was hardly regarded as being quite 'the thing' for a young lady to show Whippets she had some difficulty in doing so. However, the record shows that from 'Poppy' the first Poppy Champion was bred, a pure white which became Ch. White Poppy. This bitch won the C.C. and Best of Breed at Cruft's in those days when she was in the veteran stage. From Poppy came Poppette, sired by Ch. Watford Playful, and from that bitch came the famous Ch. Silver King, a dog which was never beaten by dog or bitch. He sired, among others: Ch. Poppysilver, Ch. Willesberyl, Ch. Silver Knight, Ch. Una and Ch. Willesbelle. Many of the 'Poppies' have found buyers from overseas; India, Australia and America have all imported from this kennel.

Coming to the post-war period, Mrs Martin achieved fame with her black Ch. Poppy Tarquin, and today is just as enthusiastic about what she has 'coming out', as she was way back in pre-World War I days. There is no doubt that when thinking of South Wales and Whippets there is one name which will always stand out, not only for what it was, but also for what it is, what it has done and what it is still doing—Poppy.

In most walks of life one finds an outstanding personality, and we certainly have this in the popular owner of the Springmere Whippets, Miss Stevenson. A well-known figure in Great Danes, she turned her attention to Whippets in 1937 when she was sent by her mother to find a dog to keep the rabbits down. It was natural that Miss Stevenson's thoughts turned to a Whippet and the purchase of parti-coloured bitches, grand-daughters of Ch. Boy Scrounger, from Mrs Graham, in the New Forest, was the result.

From these two bitches have come all the present Springmeres in direct tail female. The bitch line has never been changed, for Miss Stevenson, very rightly, believes that the foundation of a sound winning kennel is a good bitch line. It is interesting to note that Miss Stevenson sold a bitch to Mr Sam Skelton, and from her he bred many good winners. The bitch which was retained was Springmere Flip, who proved a wonderful brood and has many famous winners connected with her name. Miss Stevenson recalls that under Mr Jesse Prowse at the Paignton Show, before it attained its present Championship status, she won her first prize cards. Three Champion dogs have been bred under the Springmere colours: Fanfare, Only Too True and Only One. The greatest thrill Miss Stevenson has had, she claims, is when she won his third and qualifying C.C. with Ch. Only One under me. Hand-reared and nursed through the worst case of hard pad Miss Stevenson has ever experienced, given up for lost by the vet, but saved by a family doctor, it is not surprising that Ch. Springmere Only One became Miss Stevenson's favourite dog out of all the many she has owned through the years. Miss Stevenson takes great pride in the claim that her three Champion dogs have been under nineteen inches.

The present star of the kennel is Springmere Herald, a son of Ch. Springmere Only One who has an excellent all-round record. Miss Stevenson emphasizes the fact that the encouragement she received from Mr Jesse Prowse and the late Mr Taylor of the 'Yentocs' Kennels did much to sustain her determination to build a first-rate kennel of Whippets.

10

Common Ailments

I NEVER place much faith in the novice being able to diagnose illnesses and I advise, most emphatically, that when a dog appears 'off colour' if, after a few hours it still seems that way, there is only one safe course to adopt, and that is to call your vet. I recall an instance where my own vet, after examining one of my dogs, turned to me and said: 'Now this is a case where you give your vet a chance,' and he immediately began his treatment and gave me my instructions. He seemed in a high good humour for some reason or other, which was explained when he said to me: 'What I can't make out is *how* you spotted this so very early.' All I could tell him was that it was because I *know* all my dogs, I know every little whim and fancy, and I can tell immediately if they are normal or not, whether they are annoyed or extra pleased or what-have-you. That particular morning when I 'opened up' I noticed that I did not get the usual bouncing greeting from this particular animal, which I come to expect from all my dogs. She wasn't 'smiling' when she saw me, and so I took her temperature. It was 104° and I naturally called my vet. I was assured that it was solely because I had acted so promptly in the very earliest stages that we saved, that is, my vet saved, from almost certain death, a dog which afterwards became a very famous champion. It was just *knowing* my dog, and most certainly not because I possessed any medical knowledge beyond that which common sense and experience has taught me. This brings me to the first thing everyone who runs a kennel should make certain of doing, namely to buy a thermometer (two, so as to have a spare in case of accidents). The next thing is to learn how to read it correctly and how to use it. Please do believe me when I say that this is most important. If you do not possess a thermometer make a note now, on your shopping list, to get one *today*. It will repay you one day, believe me. Get a short-type clinical thermometer, one with a thick blunt end which can be read quickly and clearly, and not one of those very slim brittle types which can so easily snap, and often do.

A dog's normal temperature is 101·5°F. (38·6°C.). After violent exercise temperatures rise quite a bit and some need half an hour or so of quiet and rest before they become really normal again—so bear this in mind. Before using a thermometer make certain that the mercury is down to 96°, by shaking it down if necessary. If you cannot use a thermometer have a word with your vet; he will soon put you right. Before inserting the thermometer into the rectum of a dog smear the end with 'Vaseline', and if it is difficult to insert don't use force but move the dog's hindquarters gently from side to side. You will then have no difficulty in getting the thermometer to slide in. I use a 'half-minute' thermometer myself, but I always give it a full sixty seconds before withdrawing it and taking the reading. If the dog's temperature is above normal—no matter if it is only one degree up—separate it and take the temperature again about four hours later. If it is still 'up' or gone higher, get on to the phone to your vet at once. It's no use delaying these things, twenty-four hours may make all the difference. Although this is a chapter on 'ailments' I am not going into any more detail than is necessary to give the novice some idea of the various illnesses and diseases, and to touch upon a few matters relating to general health.

Attention to the early warnings of illness is the safest and surest way to avoid the ravages of real disease. We have discussed diet and exercise earlier on, but a few additional words upon toning up may not be out of place here, plus a little explanation of the smaller troubles which in themselves do not amount to real illness.

Among these, minor digestive disturbances are the most common. Loss of appetite is something that should always be noted and looked into when it occurs. It may be nothing, it may be the forerunner of something serious. If the teeth are in good order and there is nothing wrong with the dog's mouth, it usually means that a mild stomach disturbance is the cause. I do not advocate the use of castor oil, it is too irritating to a dog's stomach. Syrup of figs (I use Boots' preparation) or liquid paraffin is much better. One dose will often put matters right. Keep an eye on the dog for a few hours and put it by itself while you have it under observation. Milk of magnesia too is a good medicine to use in this connection. The common cause for many 'tummy upsets' may be attributed to not soaking the biscuit meal thoroughly and giving it to the dog in a half-soaked state. This is bad, *so always see that the biscuit meal is well and truly soaked before mixing the meat and other additions with it.*

The many well-known brands of condition powders are useful as a general and mild conditioner, and in general debility the use of a few drops of Phospherine each day for, say, a couple of weeks or so, often has a very beneficial effect. The dose for a Whippet should be about five drops to a teaspoonful of warm water. If a dog loses 'condition' and appears to be on the thin side, but not to such an extent that it causes alarm, it is usually a sign that he requires a little more vitamins, and a daily dose of cod-liver oil will do much to tone him up and put on weight. Halibut oil is rather better for puppies, as it is more easily digested and is a very good safeguard against any tendency to rickets. When a dog appears 'out of sorts' and you notice that he is constipated, Syrup of Figs or Rhubarb tablets are excellent in their effect, and the tablet form makes them very easy to administer.

The old-fashioned idea that a cold nose denotes a healthy dog should be utterly disregarded, but if a dog has a dry nose, and, in addition, is off colour, a mild dose of almost any good iron tonic will usually restore things to normal.

Fits in Puppies. These sometimes occur and are very frightening to the novice, as indeed they need to be. The cause may be either worms or teething. Puppies, however, should never be allowed to get infested to such an extent that they fall prey to fits. Action must be taken at once to rid them of these parasites, but, in a bad case I would most certainly advise the veterinary surgeon being consulted—and immediately. A puppy when suffering from fits must be kept very quiet in a cool, darkened room pending the arrival of the vet. Remember always that fits are *not* a disease in themselves but a symptom of some other and more definite trouble. Don't delay, whatever you do, in getting expert advice.

Car Sickness in Young Dogs. It is not often that Whippets suffer from this annoying disability to any extent, but some do when they have their first car journeys. The thing to do is to see that they gain confidence as soon as possible. A good plan is to take them for short journeys daily, when it will generally be found that they speedily get their 'sea legs'. Where car-sickness persists, it is as well to obtain from your vet some of the tablets which are specially prepared for this trouble, and act as a sedative. Use these carefully, according to the instructions, because I know of a well-known exhibitor who over-dosed the young dog she was taking to a show, with disastrous results. When she arrived at the show the dog was sound asleep and nothing she could do would arouse him. He slept in the car right through the show and right on through the night and only came back to normal late the following morning. He suffered no ill effects I was assured, but had an enormous appetite. History does not recall whether or not he was cured of car-sickness, but it was not a very profitable show day; so use any tablets you may get strictly according to instructions.

Diarrhoea. This is a frequent complaint among young puppies. A chill, a sudden change of food: these are the usual causes. A mild dose of liquid paraffin may prove helpful, but if the condition of the bowels remains unchanged attention must be given to the diet. This should be white of egg in milk to which a little glucose may be added with advantage. An old-fashioned remedy, however, is Salicylate of Bismuth which is obtainable from any chemist. Mix rather less than half a teaspoonful with water or milk (a job calling for patience) and give from the teaspoon. Diarrhoea in an adult should be viewed with some misgiving as it may be a symptom of something more serious. It should be carefully treated. If the dog does not respond very quickly your vet should be advised as soon as possible.

Enteritis. The symptoms are vomiting and excessive thirst. A high temperature may also be present. Although this complaint may be caused by some irritant in the stomach, *no* violent purgatives should be given. The dog should be kept warm and quiet. No water should be allowed, except a little barley-water or milk, or again, egg and milk if he will take it. If vomiting persists don't delay in calling your vet.

Inflammation of the Eye. A foreign body in the eye may cause this, and it may be under the lid. If the eyelash is gently taken between the thumb and a round piece of wood, such as an ordinary lead pencil, it may be gently turned back and the object located. Never try to probe out the 'body' no matter what it happens to be, but wash out the eye with plain water. The use of Golden Eye ointment will generally prove satisfactory, but if there is still much irritation, causing the dog continually to rub his eye on his bedding, send for your vet. If, however, the irritation is being caused by some foreign body getting into the eye and scratching the lid, the use of the Golden Eye ointment will generally relieve and clear up the trouble.

Sprains. Whippets, owing to their natural activity, occasionally suffer slightly from sprained legs, and this must be treated immediately it is noticed. Heat will be apparent, and the dog will show signs of suffering pain. Swelling will quickly develop. The dog must be kept quiet, and warm-water fomentations applied to the injured part. Recovery is generally rapid once the inflammation is reduced, and when it has been completely cleared, usually within a few days, gentle massage and the use of a stimulative embrocation should be the treatment. A sprain should never be left and disregarded in the hope that it will clear itself up. If bandages are called for, this should receive the attention of your veterinary surgeon.

Rheumatism. This is a painful complaint which usually affects the muscles of the shoulder, neck and back. Once termed Kennel Lameness it was particularly common in Greyhound kennels. The dog will cry out as if in sudden pain, which it is of course, when moving or when touched. It will show the same symptoms even when standing alone and untouched. It will also be noticed that the dog will wear a definitely 'worried look' on his face as if he is puzzled to know why he is being hurt and is unable to understand it. This 'worried look' is a definite symptom, and is not a sentimental piece of imagination on the part of a fond owner' it cannot be mistaken. In this form, i.e. in the neck, shoulders and back, this complaint may be noticed in Whippets, but there is another development of rheumatism which is articular, when the joints become very swollen. Cold and damp kennels will bring on this complaint, also through the dogs being left for any length of time in a cold wind or draught after being exercised. In these days it is far better to consult your vet than to try to treat it yourself. His treatment will usually be injections followed by regular administration of pills, which he will leave with you. Codeine tablets are often very useful in clearing this complaint in the early stages, but it must never be neglected.

Distemper and Associated Canine Diseases. Thanks to the work of the research committee organized by *The Field Newspaper* Distemper Fund, a great deal more is known of this group of diseases, which include catarrhal, gastro-enteric and cerebrospinal forms. There are four common canine diseases, viz. two virus diseases—distemper (including hard pad variety) and Rubarths disease (a liver affection), and two bacterial diseases which affect the kidneys, one, hepatitis, being contracted from other dogs' urine, in the streets and so on, and the other, leptospirosis, which is contracted from the urine of rats on food. This is not a subject for the layman to attempt to write about very fully, but happily, owners of all dogs can now ensure that their dogs can be protected against these common and potentially fatal canine diseases by consulting their vet about a course of vaccinations. When a dog has been thus treated the veterinary surgeon will issue a certificate to the effect that the dog has been immunized. Everyone owning a dog of any sort should take this precaution.

Fleas and Lice. Even the most carefully kept dogs may, at some time, pick up a few fleas which can, happily, be cleared very quickly if tackled immediately their presence is detected. It is a mistake to neglect fleas, because they can act as the host of the tapeworm cyst. Gammexane powder, well rubbed into the coat of the dog, right down to the skin, will kill all living insects on a dog. But, as fleas breed in the cracks and crevices of floors and kennels, these places should also be thoroughly cleaned and treated in the same way.

Lice. These horrible little grey beasts that may infest a dog may be cleared by a bath in which Kur-mange has been added according to the instructions supplied with the product, and marketed by Messrs Cooper Macdougal. After the dog has been dried he should be well rubbed over with methylated spirit. This will dissolve the 'gum' by which the eggs (nits) of lice are attached to the hair. A second bath should then be given on the following day, using Kur-mange as before, when the trouble should be satisfactorily cleared up. A third bath is rarely, if ever, necessary. It will be advisable, however, to use a close-tooth comb and keep a sharp eye on the dog. If my method of grooming, which I have described earlier in this book, is regularly carried out, very little trouble should ever be experienced with either lice or fleas.

Ticks. These wretched and loathsome things sometimes become embedded in dogs which have free runs through grass and, when seen, may easily be removed by using a small pair of tweezers. Get the tweezers well into the head of the tick and see that it is nipped out completely. I have kept dogs in Aden, where camel ticks literally swarmed over them, but I experienced very little difficulty in removing them, in spite of what some may claim. Ticks are revolting, do little harm, but are disgusting things to find in a dog's coat, and it is a nauseating job to have to remove many of them. At least I used to find it so.

Rats and Mice. I have known of owners who simply ignore the presence of a 'few rats' around a kennel, and when it came to mice they gave it no thought. This is an exceedingly foolish and old-fashioned attitude to take. If ever there is the sign of a rat in my kennels I will go to almost any length to have it destroyed. Rats are *fatal* to have even *near* a kennel, and never believe anything to the contrary. The deadly leptospiral jaundice, one of 'the deadly three' canine diseases, is contracted from rat urine, and, I believe, mice urine too. Even a 'travelling rat' passing through an outside run can contaminate any odd bits of food such as an old bone lying about, with disastrous effects on your dogs. The moral is to see that there is never a scrap of anything eatable left down anywhere at night; *anything* that might attract a rat or a mouse *must* be removed. I strongly recommend a couple of 'barn cats' around the kennel. I have two which are pearls beyond price, and they get on well with the dogs by simply keeping out of their way. The dogs take no notice of them, and this, I think, becomes general in most kennels. You can't have good cats *and* rats or mice, and I much prefer cats.

Stings. Dogs that snap at wasps, as Whippets will, invariably scare me, for a dog that gets stung on the tongue can be a dead dog unless he is reasonably quickly treated. I had one of my best-known dogs stung in the face at a recent summer show and her face swelled alarmingly. She responded very quickly, however, to the kindly administrations of a veterinary surgeon, a lady who was exhibiting in another ring, so that she (my dog) within an hour won Best in Show. I mention this only to reassure those who may be fearful of their dogs getting stung. A bee leaves its sting in the skin, whereas the wasp does not. When the sting is located, remove it—a simple thing to do—and apply either T.C.P. or the old-fashioned blue-bag, or a cut onion. If the dog is stung in the mouth do *not* use the blue-bag but *do* use the onion or the T.C.P. The application of a little bicarbonate of soda rubbed in by the finger will relieve the pain. It is not a bad idea to add a small bottle of T.C.P. and a small package of bi-carbonate of soda to your show-bag when going to summer shows, for both are useful items to have handy.

If a dog is badly stung on the tongue a rapid swelling will take place, and it may be severe enough to cause a risk of the dog choking. Rush him to the nearest vet immediately. If for some reason there is some delay in getting expert attention, and the dog becomes distressed, use the handle of a long spoon and endeavour to keep the tongue down so that he does not suffocate. It is essential to get the services of a veterinary surgeon without fail.

Wounds and Torn Skin. The skin of Whippets, unfortunately, can be very easily torn, because it is so thin, and they can suffer quite a lot of damage from being 'nicked' on barbed wire. Such wounds call for quick treatment, when they often make the most amazingly clean and quick recoveries. If wounds bleed freely it is usually an indication that it will heal quickly and cleanly. A deep puncture calls for careful treatment, and it is essential that it is healed from the bottom of the wound so that any infection is not sealed within the cavity. If the cause of the wound is still present it must be removed from the flesh, the bleeding stopped and the wound cleansed. A weak solution of T.C.P., or a similar mild antiseptic, is useful for this, but Lysol or carbolic must never be used in any circumstances. Your vet will doubtless supply penicillin powder or ointment, and his instructions should be most carefully carried out. He will no doubt supply you later with some sulphathyzamide powder, which will speed up the 'drying' of the wound, and these are excellent items to have in your kennel medicine store.

The foregoing are only a few of the troubles that may arise in any kennel, and they are merely touched upon in order that they may be recognized and quick treatment given until such time as expert knowledge is at your command—in other words the arrival of your veterinary surgeon, your dog's best friend, and yours too!

Accidents and Shock Treatment. So seldom does one read anything about on-the-spot treatment for dogs which meet with sudden accidents away from home, perhaps out at exercise and so on, that a few hints will not be out of place here.

Most severe accidents are road casualties, and while it is hoped that no Whippets are ever taken out on or near roads unless on leads, should an accident occur the dog must be moved at once to the path or the road verge. If the dog cannot stand, it must be carried on a coat or something which you can use hammock-wise. The animal *must* be covered and kept warm. In a built-up area no householder will deny you the use of a telephone to call the vet, and if you do not know of one locally, phone the police station who will furnish the phone number of one. If a limb is broken, a temporary splint should be used. These can be two strips of wood wrapped, in an emergency, in handkerchiefs or a scarf, and gently bound on each side of the limb pending the arrival of expert attention.

Blood which spurts from a wound indicates that an artery has been damaged. Apply pressure on the artery between the wound and the heart. If a limb is thus injured, apply a tourniquet, a handkerchief tied very tightly will suffice for a time, and this may be tightened if necessary by inserting a pencil or a stick under the bandage and the flesh, and turning to tighten the bandage.

A severe accident, or a fight, may cause a dog to suffer from shock. This is serious because the heart is affected, if only temporarily. Send for your vet of course, and while waiting for him put the dog in a box or basket, cover it with a soft blanket or shawl and add a couple of filled hot-water bottles, one near the underpart, as close to the heart as possible. The second should be at the back of the animal. If it can swallow, give it sips of glucose and warm water (one teaspoon to two tablespoonsful in strength) and add a teaspoonful of brandy or whisky.

A dog suffering from shock or damage may snap, and it is advisable to use a silk stocking in a case like this, but don't bind the jaws too tightly. As soon as the dog recovers and recognizes its owner the stocking may be removed as it will not then bite.

The main thing at all times is to keep an injured dog as quiet and as warm as possible pending the arrival of the vet, and by whatever means this can be done will be right.

II

The Whippet on the Continent and in America

In America there is growing interest in Whippet racing. Really excellent tracks, far and away better than anything we have for Whippets in this country, are in evidence and the sport seems to be creating quite a lot of public interest, according to reports I have received from time to time.

In Holland the breed has improved tremendously during recent years and from the time I judged Whippets at The Hague a few years ago up to my recent visit to Holland in August last year (1959) to judge at Nijmegen, I thought the general improvement was most marked. In Australia the breed steadily improves, both in quality of exhibits and numerically in entries, while in Germany, Switzerland, Sweden and Denmark the Whippet is a very popular dog. Kennels as we know them here are not the general rule on the Continent, except those of the really big exhibitor, the dogs, as a rule, living in the house with their owners. I am assured that it is mainly on account of their size and their natural characteristics, which make them such a splendid house-dog, that Whippets are ousting the Greyhound from popularity on the Continent, both as a track-dog and a show-dog. Licences, too, are much higher on the Continent than over here. It should never be forgotten that rabies is still rife in Europe and it is nothing out of the ordinary for an area to be closed for all shows for that reason. We have much to be thankful for regarding our canine activities in this country, although I am afraid we don't always appreciate it as we should.

In Europe the system of judging the breed differs from ours in some ways, but it is quite easy to pick up. Rings and benching are the same, the latter being better constructed and more solid than our type. In place of our Kennel Club's Challenge Certificates, they have their C.A.C.I.B., which is an award for the best of each sex. A dog cannot become a champion as quickly as it can in this country owing to certain age restrictions. I do not propose to confuse my readers with a mass of detail here but I would mention that a judge at a Continental Championship event is required to report on *every* dog shown under him. The awards may be Excellent, Very Good or Good. In a class of, say, six, all could be marked 'Excellent', or all 'Very Good' or all just 'Good', if the judge so rated them. They would compete for the C.A.C.I.B. later, of course.

I think perhaps if I had to state which I consider the best kennels I have ever seen outside England, I would have to vote for Madame Donath-Seeuwen's of Den Dolder, Holland. From the photograph (facing page 80) you may obtain some idea, but to see them in their entirety—well, it really is impressive. Built on a sandy soil, with a wonderful wooded background, I don't wonder the hounds and dogs live such happy and contented lives. During the 'occupation' of her country, Madame Donath-Seeuwen daily risked her life and all she had by continuing to look after her kennel inmates, and brought most of them through those difficult times by hiding them in the woods and by all sorts of subterfuges. My wholehearted admiration goes out to her for all she did and I know that I would never have had the courage to do as she did. Madame Donath-Seeuwen, for all her inherent modesty, is a very skilful person when it comes to dogs, and that, coupled with her amazing love of them and her natural kindness to them, is really something to be seen to be fully appreciated. She has, I suppose, easily the largest kennel of Greyhounds and Italian Greyhounds in Europe. Every inmate of them is as fit as it can be, and it is amazing to have pointed out old retired show-dogs, which are fifteen, sixteen and even seventeen years old, for no dog in this kennel is ever 'put down' unless it is to save it from pain and suffering, and I do not think this has happened more than twice during the many years this kennel has been in existence. I was most touched with many little everyday happenings I witnessed at this lovely place. Nothing that could add to the dogs' comfort and well being is overlooked, and yet not the slightest thing that is merely silly sentiment is permitted. Madame Donath-Seeuwen is very fortunate in having as her kennel manager Mr A. Staffhorst. Mr Staffhorst does not speak English and I do not speak Dutch, yet I can go round the kennels with him at any time and know exactly what he is 'saying' for he is that type of 'good doggy man', his actions speak louder than his words. Now that Whippets have been taken up so enthusiastically I feel quite sure that we shall soon hear much of the winners from this kennel. Ch. Wingedfoot Hildegarde is, of course, the foundation bitch, and already she has 'done her stuff' in no small degree as the photograph of her, together with her twelve-day-old puppies by Ch. Wingedfoot Wild Goose (facing page 65) shows. It is a very fortunate dog indeed which joins this kennel at Den Dolder.

For those interested in racing on the Continent, a circular track of 350 metres (1 yard equals 0.914 metres) or, as we would say, 380 yards, is usual, and the dogs start from traps. The old style of starting from hand and running to the rag is completely unknown. This is not surprising, as what I have always regarded very much as an art, i.e. hand slipping, is completely out-of-date there from what I hear.

For those who like to compare records and times, at the last Amsterdam Meeting, held in September, 1959, 24.65 seconds (i.e. for 380 yards) was the winning time, and was put up by a bitch named Reni van Us Honk. The photograph taken at Amsterdam track (facing page 80) gives a very good impression of Whippet racing as carried out on the Continent. I think it will be agreed that the dogs put up very creditable performances on the Continent.

With reference to American Championship Shows, the following will give a very good idea of what they regard as a full classification for the breed in that country, and was the programme laid out for the Speciality Show of the American Whippet Club—as we would say our Club Show—held in Far

Hills, New Jersey, in September, 1957. The prize money in all classes (except Veteran, Specials Only and Litter Classes) was $5, $3, $2, and $1 only. A total of sixty-five dogs made up an entry of eighty-one.

Puppy Class (Dog); 6 months and under 9 months	Drew	3	entries
Bred by Exhibitor (Dog)	„	5	„
American-bred (Dog)	„	4	„
Open (Dog)	„	7	„
Puppy (Bitch); 6 months and under 9 months	„	2	„
Puppy (Bitch); 9 months and under 12 months	„	1	„
Novice (Bitch)	„	2	„
Bred by Exhibitor (Bitch)	„	5	„
American-bred (Bitch)	„	8	„
Open (Bitch)	„	13	„
Veteran Dogs and Bitches (aged 8 years and over)	„	2	„
Specials only	„	14	„
Litter Class	„	15	„

The smallness of the entries will doubtless cause surprise but it must be remembered that conditions in America are very different from those which we experience. The tremendous distances exhibitors have to travel in order to get to shows, the correspondingly high expenses in connection with visiting a show, to say nothing of the time involved, makes dog showing something of a rich man's pastime. The Americans are nothing if not keen on everything they take up, and showing dogs is no exception. They are a generous, warmhearted people but they all have a curious antipathy towards any form of criticism of their dogs, no matter how mild or innocuous it may be and, for that reason, it seems to me, they will not tolerate any form of critique following a show. I discussed this point with many over there and they were all adamant—they wanted *no* criticisms of their dogs in any circumstances. A show manager told me most emphatically that if he were to publish critiques on the dogs that appeared at his show he would be begging for entries at any subsequent show he put on. Now on the Continent it is exactly the opposite. I found that not only did the secretary of any show at which I was judging impress upon me that a written report was a definite 'must' in regard to every dog that came under me for judgement, but also that it must be in detail. I was also approached by many exhibitors who wanted to know reasons, not only why their dog may have been put down, but also why it had been put *up*, if it had won. They listened very carefully and, I found, prompted me on any point I might have missed, particularly on such details as the number of teeth, and other points which we might consider of no great importance. I mention this only in passing to give some idea of the difference in the attitude of different peoples.

I have often been asked for information on the type of dogs preferred in America, and so I publish here by permission the American Whippet Club Standard (dated 9 November, 1955).

First, I would say that in my opinion it is very sketchy and leaves many gaps through which any judge can happily skate. It reads as follows:

General Appearance. The Whippet should be a dog of moderate size, very alert, that can cover a maximum of distance with a minimum of lost motion, a true sporting hound. Should be put down in hard condition but with no suggestion of being muscle-bound.

Head. Long and lean, fairly wide between the ears, scarcely perceptible stop, good length of muzzle, which should be powerful without being coarse. Nose entirely black.

Ears. Small, fine in texture, thrown back and folded. Semi-pricked when at attention. Gay ears are incorrect and should be severely penalized.

Eyes. Large, intelligent, round in shape and dark hazel in colour, must at least be as dark as the coat colour. Expression should be keen and alert. Light yellow or oblique eyes should be strictly penalized. A sulky expression and lack of alertness to be considered most undesirable.

Teeth. White, strong and even. Teeth of upper jaw should fit closely over the lower. *An undershot mouth shall disqualify*.

Neck. Long and muscular, well arched and with no suggestion of throatiness, widening gradually into the shoulders. Must not have any tendency to a 'ewe' neck.

Shoulders. Long, well laid back with long, flat muscles. Loaded shoulders are a *very* serious fault.

Brisket. Very deep and strong, reaching as nearly as possible to the point of the elbow. Ribs well sprung but with no suggestion of barrel shape. Should fill in the space between the forelegs so that there is no appearance of a hollow between them.

Forelegs Straight and rather long, held in line with the shoulders and not set under the body so as to make a forechest. Elbows should turn neither in nor out and move freely with the point of the shoulder. Fair amount of bone, which should carry right down to the feet. Pastern strong.

Feet. Must be well formed with strong, thick pads and well-knuckled-up paws. A thin, flat, open foot is a serious fault.

Hind quarters. Long and powerful, stifles well bent, hocks well let down and close to the ground. Thighs broad and muscular; the muscles should be long and flat. A steep croup is most undesirable.

Back. Strong and powerful, rather long with a good, natural arch over the loin creating a definite tuck-up of the underline but covering a lot of ground.

Tail. Long and tapering, should reach to a hip-bone when drawn through between the hind legs. Must not be carried higher than the top of the back when moving.

Coat. Close, smooth and fine in texture.

Colour. Immaterial.

Size. Ideal height for dogs 19–22 inches, for bitches 18–21.

These are not intended to be definite limits, only approximate.

Gait. Low, free moving and smooth, as long as is commensurate with the size of the dog. A short mincing gait with knee-high action should be severely penalized.

Disqualification. Undershot mouth.

One final point in regard to American shows may be of interest to readers, and that is the fact that they are *not* run by the American Kennel Club but by a concern called The Foley Dog Show Organization Inc., but under rules laid down by the American Kennel Club. This system seems to work admirably, and everywhere I went in the States I heard the Foley Organization spoken of in terms almost approaching reverence. The work this concern does is obviously much appreciated by everyone connected with dog shows in America.

When one thinks of Whippets in America the name of Shearer immediately comes to mind, for the development of the breed as a show-dog in the States is mainly the work of the two famous sisters, Miss Julia and Miss Julie Shearer, of the well-known Meander kennels, Virginia. This is not a surprising fact because both the Miss Shearers are famous as stock breeders in more spheres than one. In Angus cattle they are as well known as they are as breeders of the famous Virginian bloodstock horses. Actually, as I write, details just to hand from them tell me that one of the yearlings they bred and sold in 1958 developed into one of the best two-year-olds in the United States. He won six races, five of them Stakes, and was second three times, twice in Stakes, and won over 181,000 dollars. I gather there is a great demand also for the services of their stallion Degage. I only mention these facts to give some idea of the ramifications of these two famous sisters in their selected fields of stock breeding. Miss Julia Shearer is, in addition to being a farmer on a large scale, a high official in the Angus Cattle Breeding Association of Virginia.

This is one kennel in America where I did not find an excessive heating system in full blast, although a complete system is laid on. The lay-out is very much on the lines of our own style of kennelling. The main house consists of front room, with box unit, kitchen, bathroom, where a refrigerator is kept (mostly for medicines), and trimming room, which also contains box units. There is also a bitches' room letting out into a large interior exercising run or pen. In addition there are two wings connected to the main house by archways. One is a puppy house with four interior pens of assorted sizes together with large outside runs paved in 'tarmac'; the other is along the same lines and houses Beagles, which the Miss Shearers breed in a small way in addition to their Whippets. Altogether, the whole set-up is very well thought out, and, of course, very substantially built, as well as being most pleasing to the eye. In addition to the kennels, of course, there are really magnificent stables and cattle houses. But what thrilled me when I was there was to look over what seemed like miles and miles of paddocks—all fenced by wooden rails—in which the young horses ran. In the background the distant Blue Ridge Mountains of Virginia completed a wonderful picture.

In passing, and I know it has nothing to do with Whippets, I feel I must mention something that impressed me most of all, and that was the courteous good manners of every man I met in Virginia. I have never met with such an old-world dignity anywhere—and wherever I went it was always the same. The stock in these kennels has been all bred to an ideal from a foundation bitch named Ch. Syndicate, bred from an English bitch named Towyside Teasle, mated to an English dog named Ch. Sandbrilliant of Meander, which left England in 1930. Syndicate produced eleven champions in all. Sandbrilliant himself, Miss Shearer claims, started the breed winning—as she says—'on the big time' in America, and surprised the canine world by doing the impossible for Whippets at that time, namely winning a Hound Group at a big show. From that foundation have sprung all the present-day Meanders. A great feat of breeding indeed.

12

Whippet Racing

SO MUCH is being heard today about the revival of Whippet racing in America, and so many enquiries have reached me, that I set out here the past history of the sport in that country as well as details of the present activity. I am greatly indebted to my good friend Mrs T. Wendell Howell, of the Great Circle Kennels, San Francisco, California, for the wealth of detail she kindly forwarded to me. The revival of the sport in America owes much to the enthusiasm of Mrs. Howell.

Whippet racing in the United States was introduced by the Lancashire textile workers who went to the New England mills at the beginning of this century. The sport rapidly caught on and attracted great crowds. Mr. Charles Draper, a wool merchant of Boston, Mr Bayard Tuckerman, Miss Warren, Mr George West, among others, were the prime movers in introducing this sport and creating widespread interest in it. Reports are that Whippet racing, attracting great crowds of betting folk, flourished in particular in the suburbs of the staid and solemn city of Boston, before World War I. The racing stock was of British origin and further imports were made when top racing dogs were required from time to time. The coming of World War I put a sudden stop to the sport and it was very slow to revive.

A Mr Tuffley and Mr Stewart Eddington, and one or two more sporting gentlemen, started a very successful race track for Whippets in Cleveland, Ohio, which operated for a number of years between the Wars I and II. Mr Charles Stewart imported from England a top-line racing bitch named Critic, and it was

Rhodesian Ch. Wingedfoot Beau Brocade, with the author, meets the Rhodesian Premier, Mr Ian Smith

Sid Myers

Rhodesian Ch. Rhapsody of the Tinderbox

Int. Ch. Wingedfoot Fieldspring Bryony

Ch. Laguna Lucky Lad

Int. Ch. Wingedfoot Fieldspring Bryony at eight months

Allways Wingedfoot Running Fox at seven months

C. M. Cooke

W. L. Beara and the author

Sally Anne Thompson

Ch. Samarkand's Greenbrae Tarragon

Diane Pearce

Ch. Beseeka Knight Errant of Silkstone

then that for the first time Canada challenged America at Whippet racing. Record has it that Mr Tuffley and the Cleveland group took the honours on two occasions, one of which was in 1925 when the then H.R.H. The Prince of Wales visited the city and was so charmed with Whippet racing that he had special bracelets made for the lady members of the club.

In California about this time, Whippet racing was staging a come-back, largely inspired by a Mr Freeman Ford of Pasadena. This gentleman became so keen that he engaged a Mr James F. Young of Canada to come to California and start breeding Whippets for the track there, in addition to racing them. Mr Young brought his Canadian-bred Strathcona Girl, Soprano and many others with him and, during the years from 1925 to 1929, built Mr. Ford's kennels to a peak that made Whippet racing in Southern California an outstanding sport. The club was exceedingly well organized and attracted such owners as Mr Arthur Rankin, Miss Mabel Norman and many other film stars and directors—all of whom ran their own dogs. Mr Donald Hostetter, the present President of the American Whippet Club, was an enthusiastic junior owner in those days. Santa Barbara became a centre for the sport and it was here that Mr Arthur Wright made history with his imported dog from England, Willesbeau, and several others. At this time Whippet racing became so popular that the Kezar Stadium in San Francisco, to which Mr Young and others from the southern part of the State came with a string of racing dogs, was filled to capacity on Sundays. Betting was a great attraction, and at that time parimutuel wagering on dog racing was legal in California. In 1934 a law was passed under Governor, now Chief Justice, Warren that put a stop to betting on the dogs. This, of course, was directed at the Greyhound tracks, but it also caused Whippet racing to fall off. In Florida, Colorado, Oregon, Massachusetts, Maryland, Rhode Island, New Mexico and Arizona, legal Greyhound tracks exist under parimutel laws. The depression of 1929 brought another check to Whippet racing, and when Mr Ford died a few years later the Southern California Club broke up. There was a rabies scare in Pasadena and this prevented bringing racing dogs to the Brooklands Park track. Whippet racing continued at this time only in Baltimore where a successful circular track had been operating for some years. Local pressure and internal quarrels eventually put this track out of business in the early 'thirties. The basis of the American show stock, I am assured by Mrs Howell, is in great part derived from these Baltimore track Whippets, as they were the first to obtain American Kennel Club registration as the result of the great efforts made by Mr Louis Pegram and Miss Julia Shearer.

During the following decade and a half, when there was no racing, a great number of outstanding show Whippets were bred in America. Wins in Hound Groups were frequently recorded and even B.I.S. wins became almost commonplace. The Whippet Speciality shows began to draw larger entries and interest in the breed gradually grew. As in this country, the fading away of Whippet racing did not kill the breed, and the exhibition side began to take its place.

In 1953 a small number of enthusiasts got together in California, and Whippet racing began again. Among those who were actively engaged in reviving the sport were Mrs Howell, Mr and Mrs Charles Pinckney, Miss Virginia Archey (now Mrs Drew Mullan), Mr and Mrs Gregory Stout, Mr Andrew Delfino and Mr and Mrs Eugene Cropper. Later, others joined in, and an electrically operated starting-box unit was obtained and a lure machine manufactured. Racing began again at Golden Gate Park, San Francisco. Ragged racing and many breakdowns were often experienced, in fact more often than not. But such was the enthusiasm and determination to succeed that, gradually, better equipment was obtained, dogs worked and trained harder, fighters weeded out, and racing began to take on a new shape.

The next move was to exhibit the racing dogs and race them later at shows where space and facilities were available. Much work was done by these enthusiasts and much credit is due to them. In 1956 a Whippet Speciality Show was revived in connection with the San Mateo All Breeds Show, and a race meeting for Whippets was put on. This met with great success, for which the help and guidance of Mr Young, whose enthusiasm seems not to have diminished one iota, was largely responsible. This gentleman made all the old records available to the new enthusiasts and presented the newly formed club with a fine stop-watch.

In 1957 Mrs Wendell Howell took a team of Whippets to the International Show at Chicago. Enthusiasm for Whippet racing in the Mid-West was now fast reviving but nobody seemed to have any clear ideas how to get it started along the proper lines. Mrs Howell tells how she well remembers scribbling diagrams and working out dimensions of starting-boxes and a general outline of lure machines on the back of a menu at the famous Stockyards Inn where the enthusiasts had foregathered. (Incidentally, this remarkable place, the Stockyards Inn, is one of the most famous places for steaks in the whole of America.) In August of that year, Mrs Howell took her station-waggon loaded with Whippets and starting-boxes (which she says became her own bed for the the trip, and knowing this amazing young lady I can well believe it) and set out for Illinois. There, under the leadership of Mr and Mrs Eugene Jacobs, she found a going concern in connection with Whippet racing. They used no starting-boxes, but slipped their dogs in the old-fashioned English manner. They had, however, produced and perfected a very fine lure machine, which apparently was the main reason why the local dogs showed the visitors a clean set of pads in all races. The following spring, again at Chicago, the first National Whippet Races were run. A great fancier, of whom everyone speaks so highly, Mrs Ellis, the owner of the Stockyards and President of the show, had put down, indoors in the arena, a dirt track, 200 yards long. The cost of this was very high indeed, as can well be imagined, but our American cousins are nothing if not enthusiastic when they 'get going', and Mrs Ellis was unstinting in her co-operation. It is pleasing to be able to record that more than 2,000 people came to the Stockyards specially to see the Whippet racing, and so the venture was highly successful. But what enthusiasm and what courage—I take my hat off to them indeed.

In April, 1960, the third National Whippet Races were held.

California had yet to win the crown at the 'Nationals', as they are now called, but Mrs Howell's import, Ch. Wingedfoot Dominic, won the event, which naturally gave me a great thrill.

To sum up then it would seem that a strong wave of enthusiasm for Whippet racing is spreading across the United States, and this time from the West to the Eastern seaboard, where it all began. There is some alarm among some of the exhibitors that breeding for speed may impair the type necessary for show but, as it is claimed that the fastest track dogs in America, with few exceptions, are show-bench Champions, B.I.S. winners and Best in Group winners, these fears are subsiding. Finally, to set a seal on the racing activities, the American Whippet Club has bought a set of racing equipment, and this, to me, seems as though we shall hear more of the racing side of things from America as time goes on. All of which I am sure must be very gratifying to Mrs Wendell Howell and her band of racing enthusiasts.

And now for a few words in regard to something that I feel we in England do not understand in regard to America and their Whippets. We often speak, and perhaps a little contemptuously, without meaning in any way to do so, about the *size* of the American exhibit. From the standard it will be seen what a difference there is between the English and the American measurements.

As I have said in my early chapter on the origin of the breed, dogs are largely the creatures of environment. In England we used Whippets for hunting our native 'bunny', while in America they hunt what they call the jack rabbit. I don't think many of us understand the difference between our animal and the American version, nor do we appreciate the difference between our fields, hedgerows and woodlands and their deserts. Let me explain. The American Whippet of the West lives and breathes for the jack rabbit. This animal is indigenous west of the Rockies and in the plains of the Western Mid-West. He behaves far differently from the cottontail and the hare. When chased he stays in the open and seldom, if ever, goes to ground. The terrain on which he lives is unlike anything encountered in this country and, therefore, the sport of hunting jack rabbits is peculiarly adapted to the larger American dog. In fact, they have to be bold and strong in order to stand up to what is demanded of them. The time to hunt jacks in the Nevada desert is at sunrise in summer, on account of the heat later in the day. The dogs are called upon to hunt among high sagebrush which tends speedily to unsight them. They can, however, run a jack for miles without danger from barbed wire or highways. Jacks in those parts are very large, weighing up to 15 lb, and they are very fast. It takes more than one dog to run a jack down, and they hunt in teams. The jacks in the rolling country of Colorado and Oregon are of a different type, just as speedy, they invariably run uphill, at the outset, and as far as possible. In the pasture country of California Whippets run down and kill on an average three out of every five jacks they put up. A jack, once turned, and that is the art of hunting it, it would seem, runs in a square, and I am told it is very thrilling to watch. Here I am going to say it wouldn't, at all events, be to me, for reasons I have given in an earlier chapter, but that is neither here nor there. The plains of Texas are full of jack rabbits and I am assured that they are as fast and as big as everything in Texas is supposed to be.

Why I mention the foregoing facts is so that readers may understand why, since they delight in hunting the jack rabbit with their dogs, and since he is so different from our own 'bunny', our American friends *like* their dogs to be of a larger size than ours. It is not the fact that they *cannot* breed them smaller, but that they *do not want them* smaller. Incidentally, I was informed while I was in America that nobody wants to eat a jack rabbit, for he is a hard and stringy animal and not to be confused in any way with our English hare.

And now one final item which may interest my American readers in connection with their old-time Whippet Racing.

Records here show that Mr Billy Onions of Gateshead and Mr Jim Pendlebury of Leigh sent dogs over to the U.S.A. to run in the famous Pasadena Derby. Two bitches went, namely, Nellie from Leigh and Sidlow Foureyes, and both ran in the nomination of Mr. Douglas Fairbanks (Senr) and Miss Mary Pickford. One of these bitches won the event, and it is on record that the handlers both wore bright red coats throughout the entire trip so that the colour stood out for the dogs all the time, thus bearing out my contention that the old-timers put a lot of faith in their belief that dogs do see colour, a theory to which we do not subscribe today—at least some of us.

From time to time we hear much about a revival of old-time Whippet racing in England, and while I understand that in certain parts there are meetings held, I feel that those who know only present-day Whippet racing know very little about the sport as it used to be conducted. The training of present-day dogs as compared with that of the old-timers is as different as chalk from cheese; so, no doubt, are the racing times of the dogs. There are many reasons for it. In pre-World War I days Whippet racing was a most popular sport, as I have previously mentioned, and while it was known and promoted in the South of England, and in the Midlands and in Wales, it was confined for the most part to the colliers of Yorkshire, Durham and Northumberland. The training of the dogs was most carefully carried out. I have kown dogs which, during the racing season, were kept almost entirely in the dark when they were not being 'walked' over their two five-mile training distances per day—ten miles each day they did, hail, rain or shine—they were virtually deprived of their normal liberty. They were rarely, if ever, attended or fed by other than the same person. That same attendant was the one to whom they ran in their actual racing heats. In other words, they knew one man and one man only for the most part. They were treated very kindly, and most beautifully fed, but they were racing machines and for that purpose they were kept.

Another thing was that they were never allowed out even on exercise without their box muzzles on in case they should pick up anything while they were out. I have known dogs which were regularly 'strapped' with spirit, sometimes even whisky, and they were not even fed with ordinary beef which could be obtained from the normal butchers' shops. Some of the best dogs fed exclusively upon Scotch beef which was sent down especially for them. That was how the top-line racing dog was looked after when Whippet racing was at its height. Some people believe that live rabbits were used in the old-time racing, but this was not so, for many reasons. It is true that there used to be some attempt made at rabbit coursing but this was soon stopped and amounted to nothing, according to my recollection and information.

No, Whippet racing in the old days was 'to the rag' and very exciting it all was. The tracks were usually about 200 yards long and the times for that distance somewhat under twelve seconds for fairly good dogs. The actual record was, I believe, held by a dog at a Yarmouth meeting, but I have forgotten the actual time—I believe it worked out at about forty-four miles an hour, or something like that. Whippet racing was not conducted upon the strict lines of the present Greyhound racing and, therefore, not a lot of faith can be placed on some of the reported record times, although there is no doubt some remarkable times were put up. A great deal depended upon the prowess of the starter of the dog, the slipper. He stood on the stipulated mark for the dog, and holding him by the nape of the neck and the hindquarters, literally threw him as far as he could, but with such skill that the dog always hit the ground with all four feet in such a position that he bounded forward from the ground like a shot out of a gun. It is difficult to describe, but first-class slippers were always in great demand, and very expert they were, too. The actual starter of the race stood behind the slippers and started the race by firing a pistol. What is more, some slippers were so alert they could almost anticipate the firing of the pistol by watching the starter's finger tightening, and thus, upon occasion, 'beat the pistol'. Most starters who knew their business held their starting pistol behind their backs and fired it from that position. We have with us even now old-time starters who will vouch for this, odd as it may seem. Split seconds counted for much in the old-time Whippet racing days and some of the dogs carried a lot of money, as well as their coloured racing ribbons.

One of the most extraordinary sights was to see the dogs literally leap over the finishing line, and hurl themselves at the rag or towel, which was frantically waved by their handler or owner, and seize it between their teeth, then to be swung round and round, shoulder high by their handlers, the dogs hanging on with their teeth like grim death. They just loved that swing, and I am sure that is what many of them ran for. A racing Whippet of the old days was a happy, fit dog, living to run and bursting with good health and energy. I, as a lad, used to exercise a dozen at a time, and I loved them, and they me. Now I must add something which may shock many people. It is this, I am quite sure that all the old-time Whippets used to move with a definite high-stepping hackney action in spite of all we say about that movement restricting speed. I am also certain that no Whippet starting from 'boxes', as they do, I believe, today, could have lived with a good dog of the old days being 'thrown' by a first-rate slipper. I am just as confident that it was the betting on the dogs which led to the pastime falling into disrepute, and I remember that famous all-rounder judge, Mr Syd Simpson, who was killed in an air raid on Birmingham during World War II, talking to me very severely when at one time I was trying to resuscitate Whippet racing in the early 'thirties. He pointed out the many evils which 'betting on the dogs' brought about by meetings held impromptu at the pit-heads on pay-days, and I recall his words to me on that occasion, 'And so you see, lad, those are the days none of us want to see back again, so you drop it, and be content with showing a really good dog.' He was a wise man was Simpson, and a great Whippet lover and judge, and maybe he was right.

Reading through what I have written up on the subject of old-time Whipper racing, I thought it might be a very good idea to get some comments on it from a really experienced man, one who had a considerable connection with such racing in the old days. So I wrote to him and he promptly replied. My correspondent will be well known to many of my readers as a Championship Show judge of the Breed and a life-long lover of the Whippet, Mr Gwyn Owen of Tredegar. This is what he says:

Never has a sport which had so many followers received so little public support nationally as Whippet racing, or, as it was better known, 'Rag racing'.

I have often wondered if it was because of the stories which were circulated about it to the effect that the home and the children were sadly neglected for the sake of the racing dogs. That these stories were told, repeated and believed by many can never be denied. It is true that his dog often became the owner's first thought in many ways, and the racing dog's welfare became a major part of his life, but in my experience, this enthusiasm was fully shared by the wife and the children. So much so, that very often their treatment of the dogs, so kindly meant, often jeopardized their chances of winning races worth, as they were in those days, anything from £20 to £100 and more. Bob, Kate and Jack—the dogs—did not lack for much on the part of the family, believe me!

It was a regular thing for the owner's wife or mother to make rugs for the dogs, and the great pride they took in their work was remarkable. Each dog had to have his own warm exercising coat, his 'night sleeping coat' and his 'very special occasions coat'. These latter were often brilliantly designed, for the dog to wear when he went to the races. There was a great deal of competition in turning the dogs out smartly and this was all done by the women and children, and a great deal of pride went into this particular work. There was also the actual 'rag' to which the dog ran. The white towel—and no modern washing powder could have made them more white than they were washed in those days! The idea was that the more the dog could *see* his 'rag' as his owner ran down the track whistling and calling—yelling if you like—the better chance the dog had of making a bee-line to it. There was not any thought given to the question as to whether dogs could see colours or not in those days, the natural assumption was that they most certainly could. It was only natural therefore that some towels were brilliantly patterned and coloured, and, as I say, this was the 'family side' of the game.

What used to happen was that a pup would be purchased, possibly from some famous and noted fast strain, and, when introduced into the home, would be met with (from the wife): 'I don't want that thing here—take it out. I won't have it' or: 'What have you brought that here for? What will the neighbours think we have come to? Whippet racing indeed! Take it away!' All of which emphasizes the fact that it was not regarded as 'the thing' to indulge in 'Rag racing' in some quarters. There was no social uplift about it, I'm afraid. This sort of reception would last for a few hours, but when the owner came home from work next day he would more than likely find the little pup, looking like a fat little ball, rolled up in its own special box in front of the living-room fire! His wife would explain to him that 'the poor little thing looked so skinny and half starved that we have been feeding it up a bit, but it's not going to stay' and so on and so on. In other words the little Whippet had, as it invariably was, been accepted and was now part of the family. I never knew anybody who could resist a little Whippet puppy and I don't think anyone else has either. So the embryo racer started. From then on 'the family' would receive their instructions and start its training. Firstly for house manners, then going on the lead, and so on. Later would come the introduction to the rag—the kids taking this on in play with the rapidly growing-up pup. The children would be encouraged to take pup out for walks and to give him little runs of twenty-five yards or so, always 'to the rag'. The day would come eventually when he became strong enough and keen enough to be taken in hand for serious training. This had to be very gentle at first because this could be the 'make or break' part of a young racing dog's life—this early training. At the age of about eight months or so, the puppy would meet dogs of about his own age, and would then be run by himself between strings, representing the racing nets to which he would be introduced later, over distances of fifty yards or so. He would be encouraged by the 'rag' and whistle and so gradually learn the game. As he progressed so the distances would be increased. It was a careful and gentle training and much patience was required to develop the 'flyer'. As he progressed, the young dog would be run *with* other dogs of his own age and so, gradually, he would come to the stage when he could be relied upon to run a straight race, be a non-fighter, and, best of all, never be a 'chaser', that is to say, one who just ran after the other dogs and played the fool. The young dog was trained to get to that 'rag' as fast as possible and to have nothing else in his mind but that. He was trained never to even look at another dog, to take not the slightest notice of them—just to get to that 'rag'. By now he would be going down the actual track, still only over short distances eighty to one hundred yards—under racing conditions. Next he would come under the 'timing clock'—thus, gradually, step by step, patiently and carefully was he built up to become the perfect racing machine—with one thought in mind—to get to that 'rag', that towel. How he loved to swing on that towel! Don't let anyone make any mistake about it, Whippets *loved* their racing!—*and* the swing on the towel!

As the dog's training advanced, all sorts of special tests were set for him. He would be started behind faster dogs to see if he had the courage to continue when he was being left further behind. He would be started in front of slower dogs to see if he would still go even when out-distancing them, or if he would turn and wait for them to come up and play the fool with them. He would be started behind slower dogs to see if he would pass them, ignore them, and continue his race and never slacken his speed. He was trained from every angle until, at last, the day came when he was entered for his first handicap. But before he came to that he had to be the sort of dog who could hold the handicap which had been given him. He would be entered in the right sort of race at some local meeting, and this type of meeting was often arranged for the puppies which were 'coming on'. So much for the dog.

Now a very important point in Rag racing is the selection of the slipper. The man who holds the dog whilst his owner runs down the track waving the rag, and who lets the dog go. This training with the slipper was a most important part of the young dog's education. The owner had to watch most carefully in the early days of this part of the dog's training to be absolutely sure that Dick (say) could put the dog down on his feet further down the track than either Harry or Bill. What is just as important, if not even more so, if he could put the dog down 'right into his stride' as he touched the ground. A split second lost here through a clumsy 'landing' would mean a lost race. Slipping was so important that, in the days of big handicaps, slippers were engaged in the same way as jockeys are for racehorses today. Big fees were demanded and willingly paid to first-class slippers. It was thought by some to be a very good thing to have one's dog trained so that it would run to anyone holding the 'rag' in order that the actual owner could slip the dog. It was, however, often taken as a sign in those days that, when an owner was slipping his own dog he was not 'out to win'. I tried to copy a very famous slipper once, and, to my cost, found it was not for me!

(*Author's note:* I feel I must break in here as I happen to know that Mr Gwyn Owen was regarded as a very fine slipper and I know of one occasion, when slipping a dog, Mr Owen tore all the nails off his right hand—I know because I saw the hand afterwards. I also know that such was the concentration Mr Owen used to put into his work that he invariably used to finish flat on his face, at full length, when he slipped a dog. I feel he is being too modest in his remark above.)

Mr. Owen continues:

In the old days there were many things done which are better not written about I am sorry to say, such as 'holding'—that is to say not slipping immediately 'on the gun'—slipping the dog *into* the nets was another questionable trick, treading on the feet of a dog to lame him and so on. There were also cases of 'ringers' being entered—that is to say a dog entered under a wrong name, duplication in other words, and many other miserable tricks not worthy of mention. When it was found that a dog 'went' better for one person than another, as was often the case, it was generally the custom for that person to be kept clear away from the dog for several days prior to a big handicap being run, and then for that person to appear with the towel for the dog to run to just immediately before the start. The joy of the dog when seeing his favourite appearing before him was a great incentive for him to 'get down the track to that rag'. All these little details were carefully thought out and put into practice in the old days of true Rag racing.

The sport however was often brought into disrepute by outsiders who were definitely more interested, in fact *only* interested, in the betting side of Rag racing. It also affected working conditions of some of the men who owned well known racing dogs and whose foreman, for example, had an interest in the sport also. All sorts of complications could, and did, arise, at work. Many a school teacher too would ask Billy, Susan or Johnny after class was over 'when father's dog was going to run again' and so on—and the kids played on it well! There were upheavals too after form had been upset after some races and the owner would be hard put to it to look after his dog! All of which did the sport no good.

It would be grand to see really clean, and properly controlled, Rag racing again and I am sure there are people who could get it going again—really capable people who could handicap a dog properly. I feel that there are dogs even today which, with the proper training, could put up a good show when compared with the stars of thirty and forty years ago. Yes—it was a grand sport and when it was run properly I loved it.

Thank you, Mr Gwyn Owen. I think it will be obvious, from

what he has said, that Mr Owen has endorsed much of what I said previously and also what Mr Syd Simpson said to me.

I will say in conclusion that I have walked with Mr Gwyn Owen over the hills round his home and have been shown where the local track used to be, and as we walked he talked of famous races he had witnessed there. Listening to his detailed description of various events, still so fresh in his memory, one could almost see the flying little bodies of those gallant little dogs, now long since gathered to the Happy Hunting Grounds, hurtling down the track encouraged by the shouts and yells of the miners. It was easy to live it all again through the enthusiasm of one who dearly loved the game, as he has told us.

13

The Whippet Today

by Kay Smith/Douglas-Todd

CHARLES DOUGLAS-TODD having departed in 1968 to warmer climes, has not now ready access to breed records, and so I have found myself in the enviable position of tracing the progress of the breed through the past decade and into the '70s. For someone like myself with a naturally inquisitive mind this has proved a fascinating study.

Over the past decade the Whippet has risen steadily in popularity, reaching a peak of over two thousand registrations at the Kennel Club during 1965 and again in 1969 and 1970 and, although numbers have fluctuated slightly, maintaining a high average over the period. The slight drop in registrations which was apparent in 1971 may well be accounted for by rising costs in foodstuffs, veterinary fees and wages for kennel staff, these in their turn necessitating a limit to one's breeding programme. This drop in registrations is visible in many of the more popular breeds during the same period.

A study of breed records during the past ten or twelve years makes it very obvious that breeders, on the whole, have subscribed to the idea that careful line breeding pays dividends and this in itself is surely a compliment to the wisdom of Mr Douglas-Todd. The older and more experienced breeders, it is true, were already aware of this and had carefully mapped out their breeding programmes in advance, but those less versed in 'the dog game' have been quick to note the advantages of following the author's good advice.

Sadly, several of the more prominent and successful breeders of the early post-war period are no longer with us, but many years will elapse before they are forgotten. Mrs Dorothy Lewis and her Test Whippets; Mrs Cleeve and the Dragonhills; Mrs Crawford and the Conneils—all spring instantly to mind when pedigrees are under discussion, and the Peppard colours are bravely kept flying by Mrs D. H. L. Gollan on her own. However, many new faces have appeared in the ranks and fresh honours been recorded. It is not possible to give individual mention to all of the successful kennels in a limited space and I trust that my omissions will be forgiven.

One of the first kennels to spring to mind is that of Mrs Barbara Odell, whose Shalfleet strain is a direct continuation of the Wingedfoot and Allways lines. Mrs Odell began her programme in 1955 by wisely purchasing a sound brood bitch, her beloved Wingedfoot Bartette. This bitch was a daughter of Ch. Fieldspring Bartsia of Allways and Wingedfoot Nicolette. She was mated to Ch. Wingedfoot Marksman of Allways, producing Shalfleet Sensation and Ch. Shalfleet Spellbound. The former sired two lovely daughters in Ch. Shalfleet Story and Ch. Shalfleet Springtime. Bartette mated again to Ch. Mars of Test produced Ch. Shalfleet Swordsman, an old gentleman now but yet the sire of some of the young stock in the kennel. Another litter by Bartette out of Wingedfoot Dent de Lyon produced Shalfleet Sceptre, the dam of Ch. Shalfleet Starstruck.

Mrs Odell's success is the result of establishing a sound bitch line and using this to advantage with the best dogs available, in this case dogs such as Ch. Robmaywin Stargazer of Allways, Ch. Evening Star of Allways, Ch. Wingedfoot Marksman of Allways and Ch. Mars of Test. A slight but suitable outcross was provided by Ch. Laguna Leisure, a dog with a good Wingedfoot and Allways line. In this way Mrs Odell continues to breed and exhibit excellent stock which is a credit to her dedication to the original breeding programme.

Another successful kennel which has made its mark in recent years is that of Mrs Ann Argyle. She is the breeder of the lovely Ch. Harque the Lark, the little bitch which holds the unique distinction of having notched up nineteen Challenge Certificates under nineteen different judges. Regular visitors to the ringside at our larger shows will surely know that exuberant little leap which launched her into her owner's arms at the end of each triumphant appearance in the ring. I at least always found this particularly touching and a tribute to the fact that the honour belonged to Lark and not to her owner, or maybe that it was jointly shared.

Mrs Argyle's first Whippet bitch was Evening Mist, by Bolney Short Story ex Dragonhill Skylark. This bitch was mated to Ch. Allways Wingedfoot Running Fox and produced Runway Controller, a dog which became a champion under the ownership of Mr Gwyn Williams. Mrs Argyle then purchased Wingedfoot Tu Whit Tu Whoo from Mr J. Fisher in 1959 and before showing her sent her to Ch. Runway Controller. This mating produced Harque to Beaumont, the successful stud dog which sired such winners as Ch. Harque to Rosa, Ch. Harque to Gamecock and, of course, Ch. Harque the Lark. All of these had the same dam, Rosaday of Knotknum. Wingedfoot Tu Whit Tu Whoo when she was finally exhibited became Mrs Argyle's first champion. The successes of this kennel are too well known to require further comment from me and it appears that the Harque Whippets will continue from strength to strength in the future.

No record of present-day Whippets would be complete without mention of Ch. Dondelayo Duette, the bitch which made breed history by being judged Reserve Best in Show at Cruft's Show in 1971. This is the first time that a Whippet has taken such a placing, although Ch. Robmaywin Stargazer of Allways in his day topped the Hound Group at this same show.

Mrs Knight tells me that she has owned either Greyhounds or Whippets since 1950, coursing these dogs and breeding them for work for many years but unable to take up showing because of other commitments. Although she purchased several good bitches over the years and attempted to establish a suitable strain, her efforts were dogged by bad luck. Even when two Champions were eventually produced (Ch. Swiftfoot Susanna and Ch. Oakbark Dondelayo Storming) she was unable to continue breeding plans due to the tragic loss of her foundation bitch.

In 1963 she made a completely fresh start with the purchase of a little brindle bitch from Mrs Coller. This was Linknumstar Lizard and she is the foundation of the present Dondelayo strain. According to Mrs Knight, this little bitch is small and rather plain but a superb mover and with excellent pedigree carrying a strong female line back through many champions to Lady Danckwerts' Ch. Brekin Spode. With an eye to producing the line she desired, Mrs Knight looked around and found a suitable mate for her bitch in the record-breaking Ch. Samarkands Greenbrae Tarragon, who had the type and style required. The resulting mating produced Ch. Dondelayo Rue. In due course Rue was mated to her half-brother, that great stock-getter, Ch. Cockrow Tarquogan of Glenbervie, and this now famous litter contained the three winners, Ch. Dondelayo Buckaroo, Ch. Dondelayo Roulette and Ch. Dondelayo Ruanne of Charmoll. Roulette mated back to her double grandsire Ch. Samarkands Greenbrae Tarragon produced yet another wonderful litter containing Ch. Courthill Dondelayo Tiara and the recent Cruft's Reserve Best in Show winner, Ch. Dondelayo Duette. The Dondelayos have won between 50 and 60 Challenge Certificates in a little over six years and Ch. Dondelayo Roulette shares with Ch. Harque the Lark the top honour of winning nineteen C.Cs., the record number won by any one dog in the breed.

Many of the well-known breeders who were sharing top honours during the late '40s and throughout the '50s are still to the fore, and one's mind immediately settles on Mrs McKay and her famous Laguna stock. So many of these have made their mark over the years it is difficult to extend them the praise they deserve. However, mention must be made of Ch. Laguna Ligonier who holds the record of producing more champions than any other dog.

Nor must we forget Mrs Chapman and her continuing line of lovely Whippets. This kennel is still producing worthy champions in the breed, the latest of these being Ch. Walhachin made up in 1971.

There are so very many Whippet fanciers who have remained faithful to the breed through thick and thin and none is more faithful than Mrs Eileen 'Poppy' Martin. This gallant, elderly lady has remained devoted to her Whippets for more years than many of us would wish to acknowledge, and, despite a heart-breaking experience which recently robbed her of her best stock, is yet undiscouraged and travels long distances to be present at our larger shows. Mrs Martin is well-loved at the ringside and as a judge of the breed her opinion is valued.

The foregoing pages would perhaps suggest that all is well with the breed but the point has come to remove a little of the gilt from the gingerbread. Let me first say that there is some very wholesome gingerbread as a general basis. In this connection one can but offer a personal opinion and I am sure that mine will not be shared by all. In general the breed is fairly sound and there are very many lovely and sound dogs in the country today. In fact, at times exhibitors must feel that there are far too many of these after yet another show where they were 'knocking at the door' without finding it opened to them. Classes are large and, especially in bitches, particularly strong, although why bitch classes should so often be superior to those for dogs has remained a mystery to me. However there are a few obvious wrongs which occasionally required righting.

One thing which constantly appears and which worries me not a little is the tendency for some apparently lovely Whippets to move with a decided prancing, hackney front action, instead of the long, low over the ground stride which one expects. This, as has been mentioned earlier in this book, is a fault for which there is no cure and I find it unsettling to see certain judges putting up dogs with this type of movement. It may well be that the dog with the accepted gait in that class has some more obvious fault, but surely the dog with a true front and a well laid shoulder will move in a proper fashion. I must admit, however, that Charles Douglas-Todd has said that he believes the racing dog of years gone by did tend towards this hackney-like front action, and this I have found borne out by two small Whippet bitches which I have owned and which were both exceptionally fast. I feel that in this case the high-stepping gait was the result of holding them back and making them move slowly in a fashion foreign to their natural instinct.

There also appears to be a tendency to a flatter back than is desirable in some dogs. This I feel to be a fault which detracts much from the natural grace and elegance of the breed.

Both of the above faults worry me far more than the constant argument about size. This skeleton seems to appear at some time or other from almost every cupboard. Somewhere around the middle of the 1960s the breed seemed to become considerably larger, possibly because certain breeders were finding a paying market on the other side of the Atlantic where a much more substantial dog is required. Now it appears that airing this point is at last having effect and a move seems to be afoot to return to the standard size. Certainly from the ringside the bitch classes particularly have recently appeared to be much nearer to the recognised height.

One other thing I should like to mention and this is not a structural fault. It is that many exhibitors appear to overextend their dogs when 'setting up' and with the less experienced exhibitor one finds that he or she appears to think that this means that the dog is covering more ground. This inference is, of course, quite wrong. When one speaks of 'covering ground' in connection with a Whippet, or for that matter any other breed of dog, one does not mean the distance between the front feet and the rear feet. One judges 'ground covered' by imagining a line drawn from the point of the breastbone of the animal to the buttock and one drawn from the point of the breastbone to the ground. Another similar line is imagined dropping from the point of the buttock to the ground. How far the hind feet are stretched out depends entirely on the manner in which the owner has set up his dog.

Apart from the last-mentioned point, which can easily be corrected, all the other problems must be tackled straight away if we are to retain the image of the Whippet as the small English sporting dog we all love. As one friend recently remarked, if we don't do something now, particularly with regard to size, whilst there are still dogs available correct in size and type, we shall wake up all too soon unable to find our size and type and then what shall we do? My dictionary defines elegance as refinement and grace as charm, air or bearing: with these definitions in mind, and by following Mr Douglas-Todd's advice to a new judge (which applies equally well to the novice breeder) to bank on soundness, symmetry and balance we cannot stray far from the standard we wish to maintain.

THE SPECIALIST BREED CLUBS

The five specialist clubs whose origins have been so carefully recorded in Chapter 7 have now been joined by three younger and less experienced societies bringing the total to eight.

The senior member of the latest trio, the Northern Ireland Whippet Club, saw the light of day in 1963 and this caters for the interests of lovers of the breed in the Northern part of the Emerald Isle. Nowadays it has become quite the thing for certain of our Scottish and English exhibitors to make the pilgrimage across the water to compete for honours against our Northern Irish colleagues.

In the spring of 1970 the East Anglian Whippet Club was admitted to the ranks and swiftly gained an enthusiastic following in that region. At present this club holds two shows per year and has become the first of the breed clubs to schedule a Sunday Sanction Show, which is proving a popular innovation. An Open Show is also held at the end of September. The East Anglian Whippet Club also has the honour of having Mr C. H. Douglas-Todd as their first President. With a view to establishing contact between members wherever their particular interest lies, this club has from the very first produced a quarterly newsletter which is circulated to all and this has proved an unexpected success.

The 'baby' of these societies is the newly formed Whippet Club of Wales presided over by the evergreen Mrs Eileen Martin —and who could wish for a more experienced President? The need for this new club was felt by the growing number of enthusiasts in Wales and formal application was sent to the Kennel Club on October 1st, 1970. The title of the club was granted on July 28th, 1971, since when this club has gone from strength to strength with monthly matches, organised visits by bus to other shows and their own first Limited Show on May 13th, 1972. This show, which was a great success, reflects the enthusiasm of all members.

In 1972 we saw another new innovation: this was the birth of the publication known as the *Whippet Year Book*, a book produced jointly by the East Anglian Whippet Club, the Midland Whippet Club, the National Whippet Association and the Northern Counties Whippet Club under the able editorship of Miss Gillian Ussher. It is hoped that if this proves as popular as expected it will become an annual feature on the breed scene and that the number of clubs participating in its production will increase.

As time goes by one naturally expects to find a changing scene and this is so with the Officers and Committees of the various breed clubs as with everything in our daily life. For this reason I have purposely omitted the names of the current secretaries of the new societies; the full titles of all the eight breed clubs appear in Appendix B and names and addresses of their secretaries will be found in the *Kennel Club Year Book* or may be had by application to the Kennel Club.

THE KENNEL CLUB

Over the years since this book was first printed various changes have been made in Kennel Club procedure and these changes affect the Regulations in various ways. Fees for services such as registration and transfer of dogs, export pedigrees, and fees for registration and maintenance of an affix, to mention only a random selection, have changed as also have certain of the regulations governing the showing of dogs. For instance, whereas it was at one time against Kennel Club Regulations to exhibit a dog which was known to be either monorchid or chryptorchid, it is now possible to show such a dog and the decision to fault such a condition is left to the particular judge officiating. This he will take into account along with other faults and will balance against the particular merits of that same dog.

New regulations governing the use of a registered affix are

also in force and, with very few exceptions already sanctioned by the Kennel Club, the affix must be used as a prefix when the dog has been bred by the owner and is solely and unconditionally his property, or if it was bred from parents each of which was bred by him. Otherwise it must be used as a suffix, that is to say, the last word in the name.

A change, perhaps slight but very significant, has also been made with regard to the title of Champion. At the present time the title of Champion shall attach to any dog of a breed recognised by the Kennel Club if that dog has been awarded three Challenge Certificates under three different judges, provided that at least one of the Challenge Certificates was awarded when the dog was more than twelve months of age.

The few variations in regulations mentioned here are not by any means all of the changes which have taken place and all dog fanciers, particularly those less experienced in the game, are strongly advised to purchase a copy of the *Kennel Club Year Book* which is published annually and is a veritable mine of information.

THE WHIPPET ABROAD

This popular little dog has maintained its popularity both on the Continent and in America and, as export figures show, has also increased in strength in other countries such as Canada, South Africa and Rhodesia, and farther east to Australia and New Zealand.

The American Whippet Club Standard (dated 9 November 1955) given on pages 156–7 shows us that there are several differences between the ideal of the show Whippet across the Atlantic and that which we strive to maintain in Britain, particularly as regards size. As lately as October 12th, 1971 certain revisions in this American Whippet Club Standard were approved and these are as follows:

'*General Appearance, Eyes, Teeth and Size*': Delete these sections and substitute the following:

'*General Appearance*': A moderate size sighthound giving the appearance of elegance and fitness, denoting great speed, power, and balance without coarseness. A true sporting hound that covers a maximum of distance with a minimum of lost motion.

'*Eyes*': Large, dark, with keen intelligent alert expression. Lack of pigmentation around eyelids is undesirable. Yellow or dilute-colored eyes should be strictly penalized. Blue or china-colored eyes shall disqualify. Both eyes must be of the same color.

For 'Teeth' substitute '*Muzzle*': Muzzle should be long and powerful denoting great strength of 'bite' without coarseness. Teeth should be white and strong. Teeth of upper jaw should fit closely over teeth of lower jaw, creating a strong scissors bite. Extremely short muzzle or lack of underjaw should be strictly penalized. An even bite is extremely undesirable. Undershot shall disqualify. Overshot one-quarter inch or more shall disqualify.

'*Size*': Ideal height for dogs 19 to 22 inches; for bitches 18 to 21 inches; measured across the shoulders at the highest point. One-half inch above or below the above stated measurements will disqualify.

DISQUALIFICATIONS—Blue or china-colored eyes. Undershot. Overshot one-quarter inch or more. A dog one-half inch above or below the measurements specified under 'Size'.

The reader in Britain will realise from these changes that the American Standard appears to be differing even more than previously from our own, but it must be remembered that our American cousins must obviously have their reasons for these changes and these doubtless fit conditions in that part of the globe. One suggestion for the variation in standards across the Atlantic is that the Whippet fanciers in the U.S.A. are more interested in racing than in showing and that their passionate desire to increase speed led them to cross racing Greyhounds with racing Whippets, with the natural result that size increased by leaps and bounds. This was not tied down in any way in the old standard but with the revision of the American Standard size is very definitely limited. As I say, this is but a possible suggestion and could be quite wrong.

The Canadians, on the other hand, have chosen to maintain the old American Standard at the moment and although size is somewhat larger than in Britain it does come a little closer at times. The British Standard gives the ideal size for a dog as 18½ inches and that of a bitch as 17½ inches, and yet many judges would tend to put down a bitch of, say, 17 inches as being much too small. Probably less would put down a bitch of 19 inches as being too large. Also in a class with a mixture of solid-coloured dogs and parti-coloured dogs it is easy to get a false idea of the size of any one particular dog unless the measure comes into use. Thus Canadian enthusiasts who tend towards the lower limit of their standard in size will not be too far from our own ideals.

One thing is certain though, and that is that both in the United States and in Canada there is a particularly strong dislike of such faults as bad ear carriage or tail carriage: and here I should like to stress that I feel the intending exporter of a dog must make every effort to be exceedingly frank and honest with any overseas purchaser who is buying a dog he has not seen. By all means shout your dog's praises, that is only natural, but please do also mention any obvious fault the animal may have. Possibly you may think that I am being over-zealous here, but I believe that by being completely truthful we can maintain the high regard which the British breeder has won in the past. At least, speaking personally, I can vouch for the fact that a young Whippet bitch which I sent to a Canadian breeder who has over forty years' experience of the breed (after giving my honest opinion that she had potential, although as a young puppy she was inclined to fly her ears) was exceedingly well received by her new owner and though never shown won the respect of her new owner as an excellent brood bitch and a credit to his kennel.

With regard to the Whippet in Southern Africa I cannot speak from experience, although over the past few years I have exchanged many long letters with the author himself on just such matters. So I think that I must allow Mrs Anne Allen, breeder of the Tinderbox Whippets, to tell you in her own words something of the joys and problems of owning these little dogs in Rhodesia, although lack of space has made it necessary to leave out much of what she has to say.

The author of this book, a long-standing friend of mine, both in England and now in Rhodesia, has kindly invited me to say a few words on owning and breeding Whippets in Southern Africa. Owing to the tremendous increase in popularity of the Whippet over the past few years, there are now considerable numbers in Southern Africa, and I should like to direct this article, if I may, not only to the Whippet-owners already living in places like South Africa, Rhodesia, Zambia, etc., but to those who live in, say, England and are contemplating migrating to Southern Africa and bringing dogs with them.

Having come from England to Rhodesia myself ten years ago, accompanied by English-born Whippets, I found many hitherto unknown problems entailing much trial and error, especially in health aspects. However, the last thing I wish to do is to turn this into a form of veterinary dictionary. I am no expert in that field, but I would like to mention some of the difficulties which I encountered and maybe help you, the reader, in the process.

Firstly, one must realise that if a Whippet is exported to Africa, even as a puppy, it is far more prone to diseases which exist there, however mild, than a puppy born and bred in Africa itself. Here then the advice to a would-be immigrant considering bringing out stock of his own is obvious: only bring out young, healthy animals. Also it is not, in my opinion, advisable to bring out a bitch in whelp. There are many first-rate stud dogs in Southern Africa, every bit as good as you will find in Europe.

Remember too that it will take a Whippet several weeks to acclimatise, just as it does a human; and here, of course, normal common sense must be exercised. So now let us deal with some of the health hazards with which you may find problems.

External and internal parasites can be a greater problem than in Britain. However, care in cleansing of both the dog and all kennels and bedding will normally keep these unpleasant pests under control.

Nevertheless I should like to mention one serious disease, unknown to breeders at home, which is a direct result of infestation by ticks: *Biliary Fever*, or canine piroplasmosis, is probably one of the most serious problems for the Whippet-owner in Africa. This disease of the dog occurs not only in Southern Africa but in India, many countries in the Far East, Italy and France. It is due to a blood parasite, Babesia canis, which is carried from an infected dog to a healthy one by means of a tick. One of the first things to do when you suspect biliary in a dog which is 'off colour' is to examine the gums and the insides of the eyelids for unusual paleness. Take its temperature. If it is over the normal 101·5F. (38·6C.), this is a good indication that your dog has contracted biliary. The next step is to take your Whippet immediately to your veterinarian. I cannot stress this enough: do *not* wait, thinking, 'Oh, he may be all right tomorrow'. He may well be, but, on the other hand, he may not, and valuable time has been lost.

Provided that the dog is taken for veterinary attention at once before the disease is allowed to progress, with resultant increasing weakness and ultimate liver damage, recovery is usually fast after a course of injections of Beneril is given, which destroys the piroplasms in the bloodstream. The dog will require careful nursing to restore him to his normal good health. This entails rest and quiet, a fat-free diet, which also precludes milk, an iron tonic for a couple of weeks, and plenty of raw liver.

Unfortunately there is no inoculation against biliary, nor immunity after an attack; indeed the reverse: the more attacks an animal gets, the more likelihood of permanent damage to internal organs. A Whippet, although no more prone than any other breed, having once contracted biliary succumbs very quickly to the disease. Whereas some breeds, especially the larger varieties, may go for one or even two weeks before reaching the extreme stage of weakness and collapse, a Whippet invariably reaches this stage in twelve hours or less.

A word about rabies: In Southern Africa it is compulsory under law to have all dogs inoculated against rabies, first at about four months of age and then at twelve months. Thereafter the dog has a booster injection every three years. The first two injections are accompanied by a tattoo mark on the ear and any adult dog found straying without a rabies tattoo and not immediately claimed is destroyed. The likelihood of a regularly inoculated dog contracting the disease is very rare.

The climate of Africa has a lot to commend it with regard to owning or rearing Whippets. Their coats thrive in the sunshine: in England, to get a silky, smooth coat, one must bring the dog into the warmth of the house and continually hand strap and, if housed in a kennel during the cold, winter months, the coat compensates becoming extra thick and woolly. Many of the hazards of puppy-rearing are also eliminated when one has sunshine all through the year.

A final word, especially to the new immigrant: talk to the local doggy people; you will find them friendly and helpful. Most of the dog-breeders in Africa have originated from overseas, and know the sort of problems which you have and the questions you will want to ask. Even if you have been in the dog-breeding game for a number of years in England or elsewhere, don't let pride stand in your way. Seek out the other whippeteers. They will be delighted to meet you. Compare dogs, swop stories, enquire about joining the local sporting dog associations. Whippet-owners throughout the world have one thing in common: they love Whippets, and have the interests of the breed at heart. Above all, keep a sense of humour: laughter makes the world go round. Now may I wish you the very best of luck.

WHIPPET RACING AND COURSING

Whippet racing and coursing have both increased in popularity over the past decade. Racing clubs have sprung up all over England from Northumberland in the North-East to Devon in the South-West and, of course, in their old stronghold Wales. Nor does Scotland lag behind. The Whippet Club of Scotland has a thriving racing section. Most breed clubs also schedule at least one class for racing and coursing dogs at their various shows and a number of Whippets shine in both the sporting and exhibition fields.

To the racing man, making up a Racing Champion is just as much of an achievement as making up a Show Champion. A racing dog has to compete against the best dogs in the country, that is winners from four regions. Weights of these dogs are from 16 lb. to 30 lb. and they must have a lot of stamina and perseverance to become really good racers.

Traps are used for racing and the dogs generally run after a dried rabbit skin or other type of fur pulled over the ground and termed a 'lure'. Some owners still prefer the older form of 'ragging' and it is said that a ragger is better than a dog that runs for the lure, because it tends to run in a straight line and has the advantage over the lure dog because it runs to its master.

Weight handicaps are used and a dog has to give one yard start to another dog which weighs one pound more. That is to say that a dog which weighs only 16 lb. must have 4 yards start on a 20 lb. dog or 14 yards on a 30 lb. dog. A very good 16 lb. dog can beat a 30 lb. one over 150 yards but on a longer distance, say 175 yards or 200 yards, its chances are not so good.

Here as abroad many of the best racing Whippets nowadays

are cross-bred with Greyhounds but, naturally, these dogs are barred from meetings where only pure-bred Whippets may be entered.

The Whippet Coursing Club was founded in 1962 with a limited membership of fifty. Meetings are held fortnightly on Saturdays, with an occasional midweek one, in areas mainly in Berkshire, Oxfordshire or Essex. A limited membership was made to ensure that all members had a fair chance of running their dogs during the season which lasts from September 15th to March 15th.

There is also a strict height limit of under 20 inches and a good percentage of well-known show dogs entered.

The meetings consist of four eight-dog stakes, made up of Open Dog, Open Bitch and two mixed stakes. There is a Veteran Stake (for Whippets of 6 years and over) and a Puppy Stake (for puppies whelped on or after January 1st of the year preceding the year in which the season of running begins). These two stakes usually take place towards the end of the season. The club engages a professional Judge and Slipper for practically all its meetings.

Nearly all the original Committee and members have regularly coursed their dogs with this club during its ten years of existence and to prove how tough these little dogs are, with the exception of two motor car accidents, there has not been a broken leg or neck caused whilst coursing or killing their quarry, and four or five members still have their original dogs that ran at the Club's first meeting.

Whippet coursing is, of course, an exceedingly controversial topic and I will make no comment for or against but shall leave it to the individual reader to judge for himself. It is, however, and this is an undeniable fact, one more way in which the field of Whippet activities has widened over the past few years and as such merits its position in this chapter.

THE FUTURE OF THE BREED

There is little doubt at this point that the breed will continue in popularity as it has done for so very many years. History has shown that a dog of similar type and size has existed from ancient times and it is unlikely that such a type will decrease in popularity in the future. However, it is up to us, by our care in breeding only from the soundest stock and by circulating only animals of superior quality from these litters, to ensure that the popularity of the Whippet will continue unchallenged.

K.S.

1973

When one studies the Kennel Club registration figures for the years 1970 to 1975 it becomes obvious that fortune still smiles on the breed. True, there is some fluctuation, although not enough to cause concern, but, despite ever diminishing wealth at home and abroad, 1974 saw the peak figure for post-war years in registrations, and many youngsters bred in Britain still find their way abroad. Add to this fact the record of best in show and group wins achieved by the breed and you have further confirmation of the popularity of the Whippet at the present time. Indeed, for the second time in the '70s, a Whippet, Mrs Roma Wright's Beseeka Knight Errant of Silkstone (now a champion), carried off the top award in the Hound Group at Cruft's Show in 1974, thus helping to familiarise the man in the street with these happy little dogs.

The author, after an absence of more than seven years from our show rings, had taken great interest in all that he had seen since his return to Britain and had also had the chance to make his own assessment, after going over a fairly representative group of our present-day show dogs. In his opinion, Whippets have improved beyond all expectations and it was reassuring to hear a man with his wide experience speak so confidently of the future. We constantly read about the faults that are creeping in and the need to breed out this fault or that. The old argument about size has gradually stilled and has made way for other 'bones' of contention – the pros and cons of fronts and toplines, etc. – the most recent of these being good or bad movement. In respect of this latest argument one has to remember, when judging a dog of any breed whatsoever, that the feet, fore or hind, will only leave *one* line of prints and not two parallel rows. This fact was admirably illustrated by Mrs. F. E. F. Lindsay in an article on movement in *The Whippet Biennial*. Therefore one must think before labelling a dog with the criticism 'goes close'. Closeness at the hocks is something entirely different. Seemingly there are fashions even in complaints although, when one considers that these fashions are, more often than not, followed by a gradual improvement in the feature currently under discussion, this may not be altogether bad. Be that as it may, after casting a fresh eye over the present day entry, Charles Douglas-Todd offered consolation in that, in his opinion, the Whippet has never been so good.

Breed clubs around the country continue to prosper and club shows are well supported despite constant increases in entry fees and expenses. The experimental *Whippet Yearbook*, supported in the first instance by only four of the breed clubs, has matured into a much sought after publication – *The Whippet Biennial* – and the brave four have been joined by most of their fellow organisations. Not only is this useful little book in great demand at home but ever-increasing numbers go to Whippet fanciers around the world.

Over the past few years the breed has increased in popularity in many corners of the globe, not least of these being Europe with particular emphasis on the Scandinavian countries and Italy. We are becoming quite used to seeing our continental cousins at the ringside and indeed at least one of these, Mr Bo Bengtson from Sweden, could almost be termed a commuter.

The ruling body of dogdom, The Kennel Club, has also been moving with the times and there have been several important changes in procedure within recent years. The greatest change is a completely new system of registration which commenced in April 1976 and which makes provision for registering dogs at various stages, i.e. as a litter and individually. During 1975 The Kennel Club also published a new set of Rules governing the three types of licenced shows – Championship, Open and Limited – and another set covering Sanction Shows. Details of these changes have been published in the *Kennel Gazette* and can also be obtained by writing to the Secretary of The Kennel Club.

Whippet coursing and racing are more popular than ever

with many members owning dual-purpose dogs, these being seen both in the field and the show ring, several doing well in both spheres. Indeed, the East Anglian Whippet Club which started a coursing branch some years ago has given birth to a complete off-shoot now termed the East Anglian Whippet Coursing Club and members of this body course their dogs during the winter months and in summer turn to the excitement of the race track. The Whippet Club of Scotland also has proved a power to be reckoned with on the track, some members even penetrating across the border and routing the Sassenachs on their own ground. As a loyal Scot I heartily commend their spirit.

Whether or not the attempt to pass the Coursing Bill through Parliament will succeed in putting an end to club coursing remains to be seen. For several years now bill after bill has been presented only to collapse for one reason or another after the first or second reading, and the whole subject has taken on the 'cliff-hanging' suspense of the old movie serial. It is not my purpose to offer an opinion. However, I do feel most strongly that those who vote on this exceedingly controversial subject should first of all attend coursing meetings, both Greyhound and Whippet, before passing an opinion and, secondly, should consider seriously whether, by forbidding legal and organised club coursing, they will not simply open the way for illegal and brutal slaughter.

Another bogey that haunts the dog breeder at present is the threat of a heavy increase in the cost of dog licences. Most owners will admit that, with the ever increasing canine population and the many irresponsible owners who admittedly exist, something must be done to cope with the problem. However, on top of the general belt-tightening regime of today and the high cost of feeding and housing our animals, this possibility appears as the proverbial last straw.

All this gloom would seem to forecast a drop in popularity of dogs in general. Yet it seems to me that, though the fortunes of the Whippet may falter slightly under the weight of the world's woes, the breed, as it has done in the past, will surmount these difficulties and continue to thrive.

1976 K.D.-T.

Appendix A

KENNEL CLUB REGISTRATION TOTALS

1942 to 1975

1942 – 111	1954 – 696	1966 – 1774
1943 – 162	1955 – 708	1967 – 1732
1944 – 284	1956 – 845	1968 – 1885
1945 – 456	1957 – 1018	1969 – 2025
1946 – 551	1958 – 1166	1970 – 2038
1947 – 723	1959 – 1436	1971 – 1726
1948 – 623	1960 – 1528	1972 – 2003
1949 – 684	1961 – 1951	1973 – 1869
1950 – 675	1962 – 1903	1974 – 2088
1951 – 770	1963 – 1981	1975 – 1615
1952 – 676	1964 – 1907	
1953 – 746	1965 – 2045	

Appendix B

BREED CLUBS

The following breed clubs will all be found helpful to the beginner who is interested in Whippets. Names and addresses of current Honorary Secretaries of these societies may be had, on application, from the Secretary, the Kennel Club, 1, Clarges Street, Piccadilly, London W1Y 8AB.

The East Anglian Whippet Club
The Midland Whippet Club
The National Whippet Association
The Northern Counties Whippet Club
The Northern Ireland Whippet Club
The Whippet Club
The Whippet Club of Scotland
The Whippet Club of Wales

Appendix C

POST-WAR CHAMPION WHIPPETS 1946–75 (SEPT.)

Colour Key: B Black Bl Blue Br Brindle C Cream F Fawn G Grey Gl Golden P Pied Pa Parti-Coloured R Red Ro Roan Sa Sable S Silver W White

Name of Champion	*Sex*	*Colour*	*Birth*	*Sire*	*Dam*	*Breeder*	*Owner*
1946 (4 Ch. Shows)							
Mighty Atom	D	F Br	14–8–42	Tiptree George	Lovely Rosa of Luss	Mr F. Orton	Mr G. T. Silk
1947 (10 Ch. Shows)							
Pilot Officer Prune	D	W,F	11–11–45	Happy Landings	Silver Nymph	F/Lt J. Chapman	Mrs K. Chapman
Sapperley Heralder	D	F,W	20–5–46	Tiptree Pilot	Sapperley Queen	Mr B. H. Evans	Mr B. H. Evans
Seagift Sherriff	D	Gl F	8–1–45	Drummer Boy	Seagift Shadow of Bolney	Mmes K. Barnsley & D. Whitwell	Mmes K. Barnsley & D. Whitwell
Samema Dainty Princess	B	S F	17–1–41	Ch. Manorley Manala	Oxted Dainty Miss	Mr S. L. Skelton	Mr S. L. Skelton

Name of Champion	*Sex*	*Colour*	*Birth*	*Sire*	*Dam*	*Breeder*	*Owner*
Seagift Seraph	B	Gl F	28–6–44	Samema Snowflight	Seagift Shadow of Bolney	Mmes K. Barnsley & D. Whitwell	Mmes K. Barnsley & D. Whitwell
1948 (16 Ch. Shows)							
Balaise Barrie	D	F	7–9–46	Balaise Beaugeste	Samema Silvershoes	Miss B. E. A. Bottomley	Miss B. E. A. Bottomley
Golden Arrow	D	F	6–10–43	Drummer Boy	Smeaton Princess	Mr H. Wheeler	Mr H. Wheeler
Brekin Spode	B	W,P	29–1–47	Sporting Chance	Ch. White Statue of Conevan	Lady F. M. Danckwerts	Lady F. M. Danckwerts
Seagift Sylvia	B	S F	3–8–44	Seagift Seafoam	Seagift Shot Silk	Mmes K. Barnsley & D. Whitwell	Mmes K. Barnsley & D. Whitwell
Tiptree Jay	B	F	7–4–45	Tiptree Glamour	Tiptree Joan	Capt McKay	Miss M. H. Vaux
White Statue of Conevan	B	W	8–4–44	Golden Pencil	Samema Sunray	Mrs E. Conway-Evans	Lady F. M. Danckwerts
1949 (19 Ch. Shows)							
Flying Officer Kite	D	W,F	10–9–47	Ch. Pilot Officer Prune	Solo Flight	Mrs K. Chapman	Mrs K. Chapman
Sapperley Kinsman	D	F	10–4–48	Sapperley Tiptree Pilot	Joyous Greeting	Mr G. A. Watts	Mr B. H. Evans

Scribbling Pilot	D	F	27–6–47	Tiptree Pilot	Sunday Scribbler	Mrs E. Brown	Mrs E. Brown
Seagift Shadrack	D	F	15–5–47	Ch. Seagift Sheriff	Ch. Seagift Sylvia	Mmes K. Barnsley & D. Whitwell	Mmes K. Barnsley & D. Whitwell
Seagift Sunglint	D	Gl	27–8–45	Seagift Golden Dawn	Ch. Seagift Seraph	Mmes K. Barnsley & D. Whitwell	Mmes K. Barnsley & D. Whitwell
Seagift Black Diamond of Annalyn	B	B	25–11–45	Kaffir King	Fifinella	Mrs F. Peddie	Mmes K. Barnsley & D. Whitwell
Seagift Silly Symphony	B	W,F	11–11–47	Ch. Pilot Officer Prune	Ch. Seagift Seraph	Mmes K. Barnsley & D. Whitwell	Mrs M. Raynor (U.S.A.)
Shirleymoor Set Fair	B	F	12–9–45	Slippery Sam of Bolney	Shirleymoor Zephyr	Mrs J. M. Sullivan	Mrs J. M. Sullivan
Shirleymoor Zephyr	B	F	30–5–43	Regality	Gipsy Maid	Mr J. Storey	Mr J. Storey
Sweet Pepper of Peppard	B	C Br	5–12–46	Desperado of Toytown	Zanza Zita	Mrs D. H. L. Gollan	Mr & Mrs D. H. L. Gollan
1950 (19 Ch. Shows)							
Laguna Liege	D	F	12–9–48	Ch. Sapperley Heralder	Jovial Judy	Mrs J. B. McKay	Mrs J. B. McKay
Peppard Pied Piper	D	W,F Br	7–8–48	Ch. Pilot Officer Prune	Sweet Pepper of Peppard	Mr & Mrs D. H. L. Gollan	Mr & Mrs D. H. L. Gollan

Name of Champion	*Sex*	*Colour*	*Birth*	*Sire*	*Dam*	*Breeder*	*Owner*
Rolew Mile of Annalyn	D	F,W	21-12-47	Sapperley Tiptree Pilot	Lady of Fame	Mr A. G. Fachney	Mr J. Emlyn Owen
Seagift Shagreen	D	W,Sa	20-5-48	Willesbergan	Ch. Seagift Seraph	Mr J. Broderick	Mrs M. Raynor (U.S.A.)
Springmere Fanfare	D	F	29-3-48	Ch. Pilot Officer Prune	Springmere Flare	Miss J. Stevenson	Miss J. Stevenson
Sapperley Harmony	B	F,W	20-5-46	Tiptree Pilot	Sapperley Queen	Mr B. H. Evans	Mrs E. M. Walden
Seagift Sunset	B	F	14-4-48	Seagift Saxon	Ch. Seagift Sylvia	Mmes K. Barnsley & D. Whitwell	Mmes K. Barnsley & D. Whitwell
Silver Girl of Whitegate	B	S F	17-4-47	Seagift Serang	Tiptree Pearlie	Mr J. L. Cobb	Mrs F. Cobb
Tea for Teresa	B	Bl F	29-3-48	Ch. Pilot Officer Prune	Springmere Spanish Rose	Mrs K. Chapman & Mr C. H. Bryans	Mrs K. Chapman & Mr C. H. Bryans
1951 (21 Ch. Shows)							
Old Mortality	D	F	30-8-49	Ch. Sapperley Heralder	Willesbeam	Mr J. MacKenzie	Mrs F. Blandy
Wingedfoot Marksman of Allways	D	F	20-1-50	Ch. Sapperley Kinsman	Bolney Starshine of Allways	Mrs M. R. Jones	Mr C. H. Douglas-Todd

Fleeting Flyaway	B	F Br	18–12–47	Sapperley Tiptree Pilot	Blue Merle of Conevan	Mrs N. E. Sugden	Mrs M. B. Garrish
Miss Loo Loo	B	F,W	23–4–50	Dante	Wonder of Wilberfoss	Mr D. J. Meakin	Mrs M. Blackburn
Red Atom	B	R F	30–8–49	Ch. Sapperley Heralder	Willesbeam	Mr J. MacKenzie	Mr J. MacKenzie
Rosa of Ballymoy	B	F,W	9–6–48	Ch. Pilot Officer Prune	Hillgarth Senorita	Mrs J. G. Troop	Mrs M. V. Christian
1952 (18 Ch. Shows)							
Cliftongate Flak	D	F	26–3–49	Ch. Balaise Barrie	Barmoor Flirt	Mr G. E. Hutchinson	Mr G. E. Hutchinson
Pink Gin of Larchwood	D	F	19–9–49	Wyemere Collar of Allways	Samema Dainty Dancer	Mrs G. Hunter	Mrs G. Hunter
En for Nonsense	B	F	9–5–50	Ch. Flying Officer Kite	My Delight	Mrs K. Chapman & Mr C. H. Bryans	Mrs K. Chapman & Mr C. H. Bryans
Jay for Jewel	B	W,F	29–11–48	Ch. Pilot Officer Prune	My Delight	Mrs K. Chapman & Mr C. H. Bryans	Mrs K. Chapman & Mr C. H. Bryans
Poppytarquin	B	B	27–12–48	Guinea Gold	White Label	Mrs H. Webber	Mrs C. A. Martin

Name of Champion	*Sex*	*Colour*	*Birth*	*Sire*	*Dam*	*Breeder*	*Owner*
Samema Sweet Lady	B		7–11–49	Samema Rompalong	Samema Whatagem	Mr S. L. Skelton	Mrs M. V. Christian
1953 (20 Ch. Shows)							
Fieldspring Bartsia of Allways	D	W,F	19–9–51	Fleeting Hillgarth Sovereign	Brekin Willow Pattern	Lt/Col A. J. A. Arengo-Jones	Mrs M. Jones
Response of Ballymoy	D	Gl,Br	30–3–52	Sapperley Lancer	Larkspur of Thistlecroft	Mrs M. V. Christian	Mrs M. V. Christian
Springmere Only One	D	Si F	27–7–49	Ch. Sapperley Heralder	Springmere Firelight	Miss J. Stevenson	Miss J. Stevenson
Springmere Only Too True	D	Bl F	11–5–51	Springmere Only One	Springmere Flirt	Mr & Mrs S. Revie	Miss J. Stevenson
Brekin Ballet Shoes	B	Pa	14–3–49	Ch. Balaise Barrie	Ch. Brekin Spode	Lady F. N. Danckwerts	Mrs D. U. McKay
Fieldspring Betony	B	F	19–9–51	Fleeting Hillgarth Sovereign	Brekin Willow Pattern	Lt/Col A. J. A. Arengo-Jones	Mrs M. R. Jones
Satin Beauty	B	F	7–2–51	Dragonhill Socklet	Nesta of Chesham	Mrs E. E. Brownsell	Mrs E. E. Brownsell

Wingedfoot Fieldspring Bryony	B	Pa	19–9–51	Fleeting Hillgarth Sovereign	Brekin Willow Pattern	Lt/Col A. J. A. Arengo-Jones	Mr C. H. Douglas-Todd
1954 (18 Ch. Shows)							
Allways Wingedfoot Running Fox	D	F	29–12–51	Ch. Wingedfoot Marksman of Allways	Perpetual Motion	Mr C. Cotterill	Mrs M. R. Jones
Flyways Fiery of Briarcliffe	D	Si F	22–11–49	Ch. Sapperley Heralder	Laguna Lace	Mr S. Starkie	Mrs R. Hodgson
Rambler of Ballymoy	D	Si	30–3–52	Sapperley Lancer	Larkspur of Thistlecroft	Mrs M. V. Christian	Mrs I Smith
Seagift Speedlite Mustang	D	Gl F	1–9–52	Ch. Pilot Officer Prune	Seagift Simplicity	Mr & Mrs A. H. Ward	Mrs D. Whitwell
Wingedfoot Wild Goose	D	C F	14–6–53	Ch. Wingedfoot Marksman of Allways	Wingedfoot Lannette	Mr C. H. Douglas-Todd	Mr C. H. Douglas-Todd
Dragonhill Silver Ripple	B	F	30–12–51	Seagift Salix	Dragonhill Silver Slipper	Mrs D. Cleeve	Mrs D. Cleeve
Laguna Lullaby	B	F	20–11–51	Ch. Laguna Liege	Ch. Brekin Ballet Shoes	Mrs D. U. McKay	Mr D. W. Armstrong
Strange Recipe	B	F	2–11–50	Ch. Sapperley Heralder	Teribus	Mr & Mrs Revie	Mr H. Peake

Name of Champion	*Sex*	*Colour*	*Birth*	*Sire*	*Dam*	*Breeder*	*Owner*
1955 (18 Ch. Shows)							
Wingedfoot Ringmaster	D	F	12–4–54	Ch. Wingedfoot Marksman of Allways	Eh for Adorable	Mrs K. Chapman	Mr C. H. Douglas-Todd
Lily of Laguna	B	Br	15–1–54	Ch. Fieldspring Bartsia of Allways	Ch. Brekin Ballet Shoes	Mrs D. U. McKay	Mrs D. U. McKay
Mistrals Mrs Miniver	B	F	6–11–53	Ch. Wingedfoot Marksman of Allways	Fleeting Frieze	Mr A. Kersley	Mr A. G. Robbins
Porthurst Quaker Girl	B	F	27–3–53	Rajah of Thistlecroft	Rumba of Ballymoy	Mrs R. E. Ticehurst	Mrs R. E. Ticehurst
Silver Sprite of Allways	B	Si	13–5–53	Ch. Fieldspring Bartsia of Allways	Silver Dawn of Allways	Mrs M. Chesmur	Mrs M. R. Jones
1956 (18 Ch. Shows)							
Bellavista Barry	D	W,F	14–9–53	Ch. Pilot Officer Prune	Brekin Bright Spark	Miss D. Cuzner	Miss D. Cuzner
Choirmaster of Allways	D	F	28–12–54	Ch. Allways Wingedfoot Running Fox	Ch. Fieldpring Betony	Mrs M. R. Jones	Mrs M. R. Jones

Dragonhill Tweseldown Minstrel	D	F	1–11–53	Dragonhill Socklet	Miss Chief	Mrs R. N. Anderson	Mrs D. Cleeve
Laguna Limelight	D	Si F	15–1–54	Ch. Fieldspring Bartsia of Allways	Ch. Brekin Ballet Shoes	Mrs D. U. McKay	Mrs D. U. McKay
Ravenslodge Solitaire	D	W,Bl F	9–12–51	Ch. Flying Officer Kite	Brekin Brown Sugar	Miss P. Bayliss	Miss P. Bayliss
Palmercross Silver Spell	B	F Br	29–9–54	Ch. Peppard Pied Piper	Palmercross Quicksilver	Mr A. F. Naumann	Mr A. F. Naumann
Seagift Snow Maiden	B	W,R F & B	4–6–54	Ch. Ravenslodge Solitaire	Ch. Seagift Speedlite Stencil	Mrs D. Whitwell	Mrs D. Whitwell
Seagift Speedlite Stencil	B	W,B	15–7–52	Shirleymoor Summertime	Seagift Starturn	Mr & Mrs A. H. Ward	Mrs D. Whitwell
Wingedfoot Hildegarde	B	W,Bl F	27–5–55	Ch. Fieldspring Bartsia of Allways	Wingedfoot Nicolette	Mr C. H. Douglas-Todd	Mr C. H. Douglas-Todd
1957 (18 Ch. Shows)							
Bouquet	D	W,F	23–1–56	Vee for Victory	Tiger Moth	Mrs K. Chapman	Mrs K. Chapman
Evening Star of Allways	D	F	20–5–54	Ch. Wingedfoot Marksman of Allways	Ch. Fieldspring Betony	Mrs M. R. Jones	Dr A. Crampton-Smith
Hillgarth Shot Silk	B	F	6–3–55	Ch. Seagift Speedlite Mustang	Hillgarth Silver Suntan	Mrs M. F. Sheffield	Mrs M. F. Sheffield

Name of Champion	Sex	Colour	Birth	Sire	Dam	Breeder	Owner
Quicksilver of Allways	B	F	6–9–55	Artful Dodger of Allways	Ballagan Lightning	Mrs D. Tysoe	Mr & Mrs J. E. Kidd
1958 (20 Ch. Shows)							
Robmaywin Stargazer of Allways	D	F	28–5–56	Ch. Evening Star of Allways	Ch. Mistrals Mrs Miniver	Mr A. G. Robbins	Mr F. Jones
Runway Controller	D	Si F	1–9–56	Ch. Allways Wingedfoot Running Fox	Evening Mist	Mrs A. Argyle	Mr D. G. Williams
Boughton Modra	B	Bl F	16–6–55	Ch. Wingedfoot Marksman of Allways	Fawn Louise	Mr A. L. Dudman	Miss M. Boggia
Seagift Joystock Shana	B	F,Bl Mask	14–4–53	Seagift Sunglow	Ch. Seagift Sylvia	Mrs F. B. Thompson	Mrs D. Whitwell
Wingedfoot Clair de Lune	B	W,Bl	29–6–57	Ch. Wingedfoot Wild Goose	Int. Ch. Wingedfoot Hildegarde	Mr C. H. Douglas-Todd	Mr C. H. Douglas-Todd
1959 (24 Ch. Shows)							
Mars of Test	D	F	29–7–57	Ch. Evening Star of Allways	Wingedfoot Miss Madcap	Mrs D. Lewis	Mrs D. Lewis

Oldoaks White Rajah	D	W,F	22–3–57	Ladypark Spring Rain of Allways	Markover of Test	Mr G. Mannering	Mr G. Mannering
Seagift Fleeting Fly Half	D	W,F	16–1–58	Valentine's Gift	Pat's Pride	Mrs E. Thubron	Mrs D. Whitwell
Laguna Leading Lady	B	Pa	16–9–56	Ch. Bellavista Barry	Ch. Lily of Laguna	Mrs D. U. McKay	Mrs D. U. McKay
Robmaywin Quicksilver of Allways	B	Si F	28–5–56	Ch. Evening Star of Allways	Ch. Mistrals Mrs Miniver	Mr A. G. Robbins	Mrs M. R. Jones
Winpin Misty Moon	B	F	1–7–55	Ch. Wingedfoot Marksman of Allways	Golden Dawn	Mrs E. Winscom	Mrs E. Winscom
1960 (22 Ch. Shows)							
Blik's Ringmore Bardolph	D	F	1–11–57	Ch. Bellavista Barry	Tweseldown Mimosa	Miss A. S. J. Standring	Miss I. E. Birrell
Iniskhelltr Lovely Silver	D	F	20–5–56	Ch. Fieldspring Bartsia of Allways	Moonlight of Allways	Mrs L. Shennan	Miss G. C. Ussher
Ladiesfield Starturn	D	B,W	15–5–55	Jet de Gratton	White Swan of Teighways	Mrs W. M. Wigg	Mrs W. M. Wigg
Laguna Linkway	D	Bl F	28–3–59	Ch. Runway Controller	Ch. Laguna Leading Lady	Mrs D. U. McKay	Mrs D. U. McKay

Name of Champion	*Sex*	*Colour*	*Birth*	*Sire*	*Dam*	*Breeder*	*Owner*
Playmate of Allways	D	Pa	15–4–59	Ch. Robmaywin Stargazer of Allways	Watcherbart of Allways	Mrs M. R. Jones	Mrs M. R. Jones
Dawnstar of Test	B	F	29–7–57	Ch. Evening Star of Allways	Wingedfoot Miss Madcap	Mrs D. Lewis	Mrs D. Lewis
Teighways Tasmin	B	Pa	9–4–58	Ch. Bellavista Barry	Teighways Treacle Tart	Mr F. Barnes	Mr F. Barnes
Trevelmond Masquerade	B	F	30–5–58	Countryman of Allways	Ch. Laguna Lullaby	Mr D. W. Armstrong	Mr D. W. Armstrong
Tranwells Brekin Sally Lunn	B	F	12–6–58	Ch. Wingedfoot Marksman of Allways	Brekin Fiesta of Fleeting	Lady Dankwerts	Mrs G. K. Jackson
1961 (24 Ch. Shows)							
Fair Landing of Knotkum	D	F	25–10–58	Ch. Runway Controller	Wingedfoot Tu Whit Tu Whoo	Mr J. Fisher	Mrs C. M. Coller
Greenbrae Free As Air	D	F	31–7–58	Ch. Laguna Liege	Monky of Saxondale	Miss J. M. Maidment	Mrs O. Yerburgh
Ladiesfield Topaz	D	Gl F	19–1–59	Ch. Allways Wingedfoot Running Fox	Ladiesfield Sapphire	Mrs M. Cuttler	Mrs W. M. Wigg
Butterfly of Test	B	W,F	29–7–59	Wingedfoot Hill Billy of Test	Wingedfoot Ladybird of Test	Mrs D. Lewis	Mrs D. Lewis

Greenbrae Laguna Lucia	B	F	28–3–59	Ch. Runway Controller	Ch. Laguna Leading Lady	Mrs D. U. McKay	Mrs O. Yerburgh
Porthurst Atalanta	B	F	3–5–59	Ch. Mars of Test	Ch. Porthurst Quaker Girl	Mrs R. E. Ticehurst	Miss B. Hinde
Shalfleet Selbrook Daylight	B	G,F,W	21–9–59	Ch. Robmaywin Stargazer of	Porthurst Creme de Menthe	Mrs J. & Mrs D. Selby	Mrs N. Odell
Wingedfoot Tu Whit Tu Whoo	B	F	12–4–54	Ch. Wingedfoot Marksman of Allways	Eh for Adorable	Mrs K. Chapman	Mrs A. Argyle
1962 (25 Ch. Shows)							
Courteney Fleetfoot	D	W,F	13–10–60	Ch. Bellavista Barry	Myhorlyns Anita	Mr A. E. Halliwell	Mr A. E. Halliwell
Deepridge Masquerade	D	Pa	1–9–60	Myhorlyns Gay Cavalier	Ladiesfield Shadow	Miss E. Hawthorn	Miss E. Hawthorn
Laguna Ligonier	D	P,Br	30–6–60	Ch. Bellavista Barry	Ch. Lily of Laguna	Mrs D. U. McKay	Mrs D. U. McKay
Teighways Tiger Tim	D	P	9–4–58	Ch. Bellavista Barry	Teighways Treacle Tart	Mr F. Barnes	Mr F. Barnes
Bromholm Jonquil of Allways	B	F	21–10–60	Ch. Mars of Test	Fleeting Sticklepath Solution	Mrs K. Fisher	Mrs G. C. Ussher

Name of Champion	*Sex*	*Colour*	*Birth*	*Sire*	*Dam*	*Breeder*	*Owner*
Roanbar Hillgarth Sweet Surprise	**B**	**F**	18–8–59	Myhorlyns Shootingstar	Hillgarth So Sweet	Mrs M. F. Sheffield	Mr & Mrs E. Griffiths
Shalfleet Spellbound	**B**	**F**	9–10–59	Ch. Wingedfoot Marksman of Allways	Wingedfoot Bartette	Mrs N. F. Odell	Mrs N. F. Odell
Shalfleet Story	**B**	**Bl F**	9–3–61	Shalfleet Sensation	Ch. Shalfleet Selbrook Daylight	Mrs N. F. Odell	Mrs N. F. Odell
1964 (27 Ch. Shows)							
Ballagan Prince Charlie of Briarcliffe	**D**	**Si F**	19–1–59	Briarcliffe Bing Boy	Ballagan Twin-rivers Charlotte	Mrs A. D. Selway	Mrs C. Hodgson
Dragonhill Woodpecker	**D**	**F**	12–3–62	Ch. Ladiesfield Topaz	Dragonhill Curlew	Mrs D. Cleeve	Mrs D. Cleeve
Harque Conneil Carry On	**D**	**F**	18–8–60	Conneil Stately Fox of Knotknum	Conneil Rosaline of Knotknum	Mrs C. Crawford	Mrs A. Argyle
Samarkands Greenbrae Tarragon	**D**	**F**	8–10–61	Ch. Laguna Limelight	Ch. Greenbrae Laguna Lucia	Mrs O. Yerburgh	Mr R. M. James

Shalfleet Swordsman	D	F	20–9–60	Ch. Mars of Test	Wingedfoot Bartette	Mrs N. F. Odell	Mrs N. F. Odell
Ballagan Annie Laurie	B	Si F	19–1–59	Briarcliffe Bing Boy	Ballagan Twinrivers Charlotte	Mrs A. D. Selway	Mrs A. D. Selway
Carina Mia	B	Bl F	10–9–61	Sante Toby	Porthurst Salad Days	Mrs A. Rolle	Mrs A. Rolle
Dragonhill Curlew	B	F	1–7–59	Dragonhill Hillgarth Spring Salad	Ch. Dragonhill Silver Ripple	Mrs D. Cleeve	Mrs D. Cleeve
Fleeting Spean La Calindra	B	W,F,Bl	8–4–60	Spean Hound	Springmere Far Horizon	Mrs J. Shields	Mrs M. D. Garrish
Garganey Mistletoe	B	F	18–1–58	Ch. Seagift Speedlite Mustang	Oxslip Honesty	Mrs K. M. George	Mrs K. M. George
Harque to Rosa	B	F	4–11–60	Harque to Beaumont	Rosaday of Knotknum	Mr L. Gough	Mrs A. Argyle
Hillgarth Sunstar of Glenbervie	B	F	12–12–61	Hillgarth Snowboy	Hillgarth So Sweet	Mrs M. F. Sheffield	Mr A. B. Nicolson
Interflora	B	F	10–11–60	Ch. Bouquet	Tweseldown Menkatab	Mrs V. M. Harding	Mrs K. Chapman

Name of Champion	*Sex*	*Colour*	*Birth*	*Sire*	*Dam*	*Breeder*	*Owner*
Teighways True Love	B	W	9–4–58	Ch. Bellavista Barry	Teighways Treacle Tart	Mr F. Barnes	Mr F. Barnes
Cockrow Tarquogan of Glenbervie	D	W,F	14–7–63	Ch. Samarkands Greenbrae Tarragon	Cockrow Lady Kate	Miss F. Hudson	Mr A. B. Nicolson
Peppard Top Flight	D	P W,F	2–9–60	Ch. Ladiesfield Topaz	Palmerscross Golden Lure	Mr & Mrs D. H. L. Gollan	Mr & Mrs D. H. L. Gollan
Roanbar Star	D	W,F	11–11–62	Roanbar Cachalong	Roanbar White Fire Princess	Mr & Mrs W. Griffiths	Mr & Mrs W. Griffiths
Badgewood Sewickley	B	F,W	·23–6–62	Ch. Laguna Ligonier	Badgewood Calamity Jane	Mr & Mrs P. S. P. Fell	Mrs & Mrs P. S. P. Fell
Harque Conneil Crown	B	F	18–8–60	Conneil Stately Fox of Knotknum	Conneil Rosaline of Knotknum	Mrs C. Crawford	Mr A. Argyle
Inadown Whispering Witch	B	Bl W	16–10–62	Twinrivers Sea Holly	Selbrook Rushlight	Mr & Mrs C. C. Kerr-Peterson	Mr & Mrs C. C. Kerr-Peterson
Peppard Premium Bond	B	F Br	1–2–63	Ch. Laguna Ligonier	Peppard Tit Bits	Mr & Mrs D. H. L. Gollan	Mr & Mrs D. H. L. Gollan

Shalfleet Springtime	B	F	9–3–61	Shalfleet Sensation	Ch. Shalfleet Selbrook Daylight	Mrs N. F. Odell	Mr & Mrs J. C. Potter
1965 (28 Ch. Shows)							
Harque to Gamecock	D	F	16–7–63	Harque to Beaumont	Rosaday of Knotknum	Mrs A. Argyle	Mrs A. Argyle
Ladiesfield Bedazzled	D	W,B	9–1–62	Spean Hound	Heyville's Satan's Child	Mrs W. M. Wigg	Mrs W. M. Wigg
Tantivvey Diver	D	Br, W	20–1–63	Ch. Laguna Ligonier	Fleeting Fancy Free	Miss J. B. Clay	Mmes P. M. Robinson & M. Croucher
Telstar Moon	D	F	8–7–62	Ch. Playmate of Allways	Moonchik	Mrs K. Chapman	Mrs K. Chapman
Dancing Girl of Test	B	W,F	23–9–63	Gaynose Festival of Allways	Call Girl of Test	Mrs D. Lewis	Mrs D. Lewis
Inniskhelltr Lollipop	B	F	11–12–62	Ch. Inniskhelltr Lovely Silver	Ch. Bromholm Jonquil of Allways	Miss G. C. Ussher	Miss G. C. Ussher
Laguna Porthurst Moonlight Sonata	B	Bl F, W	30–5–63	Ch. Laguna Ligonier	Porthurst Moonlight	Mrs R. Ticehurst	Mrs D. U. McKay
Russetwood Portia	B	Br, W	1–10–63	Ch. Laguna Ligonier	Russetwood Rhythm	Miss B. V. Rooney	Miss B. V. Rooney

Name of Champion	*Sex*	*Colour*	*Birth*	*Sire*	*Dam*	*Breeder*	*Owner*
1966 (28 Ch. Shows)							
Barmaud Sungauge	D	F, W	9–10–62	Ch. Bellavista Barry	Seagift Spode	Mr J. & Miss J. M. Barker	Mr J. & Miss J. M. Barker
Danegeld Piper's Tune	D	F	17–12–63	Ch. Peppard Topflight	Danegeld Andromeda	Miss B. Hinde	Mr E. Bucklow
Fleeting Flamboyant	D	W, Br Pa	31–7–64	Ch. Tantivvey Diver	Fleeting Yamalle Aida	Mrs M. B. Garrish	Mrs. M. B Garrish
Laguna Light Lagoon	D	F Br, W	15–11–64	Laguna Lightstep	Tantivvey Oriole	Miss Clay	Mrs D. U. McKay
Poltesco Peewit	D	W, F Pa	18–7–63	Poltesco Phoenix	Poltesco Clemwade Merrymaid	Miss M. R. Ironside	Miss M. R. Ironside
Ravensdown Bright Star	D	F, W	12–1–62	Trevelmond Starsign	Samarkands Sea Nymph	Miss E. J. Fair	Mr & Mrs H. Wood
Laguna Ravensdowne Astri	B	F, W Pa	20–9–63	Ch. Ravensdowne Bright Star	Little Loo of Laguna	Miss E. J. Fair	Mr & Mrs H. Wood
Peppard Winter Queen	B	W, Si	9–4–65	Laguna Liberace	Peppard Peppermint	Mr & Mrs D. H. L. Gollan	Mr & Mrs D. H. L. Gollan
Play Fair	B	F, W	7–5–63	Ch. Playmate of Allways	Atalanta The Fair	Mrs M. Skelton	Mrs K. Chapman

Porthurst Martini Sweet	B	F, W Pa	17–2–64	Velroza Pink Gin	Shalfleet Serene	Mrs R. E. Ticehurst	Mrs R. E. Ticehurst
Swiftfoot Susanna	B	Si F	2–9–63	Dondelayo Desperado	Dondelayo Goshgones	Mr W. Knight	Mr J. Geary
1967 (27 Ch. Shows)							
Deepridge Mintmaster	D	F Br, W	21–4–66	Ch. Laguna Ligonier	Deepridge Juliet	Miss E. M. Hawthorn	Miss E. M. Hawthorn
Shalfleet Sultan of Sherimere	D	R, W	28–11–64	Shalfleet Skyliner	Shalfleet Songbird	Miss P. Powell	Mrs N. F. Odell
Velroza Pink Gin	D	W, F	6–1–62	Paul of Allways	Velroza Painted Lady	Mr & Mrs W. R. Stewart	Mrs A. M. Rolls
Wyemere Royal Prince	D	Br, W	18–6–64	Ch. Laguna Ligonier	Wyemere Miss Marilyn	Mr G. T. Silk	Mr G. T. Silk
Dondelayo Rue	B	Br	25–11–64	Ch. Samarkands Greenbrae Tarragon	Linknumstar Lizard	Mrs A. R. Knight	Mrs A. R. Knight
Gosmore Flarepath Auriga	B	Bl F, W	17–8–66	Ch. Ravensdowne Bright Star	Dorville Blue Penny	Mr & Mrs W. Walsh	Mrs A. B. Dallison
Greenbae Poltesco Dusky Maid	B	F	5–10–64	Poltesco Phoenix	Poltesco Clemward Merry Maid	Miss Ironside	Mrs E. Collinge

Name of Champion	*Sex*	*Colour*	*Birth*	*Sire*	*Dam*	*Breeder*	*Owner*
Peppard Highland Fling	B	F Br	29–5–66	Ch. Ballagan Prince of Briarcliffe	Ch. Peppard Premium Bond	Mr & Mrs D. H. L. Gollan	Mr & Mrs D. H. L. Gollan
Sky Gipsy of Glenbervie	B	Pa	12–3–65	Ch. Cockrow Tarquogan of Glenbervie	Ch. Hillgarth Sunstar of Glenbervie	Mr A. B. Nicolson	Mr A. B. Nicolson
1968 (27 Ch. Shows)							
Baydale Samfa	D	F, W	4–11–65	Baydale Silver Sable	My Juniper Girl	Mmes L. M. Blair & S. H. Fenwick	Mmes L. M. Blair & S. H. Fenwick
Laguna Leisure	D	F, W Pa	21–4–66	Ch. Laguna Ligonier	Laguna Ravens-downe Faerie Queen	Mrs D. U. McKay	Mrs D. U. McKay
Oakbark Dondelayo Storming	D	F	18–11–65	Dondeleyo Desperado	Nagrom Feola	Mr W. Knight	Mr & Mrs D. Meakin
Samarkands Sun Courtier	D	F, W	3–1–64	Ch. Samarkands Greenbrae Tarragon	Samarkands Sun Cloud	Mr R. M. James	Misses C. & B. Dinnis
Dragonhill Tawny Owl	B	F	11–12–65	Ch. Poltesco Peewit	Dragonhill Golden Plover	Mrs D. Cleeve	Mrs D. Cleeve

Harque The Lark	B	F	23–7–66	Harque to Beaumont	Rosaday of Knotknum	Mrs A. Argyle	Mrs A. Argyle
Peppard Faithful Flora	B	W,F Pa	29–5–66	Ch. Ballagan Prince Charlie of Briarcliffe	Ch. Peppard Premium Bond	Mr & Mrs D. H. L. Gollan	Mr & Mrs M. Rakison
Shalfleet Starstruck	B	F	16–2–65	Ch. Evening Star of Allways	Shalfleet Sceptre	Mr C. Bayliss	Mrs B. E. Odell
1969 (29 Ch. Shows)							
Baydale Cinnamon	D	R Br	8–3–67	Ch. Samarkands Sun Courtier	Cockrow Merle	Mmes L. M. Blair & S. H. Fenwick	Mrs J. Oddy
Denorsi Moonduster of Glenbervie	D	F	15–10–68	Ch. Cockrow Tarquogan of Glenbervie	White Gorse of Glenbervie	Mr A. B. Nicolson	Mr J. Peden
Dondelayo Buckaroo	D	Br	18–4–67	Ch. Cockcrow Tarquogan of Glenbervie	Ch. Dondelayo Rue	Mrs A. R. Knight	Mrs A. R. Knight
Flarepath Tambillo Tarquin	D	F, W Pa	2–4–67	Ch. Ravensdowne Bright Star	Ballagan Shining Star	Mrs E. Ratcliffe	Mr & Mrs D. Meakin
Gunsmith of Glenbervie	D	F	16–5–67	Ch. Cockrow Tarquogan of Glenbervie	Ch. Hillgarth Sunstar of Glenbervie	Mr A. B. Nicolson	Miss J. M. Wright

Name of Champion	*Sex*	*Colour*	*Birth*	*Sire*	*Dam*	*Breeder*	*Owner*
Sticklepath Saracen	D	F	15–3–66	Ch. Laguna Ligonier	Sticklepath Sans Souci	Mr C. F. A. Boundy	Mr C. F. A. Boundy
Cockrow Pheasant	B	Br, W Pa	10–9–65	Ch. Tantivey Diver	Cockrow Taradiddle	Miss E. M. Hudson	Miss E. M. Hudson
Dondelayo Roulette	B	F	18–4–67	Ch. Cockrow Tarquogan of Glenbervie	Ch. Dondelayo Rue	Mrs A. R. Knight	Mrs A. R. Knight
Dondelayo Ruanne of Charmoll	B	Br	18–4–67	Ch. Cockrow Tarquogan of Glenbervie	Ch. Dondelayo Rue	Mrs A. R. Knight	Mrs C. Dempster
Gipsy Moth of Glenbervie	B	Si F	16–5–67	Ch. Cockrow Tarquogan of Glenbervie	Ch. Hillgarth Sunstar of Glenbervie	Mr A. B. Nicolson	Mrs F. J. Minns
Poltesco Periquita	B	F, W	23–9–64	Poltesco Peewit	Poltesco Quiz	Miss M. R. Ironside	Miss M. R. Ironside
1970 (29 Ch. Shows)							
Mister Softie of Altyre	D	F	14–9–65	Dragonhill Hillgarth Spring Salad	Arrow of Altyre	Mrs M. Fell	Mrs M. Fell

Pimlico of Crawshaw	D	Br, W	4–2–69	Cockrow Partridge of Crawshaw	Kew Sally	Mr V. Willmore	Miss M. Wright
Topall Newbold Miguel	D	F, W	7–9–67	Ch. Ravensdowne Bright Star	Newbold Samena Queen O' Diamonds	Mrs D. M. Howarth	Mr & Mrs C. L. Goldsmith
Towercrest Flarepath Taurus	D	F, Bl, W	9–12–66	Ch. Laguna Ligonier	Flarepath Ravensdowne Vega	Mr & Mrs H. Wood	Mrs E. Watson
Deepridge Miniva	B	Si Br	1–12–68	Ch. Deepridge Mintmaster	Deepridge Miss Mink	Miss E. M. Hawthorn	Miss E. M. Hawthorn
Nimrodel Willow Daughter	B	R F	10–3–67	Ch. Poltesco Peewit	Willow of Allways	Mrs I. H. Lowe	Mrs I. H. Lowe
1971 (29 Ch. Shows)							
Denorsi Moondust of Glenbervie	D	F, W	20–8–69	Ch. Cockrow Tarquogan of Glenbervie	White Gorse of Glenbervie	Mr A. B. Nicolson	Mr J. Peden
Walhachin	D	Br, W	21–12–67	Ch. Laguna Light Lagoon	Ch. Play Fair	Mrs K. Chapman	Mrs K. Chapman
Mancot Petruchio	D	F, W	17–3–68	Ch. Laguna Leisure	Dainty Maid of Loxlin	Mr A. S. Lowe	Mr A. S. Lowe
Harque to Pegasus	D	R F	18–1–69	Ch. Deepridge Mintmaster	Harque to Image	Mrs A. Argyle	Mrs A. Argyle

Name of Champion	*Sex*	*Colour*	*Birth*	*Sire*	*Dam*	*Breeder*	*Owner*
Lowglen Newbold Cavalier	D	W,F	29–12–69	Skydiver of Lowglen	Flarepath Caprice	Mrs D. M. Howarth	Mr F. Nicholas
Garganey Bartmeus	D	Br, W	13–5–70	Ch. Towercrest Flarepath Taurus	Garganey Jenny Wren	Mrs K. M. George	Mrs K. M. George
Deepridge Minstrel	D	F, W	1–12–68	Ch. Deepridge Mintmaster	Deepridge Miss Mink	Miss E. M. Hawthorn	Miss E. M. Haswthorn
Laguna Lunanute	D	R, W	30–11–68	Ch. Laguna Ligonier	Laguna Ravens-downe Faerie Queen	Mrs D. U. McKay	Mrs D. U. McKay
Courthill Dondelayo Tiara	B	F, W	14–12–69	Ch. Samarkands Greenbrae Tarragon	Ch. Dondelayo Roulette	Mrs A. R. Knight	Mr R. N. Stock
Dondelayo Duette	B	F	14–12–69	Ch. Samarkands Greenbrae Tarragon	Ch. Dondelayo Roulette	Mrs A. R. Knight	Mrs A. R. Knight
Trevelmond Miss Masquerade	B	F	17–5–68	Trevelmond Starsign	Trevelmond Tribute	Mr T. Barron	Mr D. Armstrong
Tweseldown Whinchat	B	R F	29–7–69	Nimrodel Windhover	Tweseldown Glentopic	Lady Anderson	Lady Anderson

Witch Hazel of Raddledandie	B	F, W	1–4–68	Ch. Samarkands Sun Courtier	Tarona of Crawshaw	Misses C. & B. Dinnis	Mr G. C. Barclay & Mrs C. Anderson
1972 (29 Ch. Shows)							
Akeferry Jimmy	D	Br, W	18–12–69	Cockrow Partridge of Crawshaw	Eegee Jane	Mr S. F. R. Pendleton	Miss E. W. Newton
Charmoll Clansman	D		5–2–71	Ch. Baydale Cinnamon	Ch. Dondelayo Ruanne of Charmoll	Mrs C. Dempster	Mrs C. Dempster
Flarepath Astrinomical	D	F, W	3–10–68	Ch. Towercrest Flarepath Taurus	Ch. Laguna Ravensdowne Astri	Mr & Mrs Wood	Mrs D. Flatt
Nimrodel Ruff	D	R F	12–6–70	Ch. Poltesco Peewit	Nimrodel Wintersweet	Mrs I. H. Lowe	Mrs I. H. Lowe
Tantivvey Akeferry Crusader	D	Br	1–8–67	Cockrow Partridge of Crawshaw	Eegee Jane	Mr S. F. R. Pendleton	Miss I. B. Clay
Twigairy of Glenbervie	D	Br	26–7–70	Cockrow Woodchuck	Tarara of Glenbervie	Mr A. B. Nicolson	Mr A. B. Nicolson
Oakbark Michaela	B	F, W	18–6–69	Ch. Flarepath Tambillo Tarquin	Oakbark Michelle	Mr & Mrs D. Meakin	Mr D. Howarth

Name of Champion	*Sex*	*Colour*	*Birth*	*Sire*	*Dam*	*Breeder*	*Owner*
Peppard Royal Victory	B	W,F	9–2–70	Ch. Deepridge Mintmaster	Peppard Prestonpans	Mrs D. H. L. Gollan	Mrs D. H. L. Gollan
Sky Time of Glenbervie	B	F,W	31–3–70	Steelbridge of Glenbervie	Ch. Sky Gypsy of Glenbervie	Mr A. B. Nicolson	Mr. G. Topham
Denorsi Quick-match of Glenbervie	B	F	27–5–69	Ch. Dondelayo Buckaroo	Tarara of Glenbervie	Mr A. B. Nicolson	Mr J. Peden
Fleeting Fulmar	D	Br	26–9–70	Ch. Fleeting Flamboyant	Fleeting Akeferry Miss Emma	Mrs M. B. Garrish	Mrs M. B. Garrish
Shalfleet Sailing Free	D	F	4–6–69	Shalfleet Skyliner	Ch. Shalfleet Starstruck	Mrs. B. Odell	Mrs B. Odell
Another Rose of Glenbervie	B	W,F	15–10–68	Ch. Cockrow Tarquogan of Glenbervie	White Gorse of Glenbervie	Mr A. B. Nicolson	Mr A. B. Nicolson
Selbrook Bracelet	B	F	24–6–67	Shalfleet Skyliner	Selbrook Breeze	Mrs J. Selby and Mr D. C. Selby	Mrs J. Selby and Mr D. C. Selby
1973 (29 Ch. Shows)							
Oakbark Merchant Prince	D	F,W	5–11–71	Oakbark Pyramid	Oakbark Michelle	Mr & Mrs D. Meakin	Mrs R. Wright

Shalfleet Silver Knight of Skyeboat	D	W	24–6–71	Shalfleet Schelle	Shalfleet Silver Mink	Mrs B. Wilton-Clark (formerly Mrs Odell)	Mr & Mrs M. Rakison
Woodflame Wellington Boot	D	F,W	19–10–70	Lowglen Oakbark Masterminde	Flareparth Misty Moon	Mr & Mrs R. A. Holm & Miss P. A. Butler	Mr & Mrs R. A. Holm & Miss P. A. Butler
Fairfoot Towercrest Encore	D	F	29–3–67	Ch. Ravensdowne Bright Star	Towercrest Firedancer	Mrs E. Watson	Mrs A. J. Rollason
Gipsy Picture of Glenbervie	B	RF, W	24–5–71	Ch. Dondelayo Buckaroo	Whitebridge of Glenbervie	Mr A. B. Nicolson	Mr A. B. Nicolson
Denorsi Dancing Belle	B	W,F	16–4–72	Dondelayo Rufus of Oldwell	Denorsi Tinkerbelle of Glenbervie	Mr J. Peden	Mr J. Peden
Sequence of Shalfleet	B	RF	23–12–71	Ch. Shalfleet Sailing Free	Shadow of Andreovna	Miss M. Hall	Mrs B. Wilton-Clark
Ruegeto Gay Dawn	B	F	27–3–72	Steelbridge of Glenbervie	Carramia Honeypuff	Mr & Mrs G. Topham	Mr P. Newman & Madame Kucavicici
Pathway of Glenbervie	B	RF, W	24–5–71	Ch. Dondelayo Buckaroo	Whitebridge of Glenbervie	Mr A. B. Nicolson	Mr. A. B. Nicolson
1974 (30 Ch. Shows)							
Walkabout Waggonerswalk	D	F	19–8–71	Wingedfoot Walkabout Whiplash	Walkabout Woodbine	Mrs S. M. Thompson	Mrs S. M. Thompson

Flarepath Astrinought of Lowglen	D	F,W	1–2–72	Ch. Lowglen Oakbark Masterminde	Ch. Laguna Ravensdowne Astri	Mr & Mrs H. Wood	Mr F. Nicholas
Lowglen Cavalcade of Zarcrest	D	F,W	19–3–72	Ch. Lowglen Newbold Cavalier	Tamaline of Lowglen	Mr F. Nicholas	Mr & Mrs H. Boyle
Rearsbylea Ranjitara	B	F,W	11–9–71	Tawny Owl	Rearsbylea Rain Cloud	Mrs J. A. Cox	Mrs J. A. Cox & Mr D. Morris
Glenbervie White Frost	B	W	29–11–72	Ch. Dondelayo Buckaroo	Whitebridge of Glenbervie	Mr A. B. Nicolson	Mr. A. B. Nicolson
Denorsi Dixie Belle	B	F	16–4–72	Dondelayo Rufus of Oldwell	Denorsi Tinkerbelle of Glenbervie	Mr J. Peden	Mr J. Peden
Deepridge Mosaic	B	W,Br	6–9–72	Selbrook Brandy of Shalfleet	Deepridge Miniva	Miss E. Hawthorn	Miss E. Hawthorn
Harque Yonder	B	Br	24–9–71	Ch. Dondelayo Buckaroo	Ch. Harque The Lark	Mrs A. Argyle	Mrs A. Argyle
1975 (30 Ch. Shows)							
Beseeka Knight Errant of Silkstone	D	Br,W	2–5–73	Oakbark Moonduster	Newbold Madelina	Mmes. Lumb & Hughes	Mrs R. Wright

Nutcracker of Nevedith	D	W	7–4–73	Ch. Akeferry Jimmy	White Bud of Glenbervie	Mr Moran Healy	Miss E. W. Newton
Charmoll McTavish	D	Br	22–1–73	Ch. Baydale Cinnamon	Ch. Dondelayo Ruanne of Charmoll	Mrs C. Dempster	Mrs C. Dempster
Allgarth Envoy	D	W,F	30–5–73	Ch. Lowglen Newbold Cavalier	Shalfleet Stylish	Mr F. R. Moore	Mr F. R. Moore
Danropa His Lordship of Thurma	D	F	17–7–71	Ch. Dondelayo Buckaroo	Dondelayo Coronette	Mr R. B. Daniel	Mrs. G. Rose
Oakbark Armfield Joker	D	Ro,C	10–11–70	Ch. Deepridge Mintmaster	Patjo Madam	Mr J. Armitage	Mr & Mrs D. Meakin
Charmoll Bonnie Prince	D	Br	22–1–73	Ch. Baydale Cinnamon	Ch. Dondelayo Ruanne of Charmoll	Mrs. C. Dempster	Mrs. C. Demptser
Crysbel Skylark	B	Br,W	20–9–73	Ch. Fleeting Fulmar	Badgewood Charlottesville	Mrs M. Crocker	Mrs M. Crocker
Ballagan Flighty	B	Br	9–1–73	Shalfleet Schelle	Ballagan Gadabout	Lady Selway	Lady Selway
Denhills Delectabelle	B	F,W	16–1–73	Oakbark Pyramid	Rasaday Alisa	Mr D. Hill	Mrs A. R. Knight
Allgarth Edelweiss	B	W,F	30–5–73	Ch. Lowglen Newbold Cavalier	Shalfleet Stylish	Mr F. R. Moore	Mr F. R. Moore

Glossary of General Terms

Affix. The registered name by which a kennel is identified granted by the Kennel Club upon payment of a fee. Usually known as Prefix or Suffix.

Apple-headed. A skull which is rounded on top as in King Charles Spaniels.

Barrelled. Denoting the shape of the ribs which, when barrelled, are excessive and spring straight out from the spine—giving the body a barrel-like appearance.

B.o.B. Best of Breed award.

Blaze. A white marking running down the face. The white marking on the forehead of a horse is a good illustration.

Bloom. Sheen on the coat—denoting good condition, and general health.

Bone. A well-boned dog is one possessing limbs well rounded and giving the impression of strength and substance without being coarse.

Br. Breeder(s); the owner(s) of the dog's dam at time of whelping.

Brace. Two dogs run, or exhibited, together.

Brindle. Denoting a colour—a mixture of light and dark hairs giving the impression of darker streaks on a lighter background.

Brisket. The chest-wall of a dog, usually spoken of as brisket when regarded from the side and measured at its deepest point.

B.S. Best of Sex, denoting dog which has beaten all others of his sex.

B.i.S. Best in Show. Denotes the dog which is the best of all breeds at a show.

Butterfly Nose. When the nostrils show a part, flesh coloured or mottled, against a black or brown background.

C.C. Kennel Club Challenge Certificate.

Ch. Denotes a champion, a dog having won three C.C.s awarded by three different judges.

Cloddy. Thick-set—like a Shire horse.

Close-coupled. When the loin appears short.

Cobby. Thick and sturdy—as in a cob horse. Can also denote a neat, compact build.

Couplings. That part of the body linking the fore and hind limb joints.

Cow-hocked. When the hocks are bent inwards throwing the hind feet outwards. A very bad fault in any breed.

Crest. The upper part of a dog's neck.

Croup. The part immediately before the root of the tail.

Dam. Mother of the puppies.

Dappled. Denoting a variegated or mottled colour.

Dew Claws. The small claw found on the inside of the leg. In a Whippet should be removed a few days after birth.

Dewlap. Loose pendulous skin under the throat.

Dudley Nose. Wholly flesh-coloured nostrils—not to be confused with the Butterfly Nose.

Featherings. Long hair fringing the backs of the legs—mainly the hind legs.

Front. Usually applies to the front legs and shoulders when viewed from the front.

Gay Tail. One carried gaily over the back, or above the horizontal.

Good Do-er. A dog which has thrived well and needs no special attention to his diet.

Grizzle. An iron-grey colour.

Hare Feet. Feet which are long and narrow, having little or no ball cushion. Toes long and spread, like a hare's feet.

Heat. A bitch 'on heat' is when she is in her œstral period or 'in season'.

Height. Measurement taken from ground to top of shoulder.

Hock. Joint in hind leg between the pastern and stifle.

Pad. The cushioned sole of the foot.

Particolour. A combination of two colours in more or less equal proportions, but by no means necessary. A 'white, with brindled patches' could mean the same as particolour.

Pastern. The lowest part of the leg, below the knee of the foreleg or below the hock on the hind leg.

Pied. A somewhat old-fashioned term denoting a dog of two colours in unequal proportions.

Prefix. The registered name granted, on payment of a fee, by the Kennel Club which is used in addition to the dog's registered name, for instance 'Watford Golden Glory'—the word 'Watford' being the prefix granted to the kennel, and identifies it, for no other dog may carry the name 'Watford' in any other form.

Reserve. Usually the fourth place award in judging. It may also be applied for the runner-up for a special award, such as Best in Show, etc.

Ribbed up. Denotes a dog having good ribs.

Ring Tail. A tail which almost describes a complete circle.

Roach Back. One which arches upwards along the spine, with particular emphasis about the loins.

Second Thigh. The muscular development between the stifle and the hock of the back leg.

Service. The serving of the bitch by the stud dog.

Sickle Hocks. When the hind legs show an excessive bend at the hocks and are excessively let down, giving a crawling impression in movement—the hocks being thrust out too far behind.

Sickle Tail. The tail having an upward curve carrying above the level of the back—a gay tail.

Snipy. A weak muzzle—too long and narrow—or short and narrow

Splay Feet. Feet having the toes spread wide apart.

Stifle. The joint in the hind leg corresponding to the human knee.

T.A.F. Transfer Applied For.

Tucked-up. When the loins are lifted well up, as in Whippets and Greyhounds, etc.

Wall Eye. A combination of white and blue colours.

Weedy. Lacking substance.

W.E.L.K.S. West of England Ladies Kennel Society.

Wheel Back. Another term for roach back.

Withers. The point where the neck joins the body, about the shoulders.

Index